MONEY

a study of the theory of the medium of exchange

David Kinley

Simon Publications, Inc.
2003

Originally published in 1904 by Macmillan and Co.; London, New York

Library of Congress Card Number: 13011393

ISBN: 1-932512-11-X

Published by Simon Publications, Inc. P. O. Box 910455, San Diego, CA 92191-0455

PREFACE

THE present book is an attempt to present a systematic exposition of the theory, or scientific principles, of money. The historical and descriptive literature of the subject is already so voluminous and rich that I have not thought it best to enter that field, excepting where necessary for purposes of illustration, and in those cases I have made my references as brief as possible.

I began the work at the time when Walker's "Money" and Jevons's "Money and the Mechanism of Exchange" were the only books we had in English which purported to do what I had in mind, and I expected to have my task completed long ago. Many things have postponed this completion until now. The field which I attempt to cover has recently been occupied by Professor Laughlin's "Principles of Money" and, in part, by Professor Scott's "Money and Banking." If my own book had not been practically all written at the time of the appearance of these works, I might not have written it at all; but as so much of it was already done, it seemed best to me to finish it.

It is my hope that some new points will be found in the work, although I am painfully aware of the likelihood that what is new may not be important, and what is important may not be new. As Jevons once wrote, "I am far from supposing that the exact relations in regard to prices, commodities, gold, and capital have been hit upon. I do not believe that any of our economists have yet untied this Gordian knot of economic science, although some cut it in a very unhesitating manner."[1]

It will be seen that neither in my view of the influence of credit, nor of the relation of the quantity of money to its value, am I in accord with Professor Laughlin or Professor Scott. I take occasion, however, to express my appreciation of the high quality of both works and of the help they have both given me. The authorities to whom I am indebted are too numerous to mention specifically. The references at the beginning of each chapter will indicate in a general way where I have found my inspiration and my help.

I am indebted to several friends for help in carrying out my work. In the first place, I wish to express my warm appreciation of the kindly patience and inspiring helpfulness of my friend, the editor. Without his encouragement I doubt very much whether I would have had patience to finish the work, owing to the harassing incidents of my administrative work. Next, I am deeply indebted to my colleague, Professor N. A. Weston, who has read a large part of the manuscript and

[1] "Investigations in Currency and Finance," p. 32.

criticised it, I am glad to say, somewhat severely. His criticisms of the new points, however, were from the standpoint of accepted doctrines, and, after considering them carefully, I decided that I must let my innovations stand. To Professor Weston also belongs the credit of preparing the bibliography at the end of the book. It is designedly confined mainly to Money, to the exclusion of Credit and Banking. Professor M. B. Hammond, Professor M. H. Robinson, and Mr. L. W. Zartman, Fellow in Economics, have also given me assistance, which I am glad to acknowledge.

I hope soon to supplement this book with one on Credit and Banking.

DAVID KINLEY.

UNIVERSITY OF ILLINOIS,
March 16, 1904.

CONTENTS

CHAPTER I

The Social Importance of Money

CHAPTER II

The Evolution of Money

CHAPTER III

Coinage

CHAPTER IV

The Currency and the Principles of its Circulation

CHAPTER V

Services and Nature of Money

CHAPTER VI

The Movement and Distribution of Metallic Money

CHAPTER VII

The Static Distribution of the Precious Metals

CHAPTER VIII

THE VALUE OF MONEY

CHAPTER IX

Stability of the Value of Money

CHAPTER X

Significance and Causes of Changes in the Value of Money

CHAPTER XI

Credit and Prices

CHAPTER XII

The Measurement of Variations in the Purchasing Power of Money

CHAPTER XIII

The Standard of Deferred Payments

CHAPTER XIV

BIMETALLISM

CHAPTER XV

SOME FACTORS WHICH MODIFY THE INFLUENCE OF PRICE CHANGES

CHAPTER XVI

Inconvertible Paper Money

CHAPTER XVII

Convertible Paper Currency

MONEY

MONEY

CHAPTER I

THE SOCIAL IMPORTANCE OF MONEY

REFERENCES: Buckle, H. T., History of Civilization in England, Vol. II., p. 318; Del Mar, Alex., Money and Civilization; Harper, J. W., Money and Social Problems, Ch. 3; Jevons, W. S., Money and the Mechanism of Exchange, Chs. 1, 15; Nicholson, J. S., Money and Monetary Problems, 5th ed., pp. 16–17, 107–110; Tucker, George, Theory of Money and Banks, Ch. 3.

1. The Intimate Connection of the System of Exchange with Social Progress.—We are so accustomed to the conveniences of the modern system of exchange that we seldom reflect on its historical significance or its present importance. Yet that system is, in a way, an epitome of the history of civilization. There is no phase of life which the system of exchange, or the monetary system, has not affected; there is no byway of the life of the individual, or of society, into which its influence does not reach.

Some writers minimize the importance of the monetary system of exchange as a factor in progress and prosperity. Some, ethically inclined, and influenced by the evils which spring from the bad use of money and credit, insist that these means of exchange are not necessary to industry, and think to purify society by abolishing them. Others, with Mill, look at money as a third wheel, and tell us that "there cannot . . . be intrinsically a more insignificant thing, in the economy of society."[1] It is a little difficult to get the point of view from which a writer of Mill's logical sense could make a remark so wide of the truth. Far from playing an unimportant rôle, money is now, more than ever before, a social necessity; as necessary to the easy exchange of material goods as is writing or printing to the interchange of ideas. So interwoven with all phases of the life of society is the modern system of exchange that were it suddenly destroyed, much that is best in civilized life would be swept away; many of its noblest influences, which are commonly thought of as far removed from contact with thoughts of money, would vanish; much of the breadth of view and the toleration of spirit that comes from contact, even indirect and remote, with other peoples, workers in other fields, would be lost.

The monetary system of a country reflects its economic progress. The system of exchange is at once a cause and a consequence of the stage of economic development. With every change in the form of industrial life has come a change in the system of exchange. "Corresponding to the changes in productive methods under mechanical machinery we should find the rapid growth of a

[1] "Principles of Political Economy," III., vii., 3.

complex monetary system reflecting in its international and national character, in its elaborate structure of credit, the leading characteristics which we find in modern productive and distributive industry. The whole industrial movement might be regarded from the financial or monetary point of view."[1]

2. Adaptation of the Monetary System to the Prevailing Stage of Economic Life. — The forms of money and the whole mechanism of exchange at any time are adapted to the stage of industry and trade, and to the scale of incomes which prevails at the time. Where trade is limited, industry primitive, and market values low, we expect to find a simple and inexpensive money and a simple mechanism of exchange, with the credit system but little developed. Where industry and trade are highly organized, where business is relatively complex and expensive, and the scale of market values and of incomes high, we expect to find money of a high cost of production, and the mechanism of exchange correspondingly complex and costly. His arrow-heads, his bow, and the skins of the beasts he kills, are the natural features of the system of exchange in the simple economic life of the huntsman. Gold, in the form of a highly finished tool, representative paper money, and the manifold forms of a credit system, widely extended and intricately ramified, are the equally natural features of the system of exchange necessary to

[1] Hobson, "Evolution of Modern Capitalism," p. 7.

the complex relations of the modern business world. The people of a country with little capital endeavor to economize that little by stretching their credit. Unable or unwilling to sink labor and goods in the production of a material money, they seek to carry on their exchanges by means of its paper representatives. A rich commercial country, with abundance of capital to spare for use as money, provides itself with a plentiful supply of metallic money and rests easily and without strain, upon the basis so provided, a complex system of credit exchanges that reaches every market of the world. In short, the stage of development of their system of exchange is a measure of the industrial development of a people.

3. Relation of the Monetary System to the Scale of Incomes. — More particularly, the standard of living of a community is disclosed, more or less accurately, by the kind and denominations of the money it uses. Since expenditures depend on the scale of incomes, small incomes imply small purchases; small purchases require small denominations and a cheap money material. If goods to the value of ten cents a day represent the purchases necessary to the daily living of the larger number of the people of a country, the unit of money commonly in their thoughts is the cent. If, on the contrary, the usual expenditure of a majority of the people is a dollar and a half or two dollars a day, they think in dollars rather than in cents. To millions of Chinamen, cash, representing a fraction of a cent, is the unit of purchases for a day. To an American the dollar is the familiar unit of account. The difference in the value of the two units indicates, at least roughly, the difference in the scale of expenditure, and, therefore, of the standards of consumption, of the two peoples.

4. Division of Labor and the Monetary System.— Further, it is a commonplace remark that the modern system of production depends upon the extent to which the division of labor can be carried; but the extent to which this division can be carried is greatly increased by an easily working system of exchange, since the size of the market depends largely on the facility of exchange of products. The remark holds as well for the division of labor between different countries as between different localities within a country. In other words, money is necessary to large international trade. Without some system of exchange each country would have to provide for itself all that it needed to consume. If the mechanism of exchange, especially the credit portion of it, were to break down, the trade between countries would be so deranged that the different nations of the world would be thrown back into positions of relative economic isolation, such as characterized them before the era of modern civilization began. While it is very far from being true that Rome fell, as Sir Archibald Allison has said, because of a growing dearth of money, yet that lack undoubtedly had an influence in checking trade, lowering the standard of living, and retarding that free intercourse necessary to produce the community of interest, without which no country of extended territory can long remain intact.

5. The Monetary System and Political and Economic Freedom. — Money has undoubtedly been the means of promoting freedom, both political and industrial. Sir Henry Maine has pointed out that social progress is quickened by the substitution of contract for custom in the dealings of men. Custom has made way for competition and status for contract in the domain of economic exchange as the money economy has extended, and has left the payer of taxes and tithes and rents, as well as the seller of goods, freer because of its extension. For contracts are more readily discharged, and therefore more widely extended, with a medium of payment that is general in character and acceptability. One of the most striking historical illustrations of the impulse which a money exchange gives to social and political improvement is found in the betterment of the condition of the serfs in the Middle Ages by the commutation of the services due their overlords into money payments. "So far from being an evil, during this period at any rate, the extension of the use of money as a medium of exchange was the means of effecting great social reforms, and there can be little doubt that progress was retarded largely by a deficiency of the precious metals, especially the dearth of silver."[1]

[1] Nicholson. "Money and Monetary Problems," 5th ed., p. 17.

It is true, too, that in the later Middle Ages the growing use of money to replace exchange by barter made it easier to raise revenue for purposes of defence, and thus strengthened the cities and kings in their struggles with the feudal aristocracy. As the revenue needed grew larger, and increased taxes were in consequence imposed, the demand for greater freedom and for a larger voice in the control of the government became stronger, so that a better system of exchange indirectly increased personal freedom. Somewhat similar is the influence of money wages and rent on the condition of the negro in the South. Of the economic classes among the negroes, Mr. Du Bois paints darkly the life of the "cropper" and the "metayer," and remarks that "a degree above these we may place those laborers who receive money wages for their work," while "the renters for fixed money rentals are the first of the emerging classes."[1]

A later instance of the good influence of the extended use of money in promoting economic freedom is found in laws abolishing the truck system and requiring that wages be paid in money. Great abuses grew up in England and in certain parts of this country under the truck system. It was not only that those who lived under it suffered loss from having to pay unreasonably high prices, but, worse, that they were not free to buy where and as they pleased, and had not the power, which ready money gives, of seeking an economic escape

[1] W. E. B. Du Bois, "The Souls of Black Folk," p. 159.

from their hard conditions. Under such a system the man who is politically free may be economically enslaved; and the person who is economically a serf cannot long effectively exercise the rights of political freedom.

6. The Monetary System and Nationality. — The modern mechanism of exchange exercises an influence, too, for the promotion of national unity. Money, and the division of labor and exchange which the wide use of money implies, destroyed the self-sufficing villages of English economic history, and taught their people the advantages of mutual dependence and community of interests. The industrial and commercial unity so developed laid the foundation for an intenser common national feeling. In a similar way international comity is promoted. Like the system of transportation, the mechanism of exchange brings the people in different parts of the world into closer touch with one another. The interests of the people of different countries are united, and the facility with which the transfer of capital is made in these days is doing much to break down the industrial isolation that custom and national prejudice have fostered so long. The influence which the system of exchange exerts in bringing different countries closer together would be greatly increased by the adoption of a uniform coinage system throughout the civilized world, or at least by the great commercial countries.

The adoption of a common monetary system by

the great nations of the earth has been prevented partly by national prejudice, and partly by the inconvenience involved in making the change. Each nation is unwilling to give up its own system, and is ready to consent to the adoption of a common coinage only if its monetary unit be made the common one. Moreover, each country is anxious to get whatever advantage in trade is brought by the use of its coins in other countries. There is a feeling that German or English trade, for example, will be promoted in the Orient by the use of the German or the English coins. While there is some force in these contentions, the benefits that would accrue from a unification of the world's monetary system would far outweigh any detriment that might come to particular countries.

7. The Monetary System and Economic Prosperity. — The modern system of exchange promotes industry and trade by making the aggregation of capital easier. It enables people to turn their savings into money and, by depositing it in savings institutions, or by purchasing the shares of corporations, to concentrate under the direction of competent men the large capital necessary to the great enterprises of the present day. Still more, the modern monetary system facilitates the transfer as well as the aggregation of capital. Money is the most general form of capital, capital in the fluid state, so that it can be immediately turned to new enterprises and transferred for investment to distant places. Without this fluidity, investments would necessarily be more local in their character, and the industrial possibilities of distant places in need of capital could not be so readily developed.

The monetary system indirectly increases the total utilities available for consumption by the community. If a community effects its exchanges by barter alone, it does so at a certain cost. The introduction of money exchange, under proper conditions, will lessen that cost and thereby increase the volume of goods available for consumption. The same effect is produced in a community which already makes its exchanges with money, if by an increase in the amount of money exchanges can be effected which could not be effected before.

Not only may the introduction or extension of monetary exchange increase the net consumption of a community, by decreasing the cost of making its exchanges, but either may add directly to the available utilities. For in a régime of barter, for example, many people possess things which have no direct use to them, but have to others. As soon as this is found out, the things acquire an indirect importance to their owners, and an exchange value.

From the point of view of society money has, of course, no superiority over other kinds of goods. The belief was once common, and is still held by a good many people, that because an individual is richer the more money he has, the same is true of a country as a whole. But this is not so. The money can be used by the country, regarded as a whole, only to do its domestic business or to buy foreign goods. If any country could arbitrarily increase her amount of gold, the larger quantity, generally speaking, would simply effect the same amount of exchanges as the smaller did, but on a different price level. As a matter of fact, however, an excess of money would flow abroad for goods. The only case in which a country is richer by the possession of gold beyond her need for it for purposes of payment is when she possesses her own mines. For then she can send her surplus gold abroad in exchange for other goods, and she becomes richer, not by keeping her gold, but by parting with it. A country is no better off from having a surplus of money than is a railroad company with more locomotives than it can use economically.

8. The Monetary System and the Distribution of Wealth. — On the other hand, the monetary system of exchange involves disadvantages which appear to some minds so serious as to offset the good it does. Some people believe, for example, that money produces inequality of wealth. There is a certain plausibility in this opinion. For the possessor of money has a certain advantage over holders of other forms of wealth, because his goods are in general demand; while the owner of other forms of wealth, if he wishes to exchange, must search for a purchaser who has what he wants to buy and is willing to take what he has to offer. This fact gives the owner of money a peculiar industrial and social power, a kind of monopolistic advantage. It may be said in opposition to this view, that the same advantage lies with any one who happens to have an article for which there is a strong demand. There are occasions on which the possessor of wheat, for example, has an advantage in trade over the man who has money, that is, when the demand for wheat is strong and its supply limited. This, however, is not a sufficient answer, for any one will take money for his goods, but not every one cares to take wheat beyond a very limited quantity, if at all. If a man owns a house for which he paid $5000, he can buy other things with it only as opportunity offers. If he has $5000 in money, he can buy other things as he pleases. The market for other things is more or less local; that for money is universal. There is always a market somewhere, in some measure, for any economic goods, but the individual who has any kind of goods but money must find this somewhere and some measure. The owner of money needs not do so. Nevertheless, inequality of wealth really depends very little on the existence of money. Such inequalities were never greater than in pastoral and agricultural states, where wealth consisted of cattle and land. The rich are not rich because they have large quantities of money, for they do not keep their wealth in that form; but because they have acquired a legal title to a large share of the goods in the community.

Another disadvantage of the monetary system lies in the disturbance which changes in the value of money cause in the distribution of incomes.

Money is the vehicle of the distribution of product, and variations in its value between the times of receiving income and spending it, may change the relation of the distribution. The owner of money gains or loses, when he purchases, with every change in its value. It is true that fluctuations in the value of money may, in the long run, offset one another, so that the loss of to-day becomes the gain of to-morrow. The trouble is that the gain is not always — or perhaps seldom — made by the same persons who experience the loss.

9. The Socialistic View of the Monetary System. — Notwithstanding the evils which the use of money entails, and the impossibility of removing all of them, we may not conclude, with the socialist, that money and the monetary system could be dispensed with. Even if the socialist's dream could be realized, and all producers should turn their products into a common fund on which each would draw with equal right, it would still be necessary to have some evidence of these rights and claims, if only checks issued by the government. If the owners of these checks accepted them from one another, instead of always presenting them directly to the government warehouse, they would be, to all intents and purposes, paper money. That they would thus pass current in the absence of any other medium of exchange would be inevitable, since their currency would be necessary in order to enable each person to sell his own product for other things in such quantities and at such times as he needed them.

CHAPTER II

THE EVOLUTION OF MONEY

REFERENCES: Babelon, Les Origines de la Monnaie; Bücher, K., Industrial Evolution, pp. 67 ff.; Carlile, W. W., Evolution of Modern Money; Del Mar, A., History of the World's Monetary Systems; Jevons, W. S., Money and the Mechanism of Exchange, Ch. 4; Laveleye, E. de, La Monnaie et le Bimetallisme International, Ch. 1; Lenormant, P., La Monnaie dans antiquité; Menger, K., On the Origin of Money, Econ. Journ., 1892, pp. 239–255; White, H., Money and Banking, pp. 12–14.

1. The Conjectural Character of Early Monetary History. — There is a perennial interest in the life of early man. His habits, the instruments he used, and his ways of doing things have always been subjects of curious inquiry on the part of the antiquarian and historian. We rake over the refuse heaps of past generations to find the kind of tools with which they worked; and use the known remains of a lost language to reconstruct the religious beliefs and social customs of the people who spoke it. While many of the conclusions resulting from these inquiries rest upon a substantial basis of fact, there are some that can be classed only as conjectures. But when these conjectures are plausible, they are likely to be accepted as correct explanations of the conditions they attempt to describe long after their origin and character has been forgotten, and by people to whom it was never known.

There is no phase of the history of early institutions to which these remarks are more applicable than to money. The generally accepted explanation of the origin and development of the system of exchange is largely conjectural. It found its beginning in the *a priori* conceptions of Aristotle. It seems evident enough that the writer who would attempt to give the correct explanation of the early history of money should have at hand considerable information about life in primitive communities; but neither Aristotle nor his contemporaries had sufficient information on this subject to justify us in thinking that he or they could frame an explanation of money that we could accept as historically correct. It savors, doubtless, of economic heresy to say it, yet nothing can be clearer than that Aristotle's explanation of the origin of money is pure conjecture, and is a corollary of his distinction between what he calls the natural and the conventional modes of acquiring property. Speaking of buying and selling, he says: "The other or more complex form of exchange grew out of the simpler [or barter]. When the inhabitants of one country became more dependent on those of another, and they imported what they needed and exported the surplus, money necessarily came into use. . . . Hence men agreed to employ, in their dealings with each other, something which was intrinsically useful and easily applicable to the purposes of life, for example, iron, silver, and the like." [1]

In this passage, especially in the last sentence, we have clearly set forth the theory which has been accepted throughout the centuries as describing an actual historical evolution, but is nothing more than Aristotle's guess of what probably occurred. Being plausible and at the same time Aristotelian, it has come down to us through generations of writers, with scarcely any modification. We find Paulus, for example, saying that "a substance was chosen which, from its permanent and universal value, might become the medium of exchange, and obviate the difficulties constantly arising in the system of barter." [2] It is clear that for this passage the Roman lawyer is the debtor of the Greek philosopher.

Not only is the common theory of the origin of money conjectural, but so, too, are some of the explanations of the development of the system of exchange. Hildebrand and others have told us, for example, that the régime of barter was displaced with one of money, and that this in turn will in time give place to a system of exchange by means of credit. We are told that the extent of the use of credit in a given country may be looked upon as a test of its civilization; that as a country becomes more highly civilized it discards barter and diminishes its use of money. The pertinacity

[1] "Politics," I., 9, 7. Jowett's ed.

[2] Digest XVIII., p. 1. Quoted by Lenormant in *Cont. Rev.*, p. 34.

of this theory, which has been held by not a few, is probably due in part to its simplicity, and by its show of conformity to what is called evolution. It is too great a strain on one's credulity to believe that primitive man had as much knowledge of trade as is imputed to him in Gossen's theory that money and exchange presuppose a knowledge of the advantage of exchange in reducing cost of production. But such explanations of the origin and development of the system of exchange assume too much knowledge of trade and too accurate foresight on the part of primitive man, and a course of development that is too simple and too clean-cut. The explanation of our social progress would be beautifully easy if we could assume that every old habit and institution was to be consigned to the limbo of the forgotten and unused as soon as some new means of performing its work were discovered; and that we could always select in advance an improved means of accomplishing our purpose.

2. The Character of Monetary Evolution. — Yet criticism of such theories must not be severe, for the temptation to interpret the past by the present and to attribute to other people motives and knowledge that are our own, is a pitfall that few writers succeed in escaping. The first use of money did not arise from any agreement among men, nor has the evolution of our system of exchange been one of successive displacements of one means of exchange by another. Like other institutions, both are slow and unconscious growths from conditions and actions which existed, in germ at least, in very early times. For all three methods of trading known to the modern world — barter, money, and credit — were present in societies of more or less primitive civilization. Some early peoples traded only by means of barter, while others used barter and money, or barter and credit, or all three means; and no society has abandoned one means of exchange because it resorted to another. Illustrations of these facts may be found in some of the data collected by Herbert Spencer.[1] Among the ancient Mexicans, for example, trade was carried on by both barter and money. The money system in use was what may be called a poly-commodity system, and comprised five articles: cocoa beans, small cotton cloths, gold dust in goose quills, copper, and tin. The Shillooks, a Nigritian tribe on the White Nile, are said to have made contracts valid for one month.[2] Among the inhabitants of Yucatan there was an active trade by means of a similar money system, and goods were sold on credit, without interest; while among another South American people, the Chibchaws, interest was charged. Among the Bondas, a tribe of lower Guinea, strings of beads and cowry shells were the media of exchange, while the ordinary media of the Fuegians consisted of small pieces of damoor cloth, tin rings,

[1] "Data of Sociology."

[2] Featherman, "Social History of the Races of Mankind," Vol. I., pp. 66, 410, 424, 731, 735; Vol. V., p. 601.

slaves, and glass beads. Such cases show clearly that the evolution of the system of exchange has not been everywhere along a single line. In some cases it was from barter to money, or money and credit; but in others, credit seems to be found as early as barter, and not infrequently more than one kind of money was used by primitive peoples. If, now, it be true that all the phases of the existing mechanism of exchange were recognized in more primitive societies, in what sense can we properly say that there has been an evolution in the system of exchange? In this sense: barter, the use of money in each single exchange, deferred money payments, and cancellation of indebtedness by credit paper, while used in all stages of social development, are used in different combinations, with different emphasis on the different members of the series among different peoples at the various stages of their civilization. It is a case of evolution in which all the organs are present, even in the most rudimentary form of the organism; but different organs and different groups of organs have been developed by different descendants of the original organism because they have lived under different conditions. The conditions of their industrial life have determined whether, among a given people, barter, or money, or credit, should be the most prominent feature of their system of exchange.

3. The First Service of the Money Article.— The use of an article, or articles, as intermediate goods implies that it performs the two services of promoting exchange and expressing value. There has been a good deal of discussion of the question which of these services was first recognized. Was the first use of an article as money due to the need for a means of exchange, or to that for a common measure of value? Each view has its advocates, but the question is not of much importance, and has but little interest for the economist. Some insist that the idea of facilitating exchange must have followed the use of the money commodity for comparing values; others, that the conception of a measure of value is necessarily involved in that of a medium of exchange. As Professor Bonamy Price puts the matter: "The savages who first took to cowry shells would hardly be up to such a thought as comparing goods with one another. The given measure was the consequence, not the motive, of the use of money." This hardly seems the reasonable view, for we cannot believe that a comparison of values did not take place, even in the earliest use of a medium of exchange. Rational beings, even though savages, would hardly exchange their goods without reference to their value. The fact that the money was itself an article of consumption is sufficient proof of this view.

4. The Selection of the Money Commodity. — Of more importance than the question which service of money was first recognized, is the inquiry: What causes led to the gradual narrowing of the circle of things used as money and the final settling upon one or two? In other words, what were the characteristics of the things most suitable for the purpose? Here again we are tempted to impute conscious choice to early man. We write or speak of his choosing this or that article as the exchange medium. But this cannot be the correct description of the facts. The result was reached unpurposively. The thing which was fittest at the time to serve as a medium of exchange, became the medium; but fittest can mean only that which caused less inconvenience than other things which were used for the same purpose. The reduction of the number of things used as money came from noticing the wider acceptance of some as compared with others. That commodity for which the demand was most general established itself, without previous reasoning, on the part of its users. Among the multitude of things which men exchanged there must always have been some which, from whatever cause, were more readily or more generally sought than others. It was doubtless soon seen that these articles were the best ones for a person to get if he sold his goods at a time when he did not want things for immediate consumption. For the articles in most general demand would be most easily exchanged later on for others, and therefore came to be looked on more or less as intermediate goods. In time this circle of articles became narrower by a process of unconscious selection as experience showed which of them best served the purpose of a commodity go-between in trade. Their character as consumption goods became relatively less important, and their character as intermediate goods more so. If this process of selection could be carried to its logical conclusion, it would result in finding for use as money an article which could not serve any purpose of direct consumption. The nearest approach to such a money is bank or government paper money. Moreover, that article which by its natural divisions was best suited to the prevailing range of values, was doubtless found to be more convenient than any other. It is very likely that these two attributes, general acceptability and convenient subdivision, were the qualities that had most to do with the final determination of the medium of exchange.

5. Kind of Article Selected. — The article which, in early times, was generally acceptable was not always the same. Sometimes it was a necessary of life, sometimes an ornament. Articles which served the latter purpose were likely to be accepted over a wider area, but the generalness of the acceptability of a particular thing depended mainly on the stage of economic life a community had reached. Skins and furs were always in demand in a community of hunters, cattle in one of shepherds, dates in a date country, and wampum beads, or cowry shells, or gold, where these were highly valued for personal adornment. As soon as it was recognized by all the people in a community that a certain article could be sold at any time, it became the medium of exchange, the money of that community. The article thus took on a new function. Instead of being simply a thing for direct consumption, it became in addition an instrumental good, a means of facilitating exchanges and measuring values. There was an added demand for it, and it therefore took on a higher exchange power.

6. Subdivision of the Money Article. — But money, chosen from such commodities as men in a low industrial society had at their disposal, had inconveniences of its own. Some people probably could not get an article which was at the same time in general demand and capable of convenient division. This difficulty seems to have been met by the early use of what may be called representative money. We know that the early Greek coins were stamped with the figure of an ox, and the early Chinese with that of a shirt.[1] One form of early Russian money consisted of small pieces of definite shapes cut from the skins of animals and passed from hand to hand as tokens of ownership of the whole skins. The ox, the shirt, the skin, were each too heavy or too large to pass about. A piece of metal shaped like the horse or the shirt, or a disk with pictures of these stamped on it, or a piece of skin shaped so that it would fit a hole in a certain complete skin, all obviously

[1] Dean, "History of Civilization," Vol. II., p. 76; *Nineteenth Cent. Mag.*, Vol. VI., p. 789.

mean that they entitled the receiver to expect goods of a value equivalent to that of the horse, or the ox, or the shirt. The value of the metal itself was, perhaps, not prominent in the minds of the exchangers at first, so that the money was representative. Not for some time was the value of the money thing taken for the measure of the value of the goods it bought.

Experience taught men in time that the metals, of one kind or another, served as a medium of exchange better than anything else that had been tried. For the metals, as Menger says, possess in higher degree than any other article the attribute of universal salableness. As the standard of life rose and the range of prices became higher, a more valuable unit was needed, and this need gradually led to the use of the most valuable metal available. Curiously enough, when the stage was reached where the most valuable came into use, it was found necessary to return to what has been called the poly-commodity system. The most valuable metal was not divisible into convenient units of small enough value to suit the scale of prices and the range of incomes. So modern man uses gold for his larger payments and more valuable exchanges, and one or two, or more, other articles for payments of value too small to admit of the use of the dearest metal.

7. Influence of the Market on the Evolution of Money.— The principal influence in the evolution of the money commodity was, of course, the growth of trade in volume and complexity. Indeed, it may be said that the development of the money system depended entirely on the development of the market. Barter was the earliest form of trade, because it is the form peculiarly suited to that stage of trade in which exchanges were few, local, and between individuals who wanted articles for direct personal use. In time, trade between individuals gave place to local markets on the borderland between tribes, and these markets, in some cases, became regular established fairs, in which the traders found profit by bringing the products of different localities to these centres of trade. This class it was whose experiences of the inconveniences of barter, and of the use of several things as money at the same time, gradually led to the various steps of progress that have been briefly described. So long as there was no separate trading class and no market in the community, individuals could as well as not use any one of a variety of goods to pay for their purchases. In local markets the adaptation of the single money medium would be a matter of great convenience, and in trade between different communities it would be almost a necessity.

8. The Complex Character of the Mechanism of Exchange. — We have seen that barter and credit, as well as money, are found as means of exchange in communities of a low degree of civilization, so that we cannot accept Hildebrand's cut-and-dried theory of simple steps from one to another of the three means. Of course the credit methods used in undeveloped communities were of a very simple character. We cannot in any case speak correctly of the existence of a credit system in such cases. So far as credit was used at all, it assumed the form of debt between individuals with direct personal payment by debtor to creditor. Cancellation of indebtedness was unknown, for the clearing system, even in its simplest form, belongs to a comparatively higher stage of civilization. The sphere of barter in the modern world is still somewhat extensive. In the country districts of even the most highly civilized countries the farmer still brings his produce to the country storekeeper to exchange it for what he needs, and the world is far from having abandoned the payment of labor in kind. But as the different countries become more thickly settled, and society becomes more integrated, we may look for still greater restrictions of the sphere of direct barter. Perhaps in the far future barter will cease to be important as compared with the total trade of the world. But here, as in many other cases, the simple method discovered by the world in its infancy will always prove serviceable, and perhaps necessary, to the world in its maturity. It is the simple which is universal.

CHAPTER III

COINAGE

REFERENCES: Evans, G. G., History of the United States Mint and Coinage; Hepburn, A. B., History of Coinage and Currency in the United States, Pt. I., Chs. 1, 2, 3; Jevons, W. S., Money and the Mechanism of Exchange, Ch. 7; Knies, K., Das Geld, 2d ed., pp. 192–210; Laughlin, J. L., Principles of Money, Ch. 2; Liverpool, Lord, Treatise of the Coins of the Realm; Muhleman, M., Monetary Systems of the World; Nicholson, J. S., Money and Monetary Problems, Pt. I., Ch. 3; Norman, J. H., The World's Metal Monetary Systems, pp. 8, 12, 45; Ridgeway, W., Origin of Metallic Currency and Weight Standards; Scott, W. A., Money and Banking, Ch. 5; Watson, D. K., History of American Coinage; White, H., Money and Banking, 2d ed., Ch. 2.

1. Natural Objects as Monetary Units. — Man naturally turned for his first money to something ready to his hand. The earliest forms of the medium of exchange were, therefore, natural objects, and the diversity of the things used for the purpose by different peoples is almost as great as that of the portable natural objects available. It was necessary, however, to find articles whose units were of as nearly equal purchasing power as possible, and also capable of subdivision to make purchases of different amounts. The first of these needs gradually led to the selection of natural objects which were approximately uniform in size, shape, and color. The need for money units of different purchasing power led sometimes to the use of different articles to furnish the necessary denominations. An ox, a cow, a sheep, would, for instance, be one gradation; and a buffalo skin, a beaver skin, a wolf's skin, another. For it was impossible to divide, for example, a beaver's skin, or an ox, or a shell, into parts to suit the amounts of different transactions. The division would have destroyed their value and their availability as money altogether. Sometimes, however, the difficulty was met by using an article, different grades of which were available. For instance, different sizes or colors of cowry shells, or of wampum beads, formed a scale of related values and served roughly the purpose of coins of denominations. In colonial times, in New England, the black wampum beads had a higher purchasing power than the white ones.

2. The Nature and Purpose of Coinage. — In time, of course, men undertook to meet the need for uniform and graded pieces of money by artificial methods. When they came to use a money substance capable of such manipulation, they made it into pieces to suit their purpose. This process of giving uniformity and thereby at the same time recognizability to money constitutes coinage in the widest sense of that word. According to Walker, the word may be defined as any method "of determining, for easy popular recognition, the quantity and quality of individual portions of that which has been adopted into use as money."[1]

But this definition is too broad. As it stands, it would include all kinds of money, of whatever material, whose character was indicated by a device of any kind, whether stamped, printed, or engraved. By the word "coinage" is now commonly meant the stamping of a piece of the metal for use as money so as to make known its denomination and value directly, or by indicating its weight and fineness.

3. The Evolution of Coinage. — It is not difficult to trace in a general way the steps in the evolution of coinage. The first effort was to give definite shape or size or weight to articles which were by nature uniform in their physical character. The cowry shells of the African negro, the wampum beads or shells of the North American Indian, the Abyssinians' cubes of salt, the Mexicans' quills, full of gold dust, square pieces of leather, and similar articles, all illustrate this effort. Nature furnished the homogeneity and cognizability which were necessary to make convenient money, and man gave shape to the articles.

The trick once learned was applied, in various ways, to all articles that successively came into use. When metal became the medium, it was made into wedges, "spikes, or small obelisks." Indeed, the word "coin" is derived from the Latin *cuneus*, a wedge, and originally meant a piece of metal so

[1] "Money," p. 164.

shaped. The modern representative of these spikes or obelisks is the bars which are used in making international money payments. Bars, it has been found, lose less by abrasion than coin, and hence are preferred for shipment.

It is not clear how ring money came unto use; but it may be that the easy bending of a thin spike into the handier form of a ring led to the change. In time the ring form suggested the plan of making metal disks with holes punched in them, probably for ease in carrying. The Chinese cash are of this form.

The transition from plain bars or disks, to bars or disks marked for recognition or guarantee, must have come early in monetary history; but the manufacture of stamped disks of the modern sort was a comparatively late development.[1] In the early days of the stamped coin only one side of the disk was marked; but the presence of an unmarked face caused loss because it tempted dishonest people to rub off or file off a portion of the metal. To prevent this, in time both sides were stamped, and at last, in order to check the dishonesty wholly, the edges were milled, and thus we come to the coin of our own days, the mechanical technique of which leaves little to be desired.

Coins have been made at different times of nearly all the commonly occurring metals. Iron, copper, lead, tin, platinum, silver, gold, and others, alone

[1] The first coins of this kind were attributed to Pheidon, King of Argos. See Grote, "History of Greece," Vol. III., 318.

or in composition, have all been used for the purpose. The choice of the metal depends mainly on the range of incomes and prices in a community. The higher these range, the more valuable the metal needed. It is for this reason that the coins in most common use in China are of copper; while in the advanced countries of Europe and America they are silver.

In a highly developed country, however, coins of several metals are needed to meet the demands of various classes with different scales of incomes and of purchases.

4. The Requisites of Good Coinage. — The requisites of good coinage are accuracy in composition and weight; convenience of shape, size, and weight; difficulty of counterfeiting; durability and cognizability. Great care is taken to produce coins as nearly perfect as possible in chemical composition and mechanical form. Gold and silver make more durable coins if they contain a definite proportion of copper in alloy, and accordingly are always so manufactured. But it is important that the proportions of the money metal and of the alloy shall be exactly the same in all coins of the same denomination. Otherwise some would be more valuable than others. This inequality of value owing to varying composition occurred not infrequently before the art of coinage was well developed. Equally important, for the same reason, is uniformity of weight in coins of the same kind. So difficult is it to attain this uniformity that all governments which coin money allow a slight variation from the exact weight prescribed for their coins. This variation is known as tolerance of the mint. In the coinage of the United States, for example, eagles and double eagles may vary one-half grain from the weight set by law. In practice, of course, this maximum variation does not often occur.

If coins always passed by tale, slight differences in weight would be of little consequence. But they pass this way only in the country in which they are coined. In the payment of foreign debts they pass only by weight. It follows that if the coins of the same denomination differ much in weight, the heavier are picked out for melting or for export. For the owner of the coins can either sell them as bullion or pass them by tale. If they contain so much bullion that they are more valuable in that form than for payment by tale, they will be melted or sent abroad. Either operation depletes the circulation of the country.

The best shape for coins is that which allows for the least loss from use and from fraudulent alteration, and at the same time affords most convenience in handling. Most coins nowadays are circular, but square, octagonal, oblong, and cubical coins are not unknown. The circular is the most convenient.

A good coin should not be too large nor too small for convenient handling. A five-dollar piece of silver would be clumsy, and our old one-dollar gold piece was too slight.

In order to prevent counterfeiting, the device on a coin should be difficult to imitate, but in spite of the high state of the art of coinage this result is hard to reach. The coin should be hard and tough enough to reduce loss by abrasion to a minimum, and yet malleable enough to take sharply the impression of the die. The durability of the coin is generally promoted by putting a rim around it somewhat above the face so that when the coin is laid down it rests on this rim. Finally, the shape, color, and device should show at once what the coin is and what its value. The device should be simple and legible.

5. Government Versus Private Coinage. — Coinage is now everywhere regarded as an attribute of sovereignty and is done by the government, although, historically, it did not originate with governments. Doubtless the fact that coinage could be so easily made a source of revenue had much to do with the early claim of governments to its monopoly; but there are better reasons for the monopoly than a custom derived from the claims of kings and overlords to exact tribute from trade. Since coins circulate among people who have no means of verifying the accuracy of the device upon them for certifying their weight and fineness, it is desirable that the devices shall be the same on all, and shall be made by an authority in which every one has confidence. The sovereign power is the only one that fulfils this condition. Moreover, if coinage were left to private enterprise, the difficulty of verification would make fraud easy. Light weight and spurious coins would be put into circulation, to the damage especially of the poor and ignorant. With competitive coinage more, perhaps, than in any other business would it be true that the character of competition sinks to the level of the most unscrupulous competitor. Finally, if a profit is to be made from coinage, this profit in equity belongs to the people.

6. The Charge for Coinage; Seigniorage. — Bullion may be turned into coin by governments either for their own account or for individuals; and they may do this free of charge or at a price which exactly covers the expense of coinage or which exceeds it. If the coinage is on government account, it is said to be limited; if it is done for any individual who offers bullion for the purpose, it is called free coinage. If the work is done without charge to those who offer bullion, the coinage is gratuitous. If a fee is exacted equal to the expense incurred, the charge is called brassage;[1] if in excess of this expense, it is called seigniorage. However, the name "seigniorage" is commonly used for both charges, and not infrequently describes simply the government profit on coinage whether the work is done for individuals or not.

The practice of charging for coinage varies. Most nations exact such a charge, but those most

[1] In compliment to Sir Thomas Brassey. Seigniorage derives its name from the old feudal exaction by the "seignieur" of a tribute from trade.

advanced try to keep the charge equal to the actual expense of the work. To charge more than this is wrong to the owner of the bullion, deceives the public, and leads to the evils of a debased currency. England is the most conspicuous, perhaps the only important, country in which no charge of any kind is made for the coinage of the standard metal.

7. The Arguments for and against a Charge for Coinage.—Several arguments are advanced in favor of brassage. In the first place, it is urged that a coin is a manufactured article, and that to charge for its making "puts the cost of coinage where it belongs." It is questionable, however, whether this is strictly true. The convenience to the public at large, and to traders and producers other than the bullion owners, which comes from the existence of coin is very great. It is a fair question whether they should not pay part at least of the cost of manufacturing the coin.

A second argument advanced by the advocates of brassage is that if there is a charge for coinage, coins are less likely to be exported than bullion to discharge a foreign indebtedness, because with brassage the metal would be more expensive as coin than as bullion. Closely allied with this argument is a third point, that brassage prevents the melting down of coin by jewellers because they will not submit to the loss of the brassage charge.

Those who take the contrary view, however, and insist that coinage of the standard metal should be gratuitous, point out, in the first place, that if a charge is made, the principal measure of value will not be perfect. Inasmuch as cost of coinage will vary in different places, the same amount of gold will be embodied in coins of different values. In the second place, it is urged that if gold in the form of coin has the same value, weight for weight, as in the form of bullion, when prices change so that less money is needed, the coinage will adapt itself much more rapidly and with a nicer adjustment to the new level of prices. It is further urged that a coin of the country which makes no brassage charge is far more likely to be used by the people of other countries. That this has happened with the English sovereign is undeniable. The use of its coins in foreign countries may help the trade of a country by making people familiar with its money. "Such circulation, it is claimed, will amount to a demand for the trade of the country conducting the coinage, which it can very well afford to pay for, as truly as a merchant can afford to pay for advertisements in a newspaper, or a circus manager for having his fearful and wonderful pictures displayed along the street."[1] A fourth argument used by advocates of gratuitous coinage is, that if merchants should find it necessary to export coin, on account of the difficulty of getting bullion, they would add the loss of the amount charged to the price of their imported goods and so transfer the loss to consumers.

[1] Walker, "Money," 185.

Finally, the advocates of gratuitous coinage insist that the loss by export is less than may be supposed, for the reason that a great many of the exported coins are eventually returned. This is certainly true in the case of English sovereigns and American eagles. It has become a practice in various countries to hold imported coins for export when the tide of trade turns.

What has been said thus far about coinage and seigniorage applies to the principal coins of a country. Besides these, which comprise the standard unit and its multiples, every country needs coins of smaller denominations, submultiples of the standard unit. These are called subsidiary coins, and may or may not be made of the standard metal. Usually, even in gold standard systems, the subsidiary coins are of silver, because coins of the small value required would be inconveniently small and light in weight. Coins of the smallest denomination are usually copper.

The number of standard coins, as dollars, which may be minted from an ounce of gold, is fixed by law, and is the mint price of gold. This mint price has no relation to the purchasing power of gold. It depends entirely on the amount of gold put into the unit of money.

When coinage is gratuitous, the owner of bullion is entitled, in theory, to take this bullion to the mint and get back its full value in coin. He may have to wait, however, until his metal is coined; and if so, he loses interest on it in the interval. To avoid this delay the English law requires the Bank of England to buy all gold offered at £3, 17*s.* 9*d.* per ounce, which is 1½*d.* less than the bullion owner would get if he waited for his gold to be coined. This 1½*d.* is to cover the expense to the bank for interest and the labor of weighing and assaying the metal. When the bank is in need of gold, it sometimes foregoes part of this fee and pays more per ounce than £3, 17*s.* 9*d.* The bank is then said to pay a premium on gold. The expression is not technically correct, since one gold sovereign is not worth more than another. It simply means that the bank's need for gold is so great that it is willing to forego part of the profit on its purchases.

In the United States the owner of bullion does not have to wait for his coin, but he must pay for the alloy.

CHAPTER IV

THE CURRENCY AND THE PRINCIPLES OF ITS CIRCULATION

REFERENCES: Farrer, Sir T. H., What do we pay With? Ch. 4; Giffen, R., Gresham's Law, Econ. Journ., Vol. I., p. 304; Jevons, W. S., Money and the Mechanism of Exchange, Ch. 8; Laughlin, J. L., History of Bimetallism in the United States, pp. 26–30, 65–69, and elsewhere; The Principles of Money, Chs. 5, 12, 15; Moses, B., Legal Tender Notes in California, Quar. Journ. Econ., October, 1892; Nicholson, J. S., Money and Monetary Problems, Pt. I., Ch. 4; Report of the Comptroller of the Currency, 1896, Vol. I., pp. 57–97; Report of the Indianapolis Monetary Commission, 1898, pp. 113–130; Scott, W. A., Money and Banking, Ch. 2; Walker, F. A., Money, pp. 193–195; White, H., Money and Banking, 2d ed., p. 25.

1. Classification of Media of Exchange. — The medium of exchange, or the circulating medium, comprises all the instrumental goods used for paying debts or purchasing commodities. Payment may be made, indeed, with an article which to the receiver is a direct consumption good rather than an instrumental good, or one which he uses by passing it on for his payments in turn. In that case the article is not part of the medium of exchange.

Some of the articles which enter into the medium of exchange are generally current, or commonly accepted in payment, without any reference to any characteristic except their passableness. These articles constitute the currency. Other portions of the medium of exchange do not have a circulation which can properly be called general; they are accepted primarily because of the credit of the issuer, and are not currency. Accordingly, we may classify the media of exchange as follows: —

(*a*) The medium of general circulation, or the currency, including (1) metallic money; (2) inconvertible paper money; (3) certificates of deposit of metallic money; (4) credit paper which has a general circulation, as convertible notes.

(*b*) The medium of restricted circulation, or non-currency, including (1) credit paper which does not circulate generally, as checks and drafts, representing bank deposits; and bills of exchange, representing goods; (2) securities representing goods or property.

It is obvious, then, that the currency is not simple and homogeneous, but complex and heterogeneous. In most countries we find coins of different metals and of different denominations passing side by side with paper money, and with credit paper of private, public, or semi-public origin. There are, indeed, occasional historical instances in which the currency of a community or country has consisted of a single article. This was probably the case in ancient Lacedæmon, where iron money was for a long time used alone, while in some other ancient states copper was used by itself. Ordinarily, however, the only cases among modern nations in which we find a single thing used as money are those in which the currency consists of very depreciated paper money. For example, during our Civil War practically the only circulating medium in the United States was government and bank notes. The copper cents, and perhaps some silver, remained in use; but the fact that notes were issued for sums as small as five cents is the best evidence that coins of that denomination were out of circulation.

2. Adaptation of the Medium of Exchange to the Scale of Incomes and Prices. — It is not an accident, of course, that the medium of exchange is generally composite. It is due principally to the need of adapting the currency to a variety of grades of incomes and payments. A minor cause is the necessity for having coins convenient to handle. One kind of currency would not be convenient for payments of all amounts. A cheap metal would be inconvenient for making large payments; a dear one, for making those of small amount. The Chinese use "cash," each of which is equal in value to a fraction of an American cent, because the scale of ordinary purchases in China makes coins of that small purchasing power suitable for daily use. If we with our higher range of incomes and prices should attempt in this country to use coins of so low a denomination, we would experience great inconvenience from having to carry about large amounts of them to make ordinary payments. On the other hand, it would be impracticable for the Chinese to use gold for their small purchases.

The best medium of exchange, therefore, provides instruments of exchange of different kinds, each kind adapted, on the whole, to different scales of payments. To be sure, if paper money alone is used, it can be issued in any denomination with equal convenience; but, as we shall see, such a system involves dangers which make it extremely inadvisable. Accordingly, the circulating medium of most countries comprises metal money, paper money, and private credit instruments. As a rule, the metallic money consists, first, of the principal, or standard, money, usually gold or silver; second, of subsidiary coins, which are usually of a different metal from the standard and dependent on the standard for their nominal purchasing power. Where gold is the standard money, the smallest gold coin is usually of a denomination such as the majority of people will be able to use in their larger ordinary payments. In the United States the smallest coin of gold is the two-and-one-half dollar piece. Gold dollars were formerly coined, but were found too small for easy handling and were easily lost. In England, the smallest gold coin is the half-sovereign; in Germany, the five-mark piece; and in France, the five-franc piece.

The subsidiary coins are subdivisions of the standard coin and are generally silver and copper. The smallest denominations are sometimes called minor coins. In the United States, subsidiary coins, like the half-dollars, quarter-dollars, and dimes, are of silver; the five-cent piece is nickel, and the cents are copper. Other countries, as England, Germany, and France, use silver and copper for their smaller coins.

Paper money is used both by itself and in combination with coins. The technical advantages of paper money are its convenience to handle, its easy and cheap manufacture, and the possibility of making it of any denomination. It may be issued by the government, by banks, or by other corporations. In the United States paper money is issued both by the government and the banks. The same is true in Canada; but in England, Germany, and France the paper money is all bank money.

3. The Credit Portion of the Medium of Exchange. — Besides the kinds of medium of exchange thus far mentioned, there are certain private credit instruments which are used to effect exchanges. Broadly speaking, these include bank deposits represented by checks, bank drafts, whether written or telegraphic, bills of exchange, and negotiable securities. In so far as the last mentioned are used in making exchanges and effecting payments, they may be properly regarded as part of the medium of exchange.

Deposit currency, consisting of credits of depositors in banks, and represented in circulation by checks and drafts and similar paper, has come to play a part of immense importance in modern business, far exceeding that played by notes. Some idea of this importance may be had from the fact that, as shown by the clearing-house returns of the United States, transactions aggregating $114,068,837,569 were performed by means of this kind of currency in 1903. At various times, in England and in our own country, efforts have been made to determine the proportion of payments made by this part of the medium of exchange, by determining in what proportion it enters into the receipts of banks. All these examinations have shown that the receipts of the banks are over 90 per cent. in credit paper and less than 10 per cent. in all kinds of money. The most extensive examination into the matter was made in the United States in 1896, and secured separate returns of the deposits of people engaged in retail trade, wholesale trade, and all other businesses. It appeared from the figures that at that time about half the volume of retail payments were made with private credit currency, and more than nine-tenths of the wholesale business. After making allowances for errors and omissions it seemed from that examination that perhaps 70 or 75 per cent. of the payments in settlement of mercantile business in the United States at that time were made with checks and other similar paper.[1] Of a total volume of clearings of the New York clearing house,

[1] See Report of the Comptroller of the Currency, 1896, and *The Journal of Political Economy*, March, 1897.

of $70,833,655,940, in 1903, only 4.68 per cent. were settled with money.

4. Securities as a Part of the Medium of Exchange. — Another important part of the modern medium of exchange consists of negotiable securities, especially the bonds and stocks of corporations and the bonds of cities and states. When used as currency, these have a certain resemblance to paper money. Paper money represents or gives command over goods in general; securities represent or give command over certain general classes of goods. In other words, they avoid, although far less completely, the lack of coincidence in barter. Their use for the settlement of debts is confined, of course, to a special field, their service being mainly in the settlement of transactions in such paper itself, and, indirectly, in the settlement of the balances of international trade. We shall examine in another chapter the part they play in this latter matter. In the settlement of stock exchange transactions the sales of stock by the brokers are set off against their purchases, in the stock exchange clearing house, and the balance is paid in money or checks. Thus in New York "on the single day of January 23, 1899, there were sold 5,006,900 shares of stock valued at $350,900,000 by the transfer of only 735,000 shares and the payment of balances amounting to $724,500." [1]

[1] Charles A. Conant in *The Annals of the American Academy*, September, 1899, p. 44.

5. Standard Money, Money of Account, and Medium of Exchange. — A distinction must be made between standard money, money of account, and current money. The standard may be gold, the money of account may be silver, and the current medium of exchange may be paper. The standard money is that to whose value the value of the other kinds of money is referred for determination, but it may not be coined. The money of account is that in which prices are usually expressed, and the current money is that in which actual payments are made. In the United States, for example, the standard is the gold dollar, 25.8 grains of gold nine-tenths fine, which is no longer issued. In some parts of the country payments were formerly reckoned in a money of account spoken of as bits and shillings.[1] The public accounts of New York State were kept in pounds, shillings, and pence[2] until 1796, although the standard from 1792 was the dollar. Payments were made in various kinds of paper and foreign coins. In England the standard is the gold sovereign, equivalent at par to $4.86\frac{3}{4}$. Accounts, however, are sometimes reckoned in guineas,[3] sometimes in pounds, and sometimes in shillings, while the money actually used in payment may be

[1] A bit and a shilling were each $12\frac{1}{2}$ cents.

[2] First Annual Report of the Comptroller, *New York Assembly Journal*, Vol. XVI., p. 20. The New York pound was $2.50, eight shillings to the dollar.

[3] Twenty-one shillings.

either gold, silver, or paper. The Old English, or Anglo-Saxon, unit of payment was a pound of silver. The money of account was the shilling, and the current coins were silver pence and half-pence. Similar instances can be found in other countries.

6. Legal Tender Money. — The currency may include legal tender money and money that is not legal tender. Legal tender money is money the offer or tender of which in payment of a debt constitutes, under the law, a sufficient discharge of the obligation. The declaration that such and such a thing shall be legal tender is not necessary to its use as a medium of payment, although it doubtless facilitates that use. A legal tender law prevents uncertainty in contracts, and in a measure protects ignorant and weak creditors from being imposed on with spurious money. It does not, however, prevent people from making contracts to be settled by other means of payment.

Under a legal tender law, the standard money is usually made unlimited legal tender, while the subsidiary money is limited to payments of certain amounts. In the United States, for example, gold coins and silver dollars are unlimited legal tender. The subsidiary coins, half and quarter dollars and dimes, are legal tender to the amount of ten dollars, while the five-cent piece and the copper cent are legal tender for twenty-five cents.

7. Systems of Metallic Currency. — The system of metallic currency in use at any time depends on the development of coinage and on the scale of incomes and prices. Uncoined metal and crudely fashioned coins pass by weight; those more accurately made, by tale. A legal tender system by tale could not well be used until coinage was perfected. A single metal would serve a community with a uniform scale of incomes and prices, while more than one would best answer the purpose where considerable differences exist in the economic conditions of different social classes. Accordingly, the possible systems of metallic currency fall into five classes. Jevons [1] describes them as currency by weight, unrestricted currency by tale, the single legal tender system, the multiple legal tender system, and the composite legal tender system. Under the first of these the government simply provides a system of weights and measures, and people who have payments to make use these in weighing out, or measuring out, the metal used as money. This is undoubtedly the oldest method of payment with money. Some of our monetary terms, like the English pound, the French livre, the Hebrew shekel, the Greek and Roman talent, and others, were originally names of units of weight.

In the system of unrestricted currency by tale, the metal is coined into pieces of uniform weight and fineness, their value, or their weight and fineness, being stamped upon them, and they are passed from hand to hand on the basis of this

[1] "Money and the Mechanism of Exchange," Ch. ix.

certification. The nearest approach to this system to-day is in the use, for international payments, of gold bars made at the government mints.

Under the single legal tender system only one metal is coined as legal tender. The iron money of Sparta is an example. Such a system is suitable for a community of simple economic life. Under the legal multiple tender system, coins of different metals are used at a fixed ratio and each is an unlimited legal tender. Bimetallism is the most familiar example. Under the composite legal tender system one coin is unlimited legal tender, while others are so only to a limited extent. This is the system of advanced countries to-day.

8. Systems of Paper Currency. — There are three systems of paper money, — representative paper money, fiduciary paper money, and fiat paper money. The first is made up of notes which are receipts for metal deposited with the issuer of the paper, either in the form of coined or of uncoined metal. Credit paper money consists of notes promising to pay, with or without conditions, specified sums of metallic money. Fiat paper money consists of printed statements that the notes are of such and such denominations, or represent such and such sums of metallic money. They are always in the form of promises to pay, but are not intended to be paid. Any one of these kinds of paper money may be legal tender, and any one of them may be issued either by governments or by banks. Not infrequently both metallic and paper money are legal tender at the same time. This is the case in the United States, where gold and silver are legal tender equally with greenbacks, or government notes issued during the Civil War, and the treasury notes issued against the deposits of silver bullion under the Sherman law of 1890.[1]

9. Fundamental Causes of Circulation of Media of Exchange. — The underlying cause of the circulation of any and all of the kinds of media of exchange is confidence in their acceptability. The bases, or the causes of this confidence, are four: (*a*) belief in social stability, or the persistence of social habit; (*b*) law, or the authority of a particular government; (*c*) the credit of the issuer, whether a public body or a private person or corporation; and, finally, (*d*) direct agreement among individuals. Each of these forces promotes the circulation of a different kind of money. The persistence of social habit is the primary cause of the circulation of commodity money. As usually put, a commodity money, like gold, is more widely acceptable than any other kind because it has value independent of that which arises from its use as money. But this value can be present only so long as the demand for the article continues. To accept it in payment is, therefore, to show one's belief that the general desire to own this particular commodity is permanent; that men will continue

[1] By the currency law of 1900 these notes are being replaced with silver dollars.

to act in the future as they have acted in the past; that social habit is persistent.

The second basis of confidence which may lead one to accept a certain thing in payment of debts due him, or of sales made by him, is the stability of the particular government which issues it as money. People believe that the provisions made to create a demand for this kind of money, by way of receiving it for taxes, making it legal tender, and so on, will lead to its acceptance, although it has no direct utility and no specific value. Or else they think the law can enforce its acceptance.

In the next place, an article may be accepted in payment of debt or sales because of confidence in the integrity and stability of an individual or a corporation. The receiver believes that the issuer will redeem the article; in other words, guarantees that it will be accepted by himself, if not by some one else, in exchange for articles of direct utility. The cause of circulation here is commercial credit. Examples of such media of exchanges are checks and bank notes.

In the fourth place, the confidence which leads one to accept a given article in payment may be the direct agreement of the individuals of a certain social or industrial group so to accept it. There is hardly to be found any historical illustration of such an agreement. Some writers have written on the origin of money in a way to imply the existence of such a convention or agreement, but there is no evidence that this has ever been made. The nearest approach to it is, perhaps, the use of checks by gamblers in settling their gambling claims. A case resembling such an agreement is found, also, in the action of the nations that composed the Latin Union. If international bimetallism is ever established, we shall have another remote analogy. The cause of circulation in this case will be international agreement, enforced in each country by its own laws.

It is not a matter of concern to us at present to consider which one of these causes of circulation may fairly be considered the best on which to rest the medium of exchange. If any one of them is present, the article for which it causes a demand will serve as a medium of exchange. The first and most general principle of circulation, then, is this: The primary cause of the circulation of money is the receiver's belief that others will take it from him in turn. The area of circulation depends on the basis of this confidence which induces acceptability, and may vary from the small group, in which the cause of acceptability is the personal integrity of the issuer, to the larger group influenced by political and legal authority, or to the largest group which takes in payment only articles whose acceptability is the result of social habit.

10. Gresham's Law; its Operation and Limitations. — Although an article may be generally acceptable as money, different portions of it may have different degrees of acceptability. If coins of the same denomination differ in weight or fineness, the better ones will serve not only for ordinary payments, as do the inferior coins, but also for foreign payments or for making more valuable articles in the arts. They are likely, therefore, to be treated as bullion and used for export or in the arts. Not every one, of course, who handles coins lays aside the better ones in order to make a profit from their greater value. This is done by money dealers who handle large amounts, so that a small profit on each coin yields a large aggregate gain. Their work of selecting and withdrawing from circulation the more valuable coins is known as picking and culling the coin. So likely is the elimination of the more valuable coins from circulation to occur, if there is much variation in coinage, that it is commonly said that "bad money drives out good money." This statement of the phenomenon is known as Gresham's law, from Sir Thomas Gresham, who called the attention of modern students anew to the occurrence more sharply than any writer up to his time had done. The phenomenon was known, however, long before Gresham's time, although perhaps not scientifically formulated.[1]

[1] That it was known as early as the time of Aristophanes, at least, is shown by the following passage in the "Frogs" (lines 717 ff.): —

"Oftentimes we have reflected on a similar abuse
In the choice of men for office and of coins for common use;
For your old and standard pieces, valued and approved and tried,
Recognized in every realm for trusty stamp and pure assay,
Are rejected and abandoned for the trash of yesterday;
For the vile, adulterate issue, drossy, counterfeit, and base,
Which the traffic of the city passes current in their place."

The second principle of circulation is, then: If a money of one material is in use, the less valuable portions of it tend to remain in circulation, and the more valuable to disappear.

There is an apparent paradox in the operation of Gresham's law. Ordinarily, people are led by their self-interest to choose the commodity which is better and reject the one which is worse. In the case of money, however, they seem to keep the bad and reject the good. The apparent paradox is easily explained if we regard the owner of money as a seller rather than as a buyer. He keeps the inferior money because it will serve his purpose for payment; he sells the better goods because he can get more for them in that way. But it is not always the case that two articles which differ somewhat in quality, yet are so nearly alike that either serves fairly well the purpose of the other, will command different prices. They will sell at the same price if the demand is strong enough to need all of both, provided the price is high enough to offset the superior cost of production of the one which is more expensive. This is the case with coins of unequal bullion value. If the demand is not large enough to use all of both, part or all of the better coins will be withheld from circulation by tale, and held at a higher price as bullion. We thus find, as a limitation of Gresham's law, the condition that the aggregate of good and bad coins must be in excess of the country's need for circulating medium. To put the matter in another way, we may say that if business is so large and brisk that it needs all of both kinds of coin to perform exchanges, the demand for them for monetary purposes raises the value of the inferior coins to equality with the bullion value of the full weight coins. This cannot be exceeded because the heavier coins will not be taken anywhere for more than their bullion value. If there is any further increase in the purchasing power of coin, foreign coins or bullion will be imported, as we shall see later, and the value of the home coin will not be able to rise above the high-water mark of the value of the bullion in the full weight coins.

Again, an inferior money will not circulate in opposition to custom or public opinion. Perhaps the most notable historical instance of this fact was found in California during the Civil War. The people of California would have none of the greenbacks issued by the government; public opinion was against their use. In consequence, gold continued to be the money of California while the rest of the country was using paper. Sometimes, too, a law which requires the use of a specified kind of money may prevent its entire displacement by an inferior currency. An illustration of this is found in the state of affairs that prevailed in this country in the early fifties. Through the operation of the independent treasury law, which forbade the government to keep the public money in banks or to accept bank notes in payment of public dues, gold coin was kept in circulation in spite of the tendency exerted by the small notes of the banks to drive it out.[1]

The last illustration given suggests a wider application of Gresham's law. It operates not only when the currency is of one material, with its parts of different values, but also when the currency consists of two or more forms of money such as gold and paper, or gold and silver, provided both forms are legally usable in the payment of debts.

There are many historical instances of the loss of metal money by a country on account of the issue of paper. In our own country the most notable occurrence of the kind was the suspension of specie payment and loss of gold on account of the issue of greenbacks during the Civil War. A less obvious, but equally correct, illustration is found, however, in our monetary experience under the operation of the Sherman law of July 14, 1890. According to that law the Secretary of the Treasury was compelled to buy four million ounces of silver monthly, and to issue notes on the basis of the bullion thus secured. It was the anticipation of the friends of the measure that these notes, when they went into circulation, would increase the currency of the country and raise the level of prices. Their issue had no such result. The export of gold from the time the notes began to be issued until July, 1893, almost exactly

[1] Kinley, "The Independent Treasury of the United States," p. 62.

equalled the amount of notes put in circulation. The gold exports were $141,017,158, while the note issue was $140,661,694.

Gresham's law operates because most people are completely under the influence of habit in their use of money, and only a few keenly alive to their interest in the matter. Few people have any knowledge of the laws enacted to regulate circulation. They take a coin or a note because it looks familiar. A coin may be overweight, but most of us take no notice of the fact and seek no profit from it. The force of habit in money matters has sometimes been curiously shown by the difficulty of getting new coinage into circulation. Austria, for example, has found it necessary to coin the Maria Theresa dollar down to a very late date because the people of certain countries with which she trades have been so long used to it that they would use no other. Similarly the Spanish silver dollar has been hard to displace in some parts of the Orient.

We thus see that Gresham's law needs to be carefully stated in order to make it describe the facts accurately. It is really a law of tendency, and must be stated hypothetically. We might put it thus: If more than one form of money is legally usable in a country, and if one of these is more valuable for some other use than it is for making exchanges, then the inferior portion of the currency will supplant the superior to the extent that the two portions together exceed the need for currency in the country, provided that public opinion or any other economic force does not interfere with the operation of the self-interest of dealers in money.

Gresham's law is really a limited statement of a more general principle, which may be thus formulated: When a community in which competition is free and intelligent has a choice of means of payment, it will use the least expensive which will serve its purpose under existing circumstances. Or, still more generally: In a community in which competition is free and intelligent there is a constant effort to perform every economic service by the agency which yields the largest net results.

CHAPTER V

SERVICES AND NATURE OF MONEY

REFERENCES: Hadley, A. T., Economics, pp. 181–185; Indianapolis Monetary Commission, Report of, 1898, Pt. I., §§ 1–18; Jevons, W. S., Money and the Mechanism of Exchange, Chs. 3, 5, 6; Knies, K., Das Geld, pp. 146–237; Laughlin, J. L., Principles of Money, Ch. 1; Laveleye, E. C., La Monnaie et le Bimétallisme International, Ch. 2; Nicholson, J. S., Money and Monetary Problems, 5th ed., Pt. I., Ch. 2; Scott, W. A., Money and Banking, Ch. 1; Walker, F., Money, Chs. 1, 2; White, H., Money and Banking, Ch. 1.

1. Definition of Money determined by its Services. — The word "money," like so many other terms in economics, has different meanings, both in popular and in scientific usage. It is clear from what has been already said that no definition of money can be framed on the basis of the material of which it is made. Whatever view is taken of the nature of money must be derived from the determination of its services or functions. To these services we must now turn our attention.

The functions of money may be described as essential, or those which are necessary in all economic stages; as derived, or those which flow from, or are dependent on, the essential services; and as contingent, or those which flow from the conditions of a particular economic stage.

2. Essential Services of Money. — The essential services of money are measurement of value and facilitation of exchange. The earliest service that can be called properly a monetary service was to enable an individual to buy directly what he wanted. In other words, the service rendered was to make it unnecessary for each individual to seek a buyer for his goods in the quantities that he had to sell, who had at the same time the articles he wanted in the quantities he wished to buy. The money article remedied this lack of coincidence in barter. This service is fundamental whatever the stage of economic life, but is more important the farther the division of labor is carried. The extent to which this division can go, indeed, depends on the extent of the "general acceptability" of money. In an advanced economy, therefore, the emphasis must be laid, so far as concerns this function, on the fact that money promotes the division of labor by facilitating the distribution of its products. The money is a general exchange and circulating medium. It performs this service because it is accepted without question. It is taken because of the knowledge that others will take it in turn. There is no thought in the mind of him who has it that the ability to part with it depends on the promise of any third party to redeem it, or that it can be used for another purpose if it fails to pass. Its success in doing its work depends simply and solely upon the fact that it is in demand for the purpose of doing that work. A person who accepts money in discharge of obligations due him has no thought of recourse in case of its failure to pass.

The second essential service of money, that of measuring value, is inseparable from the discharge of the first, and doubtless is as old. Certainly if a person takes a thing in exchange for goods which have a certain value to him, intending to give away the thing he takes for some third article, he naturally expects to get something that will cause him no loss. He would not sell his goods without comparing their value with the purchasing power of the money in terms of the things he wanted to buy.

There has been some dispute as to the nature of this service of measuring value, some question whether it is truly a function of money to measure value. Some writers insist that money serves simply as a common denominator of value; that it is a term in units of which the values are declared, and does not in any true sense measure. This position has arisen partly from a wrong theory of the nature of value, and partly from an effort to find room under this theory for inconvertible paper money, and other things which perform the functions of money, but are said to have "no value in themselves." It is argued that because paper money has virtually no cost of production, it has, therefore, no value, and cannot serve as a measure of value; that, moreover, all values are ratios of exchange, and that ratios cannot be measured, although they may be compared. But value in the sense of ratio of exchange is merely relative value. If we use the word in this sense, regarding value as a ratio whose numerator is a number of units of some article and whose denominator is the monetary unit, then we may say that money is a common denominator of value. In other words, money properly may be called a common denominator of *relative* values. But relative values are simply the ratios of quantitative, or real, values. For value is best conceived of, not as a ratio, but as the quantity of marginal utility of an economic good. Now a quantity may certainly be measured, but the unit of measure must be of the same nature as the thing measured — in this case, a selected amount of value. The amount of value in a chosen quantity of any article may be this unit. Now any article, including money, for which there is an effective demand, has value; and consequently the value in a certain amount of money may serve as a unit of measure of the values of other things. When, therefore, we say that money is a measure of value, we are using a short expression for the statement that the amount of value in a unit of money may be taken as a unit of measure of the value of goods. We say, for brevity, that the money measures the value, just as we say that an arc measures an angle, although we know that strictly the unit of measure of angular space must itself be an angle.

Value is present in inconvertible paper money as truly as in commodity money, like gold and silver. Commodity money, however, has other than monetary uses. It has direct utility, and therefore value independently of its use as money. But part of its value is certainly due to the demand for it for monetary purposes. Inconvertible paper money has no direct utility and no specific value. Its value is derived wholly from the demand for it for monetary purposes. The difference between the two kinds of money is, therefore, a difference in the bases of their value. The difference is not that one has value and the other has not. Value is present in both, and can be used to measure value in other things. So far as concerns the *fact* of the performance of the function, it makes no difference that the value of the commodity money is in its origin twofold, while that of the paper money is single.

Money expresses the value of other things in prices. Price is, generally speaking, the amount of value contained in goods expressed in units of value of one article. As the thing which is commonly used for the purpose is money, we are accustomed to think of price as the amount of money which a thing will bring or which is necessary to buy it.

3. The Derived Functions of Money. — The second class of the functions of money are involved in the discharge of the essential services that have been described. They are, to serve as a standard of deferred payments, to transfer value, and to store value.

The function of acting as a medium of payment of debts is not quite identical with that of facilitating exchange. An article may serve as a means of payment without being a medium of general circulation and exchange. Wherever a credit system exists, a considerable time may elapse between the creation of a debt and its payment. As it is always desired to have the payment of a debt return an amount of goods which will restore the equities between creditor and debtor, if these have been disturbed by changes in the value of money, the article used as a means of payment serves as a standard of deferred payments.

Closely connected with the services of transferring value from time to time is that of doing so from place to place. Money serves both for the place-transfer and the time-transfer of purchasing power. Both functions require that money shall serve as a storer of value. Objection is sometimes made to classing this as a money function, on the ground that a thing which is storing value cannot be serving as a medium of exchange. But an article cannot act as a medium of exchange unless it retains its value, and this retention of value through a period of several exchanges is certainly storing value. The objection would limit money to what was in actual circulation. But is so-called idle money not money? Are the coins which the child has gathered in his little box not money? Is money money only when it is in use? To say this is to confuse the thing with its service. Steam is steam in a locomotive cylinder even when the locomotive is at rest, and the locomotive itself, though standing still, is yet a locomotive. Surely we must insist that the idle gold held by banks be called money, although for the time being it is only serving the purpose of conserving value, until the time comes when its potential force shall become active.

Since money is generally acceptable and valuable, it embodies value in its most general form. To transfer money is to transfer generic value, to pass over wealth and capital in their most mobile form. It is because it represents generic value that money is a good storer of value. Any durable article might be used to store value, but it is the value of money only that we can be sure will keep. For the demand for other things may fall away, but money is always acceptable.

4. Contingent Functions of Money. — The contingent functions of money are those which arise from the characteristics of the stage of economic life in which it is used. They are at least four in number: the distribution of social income, the equalization of marginal utility in expenditures, the furnishing of the basis of a credit system, and the imparting of a general form to capital.

Money is a distributer of the product of social industry. Without money, or its equivalent, the apportionment of the product among the various producers would be impossible in a stage of highly specialized labor, for otherwise each would have to get in kind his proportion of everything he helped to produce. Even then he would find it necessary to exchange for other things, since few men consume what they produce. Money enables each to get what he wants.

The second of the contingent services is to enable individuals so to adjust their expenditure that each unit of money spent shall bring them goods of the same marginal utility, and thus give them the largest value for their money. That is, with money each one can buy the goods that afford him the largest consumer's surplus of utility. In this way a money income brings to most individuals gains which are no man's losses.

Money further serves as a basis of the vast structure of modern credit. It is a cash reserve to insure solvency, to guarantee the payment of the balances of credit transactions. "If we have a proper cash reserve of money, we can use other things as media of exchange. . . . If we have not an adequate reserve of capital in the form of money, no credit system, however well devised, will act as a substitute."[1] The money itself is not intended for use as a medium of payment. It is used to create other media of payment, and is itself called into direct use as such only when in the round of business these other media fail to balance one another. This contingency is likely to happen at any time and, indeed, is happening all the time. Provision to meet it is necessary in order to prevent the collapse of the superstructure of credit media

[1] Hadley, "Economics," p. 181.

of payment. This use of money as a reserve for credit payments has grown greatly in comparatively recent times, and is due partly to the modern method of doing business on borrowed capital. It manifests itself in the great development of banking which the past century has seen. In earlier times the principal form of credit paper was the bill of exchange, which rested for its security on the goods it represented. Now the check, which represents the vast volume of bank deposits, is doubtless the most widely used form of credit paper.

5. Money the Embodiment of Generic Value. — Finally, modern business utilizes money, as the embodiment of generic value, to give a liquid form to capital. There is always a certain amount of capital which is actually, or potentially, free to seek new employment. It can do so quickly because it can be kept in a state of high mobility in the form of money. Does a new field of enterprise open? Money flows at once into that field. It is not, of course, meant that money, as money, is a productive agent. Money flows into the field, in the sense that it is passed in exchange for materials and machines which can be used in the new field. These either come from other uses, or, in a brief interval of time, they are made ready for use in the new field. Thus money extends production and exercises an influence to keep it at its maximum. Hence it is that nowadays a great aim in the business world is to get command over money, as general capital, in order to take advantage of any opportunity to turn that capital to productive uses in any direction.

Since money is the embodiment of generic value, it confers on its possessor a social and economic power which attaches to no other form of wealth. It gives him general command over the goods and services of others, so far as these are for sale. His market is the whole field of salable goods, whereas that of the would-be seller of other articles is limited. He has a certain monopoly advantage, arising from the universality and certainty of the demand for money.

6. Definitions of Money. — These being the services of money, how shall we define the term so that it shall be sufficiently exclusive? The word is used in various ways, and it is quite difficult, if not impossible, to frame a definition which will conform to the different uses and at the same time satisfy the demands of logical definition.

In common usage there are three general meanings, or groups of meanings, for the word money. It is sometimes used to describe all media of exchange, — gold, silver, paper, checks, bank drafts or the deposits which they represent, commercial bills of exchange, and even corporation stocks. These things all effect exchanges; in a way they all relieve the difficulties of barter. This definition, however, is too inclusive. Its error lies in including media of exchange which are not general circulating media. If this particular definition is taken, one must include several things which effect exchanges because those who accept them know that they have a recourse to recover their goods if these things should fail to pass. These articles do not attain general circulation, they do not attain the character of media of exchange because there is a demand for them for that purpose primarily. It is out of place to apply the name "money" to the whole group of things which are used to effect exchanges and make payments. The medium of exchange includes money, but its content is greater than that of money. All money can be medium of exchange; but not all medium of exchange is money.

At the other extreme is a group of definitions which would restrict money to what may be called commodity money. Those who hold this view insist that money is an article of direct utility, with specific value based on its direct use for consumption. They hold that it must have value due to a demand for it for other than monetary purposes. The implication is that in the absence of this other demand the article would not have value, and therefore could not properly serve as a measure of value. We have seen, however, that this is not correct, because the article has value if there is a demand for it, whatever the reason for that demand. Common usage, moreover, is against this use of the word. May we say that the people of the United States had no money between 1862 and 1879, because the metals had been driven out of use by inconvertible paper? That would be a hard saying and few would believe it. This view of the nature of money is certainly definite and clear-cut, and capable of easy definition; but these advantages do not balance the objection that common usage is not in accord with it.

Between these two extremes is the view that all media of exchange and payment, whose acceptance the law requires in discharge of debts, may properly be called money. Of course standard money would ordinarily be covered by this definition; but so, also, would inconvertible paper, if it were legal tender. For legal tender inconvertible paper certainly can measure value and serve as a general exchange and circulating medium. It can measure value because it possesses value, derived from the demand for it for money use. It is a general exchange and circulating medium; for, like commodity money, its acceptance does not depend upon the credit of any individual or corporation. Both kinds of money circulate without reference to the possibility of recovering their value from the payer if they should fail to pass, and their value as money depends entirely on the fact that they are generally acceptable in exchange; whereas all forms of paper currency other than inconvertible paper depend for their value upon the fact that if any one refuses to take them in payment, the holder has recourse against the issuer. This position seems sound, and we may accordingly limit the term "money" to that part of the medium of exchange which passes generally current in exchange and settlement of debts, without making the discharge of obligations contingent on the action of a third party, or on the action of the payer by promising redemption if the money article does not pass. From this point of view, legal tender inconvertible paper, and all commodities which are used as *general* circulating and paying media, are properly called money.

7. The Fundamental Cause of Superiority of Commodity Money. — Although, logically, legal tender inconvertible paper is properly called money, in practical use it is incomparably inferior to commodity money. There are several reasons for this inferiority, some of which we shall have to consider later, when we are discussing paper money. Here it is sufficient to notice that its stability of value is far less than that of gold or silver. The value of commodity money, the supply being approximately fixed, rests upon two sources of demand, — the demand for use as a commodity, and the demand for use as money. Even if the monetary use of the article should cease, it would not wholly lose its value. Now inconvertible paper money derives its value solely from the demand for it for monetary purposes. Its basis of demand is, therefore, narrow, and its value less stable. Moreover, it is accepted only within the political circle within which it is recognized as money; whereas commodity money is accepted in any place where the article of which it is made is used either for monetary or for other purposes, or for both. Of course it is conceivable that gold and silver might go out of fashion and the demand for them fall off. The likelihood of this, however, is infinitely less than is the likelihood that a government which issues paper money may fail to redeem it on demand. In the case of one kind of money, the basis of value is general and permanent; in the case of the other, it is likely to be contingent upon the continuance of the government that issues it, and upon the economic condition of that government. The instability which this difference produces in inconvertible paper is sufficient to condemn it as something which should never be resorted to by sound and honest governments.

8. Characteristics of Good Commodity Money. — We have seen that a great many different articles have, at one time or another, been used as money. There are certain qualities which the article in use as commodity money should possess in order to perform its functions to the best advantage. These may be enumerated as follows: —

(*a*) It must in the first place be capable of being exchanged in all ratios, and should be suitable to make payments in all sums. Hence it must be easily divisible and homogeneous, so that its value divisions may correspond with its physical divisions. Not only must it be divisible for this purpose, but it must be, so to speak, aggregatable; that is, portions of it must be capable of being put together into a single mass without loss of value. A diamond is certainly divisible; but two small diamonds are not as valuable as one large one whose weight is equal to that of the two, and if it were possible to fuse two small diamonds into one large one, its value would be greater than the sum of the values of the two. Neither of these conditions should exist in the case of an article used as money.

(*b*) In the next place, the article thus used must possess value, in order that it may measure and store value. As has been pointed out, this value may be due simply to the demand for it for monetary purposes. But an article of direct utility, and, therefore, of specific value, is for many reasons preferable to one whose utility is merely instrumental, and whose value depends simply on its service as a medium of exchange. As we have seen, it will have greater stability.

(*c*) In the third place, the article chosen should have a steady value. That is, its purchasing power should remain reasonably constant, from time to time, and from place to place. It must do this if it is to serve well for storing value and for acting as a standard of deferred payments.

There seems to be a certain inconsistency in speaking of an article as a standard of value and as varying in value. If an article is a standard of value, how can we regard it as variable? There is some difficulty in telling just what is meant by steadiness of value. We shall see later that there are two or three meanings of the phrase, "variation of value," in this connection. For our present purpose it is necessary only to fix in mind firmly the fact that variation is possible. It is important, therefore, that it should be reduced to a minimum, and that the article selected for monetary use should show as little of it as possible. In other words, the purchasing power of the monetary standard should not vary from any cause, except those which arise in the articles whose exchange it is used to effect. The perfect money should not vary from causes that arise in the conditions of its own supply. Of course it is not possible to secure an article that will meet this condition.

(*d*) The article used as money should also be durable, or, as is usually said, indestructible. If it does not possess durability, it will not serve as a means of transfer of value from place to place and from time to time. Moreover, it will not bear handling well, and a large loss would be incurred by the wear and tear to which the coins are subjected by daily use. It has been found that the precious metals, gold and silver, in their pure state, wear away too rapidly from usage. Coins, therefore, are usually made of a mixture of one of these metals with some baser metal, to form an alloy which has the necessary durability.

(*e*) The money article should be cognizable, or easily recognized. If it were not so, people who are ignorant of its character, or who do not see it frequently, would constantly be subjected to fraud. Business would be much hindered if it were necessary constantly to test the article offered in payment of purchases and debts. A glance must suffice, aside from a case of probable fraud, to satisfy the receiver of the coin that it is composed of the genuine metal.

(*f*) The article used as money should also be malleable; that is, it should possess the physical character suitable for coining and imprinting. It must not be so brittle as to break easily, or to take too sharp an impression under the die. On the other hand, it must not be so soft that it will not retain for a considerable time the impression stamped upon it.

(*g*) Another characteristic which the money article should possess is commonly described by saying that it should have much value in small bulk. By this is meant that it should have a high specific value. The word high, of course, is relative, and must be interpreted in this connection to mean as high as the ordinary payments and incomes of a community call for. The scale of incomes and purchases in any place determines the value of the money in general use. Copper serves in China, whereas gold is needed in the United States. In each case, however, the value of the coin is large for its bulk, relatively to the needs of the community.

It is clear from an enumeration of the characteristics needed for good money that no one article is available that possesses them all. The relative importance of one or another of these requisites is determined by the commodity which a community uses. Every community has used that which has best met its necessities, that which has satisfied the universal demand more generally than any other article could do. It is generally admitted that the precious metals combine in a higher degree than any other substance, or substances, the qualities necessary to make a good commodity money. Gold and silver are homogeneous, divisible, cognizable, and malleable. "It is clear," as Professor Jevons remarks, "that the metals far surpass all other substances for purposes of circulation, and it is almost equally clear that certain metals surpass all the other metals in this respect. Of gold and silver especially, we may say with Turgot, that, by the nature of things, they are constituted universal money independently of all convention or law."[1]

We may notice here a question to which we will find it necessary to recur. If a single substance, like gold, while possessing most of the attributes necessary to make good money, is yet lacking in the very important quality of steadiness of value, would it not be possible to use something else as a standard of value while retaining the gold as a medium of exchange? In other words, could we not separate the functions of money and assign different articles to perform the monetary services? It is not only possible, but, as we have seen, we actually

[1] Jevons, "Money and the Mechanism of Exchange," p. 53. Of course, Turgot's remark can only mean that gold and silver, by their natural qualities, best fulfil the requirements of the money substance, and hence need no law to compel their use.

do so to a limited extent. The article used as a standard may be different from the actual medium of exchange and from the money of account. Gold is the standard in this country, but in our ordinary payments we use paper, copper, silver, corn, and other things.

CHAPTER VI

THE MOVEMENT AND DISTRIBUTION OF METALLIC MONEY

REFERENCES: Laughlin, J. L., Principles of Money, Ch. 10; Nicholson, J. S., Principles of Political Economy, Vol. II., Ch. 26, §§ 11-15; Noyes, A. D., Thirty Years of American Finance, Ch. 7; Raguet, C., Currency and Banking, Ch. 4; Report of the Indianapolis Monetary Convention, pp. 145-158; Mill, J. S., Principles of Political Economy, Bk. III., Ch. 21; Ricardo, D., Works (McCulloch's ed.), pp. 79-86, 263 ff.; Walker, F., Money, Ch. 3.

1. Emphasis laid upon the Supply of Money. — How to secure for their respective countries what was regarded as their proper share of the precious metals, was long a matter of considerable solicitude to statesmen, and much legislative ingenuity has been expended at various times to accomplish this end. There have been laws hampering the exportation of the precious metals, or even forbidding it altogether; and other laws whose aim was to encourage the importation of these metals, on the supposition that the more of them a country got, the richer it became. We know now that this is not true; yet much of our monetary legislation is still colored by the old idea, and not a little anxiety is felt at times lest we may at some time fail to have on hand all the money that is necessary to do business. Nothing is more certain, however, than that a country with a sound monetary system is sure to get, and to retain, its due proportion of the money supply of the world, and that special efforts to bring about this result by mere legislation are unnecessary, unfruitful, and likely to be positively harmful.

2. The Division of the Precious Metals depends upon the Relative Demand of Different Countries. — No new principle of exchange is involved in the explanation of the distribution of the precious metals. Like other goods, gold and silver distribute themselves according to the demand for them. Wherever most is offered for them, there they will go. They will flow out from places where their value is low to places where it is high.

If gold and silver were the only means of payment in use, each country would draw to itself a proportion of the total supply determined by the state of its commerce and industry, the amount of its wealth, and the frequency and magnitude of its ordinary payments. The stock of gold at any moment, and any new supply, will be apportioned according to the relative strength of the demands of different countries for these purposes, and this division will be unchanged as long as the proportions of demand remain the same. For, since demand and supply are in equilibrium, there can be no motive to get more money, or to part with any that is on hand.

The proportions of this division of the metals are

independent of their amount. No matter what the total quantity, the proportion which each country will draw to itself is governed entirely by the strength of its demand as compared with the total demand. No country can long keep more than its due proportion. Even a country which has mines cannot retain the entire output of them, but only such part as represents the ratio of its need to the total demand. We must not infer, however, that because the distribution is not affected by the total quantity, it is not a matter of importance whether the amount of money in circulation is large or small; for it is of great importance to have an adequate amount of metallic money in a country. The point is that, whatever the actual amount, the part which each country gets is fixed in the way described.

3. The Value of the Precious Metals not everywhere the Same. — It is asserted by the classical theory of the distribution of the precious metals that if, at any moment, the distribution of the existing stock be supposed to be effected, then the metals "preserve everywhere the same value." A better form of statement would be that, the relative values of the metals once established, any change in their supply will so distribute itself that these relative values will be maintained. This does not mean that an ounce of gold will buy as much in China as in Germany or the United States. For the comparative purchasing power of the metal in two places depends, in part, upon the expense of transportation, both of goods and money, on insurance, and on the proportion of goods, not articles of international trade, which enter into the total quantity of commodities that the gold will buy in each country.

There is one price level for goods which enter into international trade, and another for goods which have only a national market. The equilibrium which results from the pressure of demand for money for these two classes of goods may be called the national price level of a country. These national price levels, acting on one another, produce the international, or world, price level. It is this international price level which is of consequence in determining the distribution of gold. There is no way of effecting changes in the relative monetary holdings of communities which have no trade, or market, relations. The law of distribution implies simply that the price level of one country is in equilibrium with that of others with which it has trade relations, so that any disturbance of prices in either is likely to cause a corresponding change in the other.

4. Changes in Prices, and the Movement of the Precious Metals. — According to the doctrine laid down by Ricardo, and commonly accepted by writers on the subject, it is through changing prices that a country rids itself of a surplus of money, or supplies a deficiency. If we suppose that, at a chosen moment, the trade of the world is in such a state that the exports and the imports of each country exactly balance, and that no country owes a debt to any other, then there is no reason to suppose that the proportions of the holdings of the precious metals will be disturbed. If, however, from any cause, the demand for the merchandise of one country increases, so that higher prices are offered for it, then that becomes a good country in which to sell goods, and a poor one in which to buy. Under such circumstances foreign goods are imported, in order to take advantage of the high prices. In other words, money has become relatively cheap, and therefore tends to go abroad, since we send abroad in payment of our foreign debts the articles which we can best spare, and which are, therefore, cheapest. The importation of goods tends to make them abundant, and therefore prices tend to fall again. Meanwhile the process is reversed in other countries. Thus an equilibrium of prices throughout the world is reëstablished, and the money of the world is still distributed among the nations in due proportion.

5. Price Changes not necessarily followed by a Movement of Specie. — As the theory is usually expounded, the disturbing cause of the existing distribution of the precious metals is supposed to be a new supply of the metals from the mines. This extra supply, going into circulation, raises the price level of the country, foreign goods are imported, and some of the metal exported. The explanation is good, so far as the new gold, if it be gold, goes into circulation without displacing other media of exchange. It is far more likely, however, to find its way promptly into the bank reserves of the great money centres, and to move abroad under the influence of international banking requirements, without influencing prices at home.

The more usual case is not that of a change in the money supply, but in the cost and supply of articles of export. When such a change occurs, and prices alter because of it, an exportation or importation of specie is not a necessary consequence. Aside from the expedients, which will be discussed later, for preventing such a movement, it will not occur in any case unless gold is the article which the country affected can most easily spare. Ordinarily, the balance of trade will be restored by readjustments in the prices of exports and imports.

Let us assume as strong and simple a case as we can, in order to bring out the relations in question. Let us take the case of two countries, A and B, isolated from the rest of the world, but trading with each other. Let us suppose that they use the same kind of metallic money, and that neither employs credit, but that all the balances of their trade are settled with specie. Suppose, now, that, on account of decreased cost of production, some of the goods of country A become cheaper. Then the price level will fall somewhat, and goods will be more largely exported. Let us suppose that the increase of exports is such as to take out of the country A the whole amount of those goods over and above the amount which, on the new scale of prices, will necessitate the use of the same volume of money as before. There is, thus far, no ground for supposing that specie will move into, or out of, the country. The goods exported are taken to country B. Here these goods have been exchanging for home products at certain rates. More of the imported articles are now offered for the goods of the receiving country than was previously the case. If we could assume that no more of the goods of country B would be given for the imports than formerly, we would be obliged to admit the possibility of a movement of specie from B to A. As a matter of fact, a larger volume of foreign goods offered for home products will draw out a larger quantity of these products in exchange. The home products will fall in price. The ratio of exchange will alter so that both countries will get some of the advantage arising from the lowered cost of the goods exported by A. The price level will fall to a point at which there will be a new equilibrium of exchange between the imports and the home products. Meantime a larger amount of goods has been sent from B to A. The price level will fall there also, with the net result that there occurs a fall in the price level of both countries, such that their average prices bear to each other the same relation that existed before, without any movement of specie.

We supposed that the whole surplus of the cheapening goods of A was exported to B. In practice this will hardly be the case. Such part of them will go to B as will cause the ratio of exchange between its home goods and its imports to come to an equilibrium, at the same point as is reached by the changing ratio of exchange in the first country between its increasing home goods and its increasing imports. That is, as before, the price levels of the two countries will come to rest in a ratio which will render unnecessary any change in their specie holdings.

The fact of the matter is that specie will be exported only if it is the cheapest article which the importing country at the moment possesses. There is no ground for saying that gold is more or less likely to be exported than is any other article in order to adjust a balance of international trade. The usual case would be that a disturbance in the price level will be met by a change in the balance of exports and imports of goods, without any movement of specie at all. If either country has mines, gold will be one of its regular articles of export; but it will be exported, not to readjust a change in the price level, but simply as part of the general current of international trade.

Even if the increase of a country's exports were caused by the production of an entirely new article of exportation, we could not say with certainty that there would be a movement of gold to pay for it. For it might simply replace articles already in use, and transfer the money demand for them to itself.

That the Ricardian explanation is too simple and sweeping is evident, again, from the fact that the amount of money which it would be necessary to export, in order to readjust the general price level, would be a considerable portion of the specie of the exporting country, but an infinitesimal part of that of the world at large. We would have, therefore, a large proportional change in the specie holdings of one country, and an indefinitely small one in those of other countries. Obviously, if it required the exportation of one thousand ounces of gold to adjust a price change of two per cent. in one country, it would take many times one thousand ounces to cause a similar change in the price level of the world at large. The remedy for the restoration of the disturbed price level is not adequate. The Ricardian theory applies in what mathematicians would call limiting cases, and only there. If all international trade were carried on by means of direct and immediate money payments, and if all countries used the same standard metal, there would undoubtedly be a movement of specie whenever a general decrease in the cost of production of goods in one country led to a fall of its prices and an increase of its exports.

6. The Ricardian Theory modified by Economic Friction. — In the case of an exportation of specie which is in fact a result merely of the disturbance of trade balances, certain assumptions must be made in order that the explanation may square with the facts. The first of these is that the flow of gold and the adjustment of prices is immediate, complete, and without expense. In no case is this true. The flow of gold is not immediate, its distribution not instantaneous. Let us suppose that a new supply of gold is added to the world's stock. Part of it will go for use in the arts, and the rest will be devoted to monetary purposes. The latter portion, if it is large, might take a long time to distribute itself among the industrial nations in such a way as to restore the equilibrium of world prices; and during the intervening period there might be differences in the price level in different countries. The distribution is accomplished only with appreciable intervals in its flow, by jerks, as it were, as the new supply passes from one market to another, from one country to another. As Cairnes remarks, "Gold and silver, like all other things which are the subjects of international exchange, possess local values."[1] It is by a succession of operations on these local values that the distribution is gradually effected.

The accuracy of the principle of the distribution of the precious metals, as usually explained, is modified, further, by the fact that the equableness, as well as the period, of distribution of a new supply depends somewhat upon the place in which it first appears. A new supply of gold in a country that is industrially backward, and in which banking facilities are but little developed, will flow out into the world less freely than it would from a country

[1] Cf. Cairnes, "Political Economy," pp. 408–410.

whose conditions were the reverse. It is true, however, that this circumstance has largely lost its importance now, because the different parts of the world are in much closer communication than they ever were before, and banking facilities and connections are far more general. Notwithstanding this fact, it costs more to get gold to countries far from the mines than to those near by. Hence the share which would fall to a remote country, according to the unmodified principle of distribution, would be larger than it would actually get, because its demand would be lessened by the expense of securing the supply.

In the next place, the rapidity and the equableness of the flow of the precious metals are affected somewhat by national, or local, customs and prejudices, as well as by legal enactment. The silver of Potosi reached the marts of the world in a different order and period from what it would have required if the laws of Spain and the economic prejudices of the country had not turned it first into the coffers of the Spanish treasury. A country whose religious ceremonies lead to a large use of the precious metals would part with a new supply from its mines less rapidly than would another country without such prejudices.

In the fourth place, different commodities and different employments would respond to the influences of the new supply of gold with varying degrees of rapidity and sensitiveness. Employments whose remuneration was strongly influenced by custom would respond slowly. The prices of goods would be found to be affected differently, according as we considered wholesale or retail trade, or markets far from, or near to, great centres of trade.

7. Influence of the Credit Mechanism on the Distribution of the Precious Metals. — All these considerations make the distribution of the precious metals very different in fact from what it would be if the assumptions involved in the principle of distribution, as commonly formulated, were true. Yet they do not invalidate the principle, for they in no wise change its character, and it could easily be stated in a way which would include and allow for all the factors of disturbance so far mentioned. The case is far different when we examine another assumption implied in the general statement of the mode of distribution; namely, that the medium of payment is homogeneous. The fact is quite otherwise; the medium of exchange is highly heterogeneous, and this heterogeneity modifies the principle of distribution, not merely by causing friction, but in a way to change its character entirely.

The chief factor in making the medium of exchange heterogeneous, and in modifying the principle of distribution, is the credit system. Credit not only alters the amount of the precious metals which a country gets, in the first place, but it acts as a buffer against sudden changes in this amount. Under the modern credit system, a country's supply of metallic money does not depend more on its wealth and industry and the frequency and magnitude of its payments than on the extent of its use of credit and the delicacy and complexity of its credit system. In countries where the credit system is most highly developed, the amount of metallic money used is relatively less than in other countries, despite the fact that it is in the former cases that the total demand for medium of exchange may be the greater. The precious metals are distributed principally according to the need for them as a basis of credit. The more complex the credit system, the less metallic money, relatively, is needed for its support, and the greater the volume of payments made with a given supply.

8. The Effect of the Use of Bills of Exchange on the Movement of the Metals. — Not only does credit change the distribution of metallic money which the classical theory would make, but it also renders unnecessary some changes which would, in its absence, occur. According to the doctrine, a rise of prices implies an excess of money, and an export of the excess. Now, it is a well-known fact that there may be a very marked change in the price level of a country, that the balance of indebtedness may be considerably in its favor, or considerably against it, without its losing or gaining any specie. Credit has supplied the modern business world with certain devices for the purpose of making the physical transfer of specie unnecessary and saving the expense of it. The first of these devices is the bill of exchange. Of course, when we speak of one country's being in debt to another, we mean that the business men of one owe those of the other. For example, some people in England owe debts to some in France, and *vice versa*. Let us suppose that English merchants owe French merchants $1,000,000, and that French merchants owe their English correspondents $800,000 of it back again. If the French merchants to whom the English are in debt can have turned over to them in Paris the $800,000 which French debtors have to pay, and if at the same time the English creditor merchants can have their bills paid in London out of the $1,000,000 due the French, then only the balance of $200,000 would have to be shipped from London to Paris. Precisely this process is effected by means of bills of exchange. The English creditors draw on their debtors in Paris, and pay themselves by selling the bills to English merchants who owe money in Paris. These send the bills to their French creditors, who collect them at home. In our example there remains a balance of $200,000 to be paid by the transfer of specie. But this need not happen. A third country, say Germany, may owe England a trade balance of this amount, while at the same time French merchants owe an equal debt to their German creditors. The English merchants need only draw bills for the amount on Berlin and send them to their French creditors, who can sell them to the French debtors of the merchants of Germany. These debtors send them to their creditors in Berlin, who collect them from the German debtors of the English. If the balance cannot be cancelled by the exchange of bills among the three countries, it may be offset by the debts of a fourth, or a fifth, and so on. So far may this process go that only a very small amount of specie may pass between different countries in the space of a year for the settlement of international indebtedness. For example, it has been computed that, a few years ago, the settlement of international trade balances required about one dollar to every seventeen of commerce.[1] Small as this amount is, it is very much larger than what is used per dollar to settle domestic trade balances.

In practice, the merchants who draw bills do not seek out fellow business men who have debts to pay in the country on which the bills are drawn. They sell them to banks and brokers, and these in turn sell them to people who have to make remittances.

If the bills drawn by the merchants of one country on the merchants of another should happen to be equal in amount to the bills drawn by the merchants of the second on those of the first, there would be no need for the transfer of money at all. Usually, however, such a coincidence does not, and cannot be expected to, occur. But, even then, the balance may not be settled by the shipment of money. There are several devices known to the business world for making such a shipment unnecessary. In the first place, the necessity of settling

[1] Muhleman, M., "Monetary Systems of the World," p. 168.

with gold may be obviated by drafts of merchants of the debtor country on merchants of the creditor country, in anticipation of future transactions. For example, if the merchants of the United States owed those of England a balance representing the excess of the value of imports over exports, they might, instead of shipping gold to London, draw on English grain importers, in anticipation of the sums which would become due American exporters of grain after harvest time. These bills, *in futuro*, simply serve to prolong the period of credit until a time when settlement can be made by the sale of goods to the creditor country.

9. Other Causes which render Export of the Precious Metals Unnecessary. — It is entirely possible, however, that such a use of bills to make a temporary settlement may fail to meet the whole of the balance due. Another means must be sought, therefore, in order to prevent the transfer of specie. It might be done by buying bankers' drafts, instead of bills of exchange. It is not uncommon for bankers with foreign connections to keep balances abroad, on which they sell drafts, when bills of exchange are not sufficient to supply the demands of debtors. They restore their balances with foreign bankers when the current of indebtedness is reversed.

If both of these means fail to liquidate the balance of indebtedness, it may be liquidated by the transfer of securities. The bonds and other evidences of indebtedness which have a world market are readily and cheaply sent from place to place. The balance of indebtedness due from English to American merchants can be quickly and easily settled, if the Englishmen or their agents sell in the New York market securities equal in value to the debt. The market for securities is, perhaps, the widest and most mobile of all markets. Hence it happens that, nowadays, a balance of indebtedness between countries is much more likely to cause a flow of securities than a flow of money from the debtor country.

However, it is conceivable that all these means should fail to offset the balance due, so that it would seem necessary to export or import some of the precious metals. This need not happen, however, for it would be possible for the debtor country to continue in debt, or to pay its debt by borrowing money from some third country. This it could do by offering a sufficiently high rate of interest. Indeed, the manipulation of the rate of discount is one of the most important of modern methods of regulating the flow of money. Creditors will continue to leave their balances in the debtor country if the latter offers a sufficiently high rate for their use; but if their need for their money is urgent, other people, feeling less urgency, will be content to lend the debtor country the amount which it has to pay. Even in this case, however, there may not be any actual transfer of money. As we have seen, the creditor country may be debtor to a third country, and may pay its debts to the third country by drafts upon its own debtor; while the third country, influenced by the high rate of discount, may not demand the payment of these drafts at once.[1]

From all these considerations, it is very clear that the flow of the precious metals from one country to another is by no means so ready and complete as the Ricardian doctrine, in its bald form, would indicate. By the devices described, a country may even for a time hold its supply of money at a level relatively higher than that of the world at large; and during that time many consequences of great importance to individuals and classes may occur, because of the difference in level.

The mode of distribution of metallic money, which has been described as applicable to the passage of such money from country to country, describes also its passage from place to place within the limits of a single country. We find the mutual balance of trade and of general indebtedness of Chicago and New York, for example, adjusted by means of direct bills on each other, or on some third place, by bank drafts, bills *in futuro*, postponed payment, and, in the last resort, the transfer of specie.

10. The Usual Causes of the Movement of Specie. — If a disturbance of credit occurs, making the uncancelled balance of credit transactions

[1] Cf. Goshen, "The Foreign Exchanges," 15th ed., pp. 129, 136, 138.

larger than usual, a larger banking reserve will be necessary, and an importation of specie will very likely take place. The movement of gold will be brought about by a rise of the rate of discount, or by the transfer of securities, without affecting the price level or the current of trade at all. On the other hand, an improvement of the banking system of a country may cause an export of specie. For the improvement implies that the country can now do its business with a smaller metallic reserve.

Again, a transfer of specie from one country to another may be caused by a change in the ratio of exchange between gold and silver if the countries in question have different monetary standards. In such a case, a rise of silver in terms of gold will exert an adverse influence on the export trade of the silver standard country. For, at the same price level, exports of its goods bring the same amount of gold as before; but this amount now exchanges for less silver at home. Hence the exports of goods from the silver standard country will fall off, and its imports increase, as will its export of silver. The net result of these movements will be a fall of prices. This fall will go on until it offsets the change in the gold price of silver. Then the export of silver will stop.

A permanent growth of the home trade of a country will necessitate a larger amount of specie and cause its importation if the banking system is already supplying all the currency which its present specie holdings permit.

DISTRIBUTION OF METALLIC MONEY

11. The Amount of Money needed by a Country. — Closely connected with this matter of the distribution of the precious metals for monetary purposes is the question how much money a country needs. The doctrine which we have just discussed tells us something about the method of division of the money supply among the nations of the earth, but it says nothing at all definite of the absolute amount of money that a country should have. There is no known way of telling beforehand how much money a country needs. The amount depends upon the population, the total amount of business, the amount of transactions done by barter and credit, the so-called rapidity of the circulation of money, the magnitude of the country's productive enterprises, the development of transportation and communication, the methods of doing business, and general enlightenment. The population of one country may use only a fractional part of the money used by the same population in another country. France, with a population approximately that of England, uses a considerably larger amount of money to do her business. If productive enterprise is great, larger money reserves are needed, as is also a larger amount of money for the payment of wages. If a million people are crowded together within the limits of a city, so that communication is easy and rapid, they need less money for a given volume of business than if they are scattered over a wide territory. If the banking habit is highly developed, if the standard of personal and business integrity is high, so that confidence is general, business settlements will be made largely with credit paper, and less money will be needed. It seems a hopeless task to try to determine either the influences of these various causes, or their mutual relations. We may say with confidence that, "other things remaining the same," the amount of money used will vary with any one of the other factors we have mentioned. But that is all.

Must we, then, abandon the attempt to reach any definite conclusions on this question? Of the actual quantity of money needed and the amount of its variation from time to time — yes; on the mode and causes of those variations, however, we may get a little light. This subject we proceed to discuss.

CHAPTER VII

THE STATIC DISTRIBUTION OF THE PRECIOUS METALS

REFERENCES: Jevons, W. S., Money and the Mechanism of Exchange, Ch. 26; Kleinwächter, F., Lehrbuch der Nationaloekonomie, pp. 343–346; Laughlin, J. L., Principles of Money, Ch. 11; Tucker, G., Theory of Money and Banks, Ch. 5; Walker, F. A., Money, pp. 48–49, 57–63, 73–74.

1. Distribution of Money in the Sense of Apportionment. — The phrase, "distribution of money," admits of a double meaning. It may signify either the movement of money from place to place, or the division of the existing quantity among different countries or groups of people. It is in the latter sense that the subject has always aroused the greater popular interest; but it is in the other sense that it has received the fuller scientific treatment. How much money a community uses, absolutely, or in comparison with other communities of the same general economic character; what is the composition of its medium of payment; what proportion of its payments are made with money and what by means of credit; and how, as a community grows, the constituents of its medium of exchange alter with reference to one another — are questions of much interest and importance, which the classical theory of distribution does not touch, and to which our existing knowledge offers us unsatisfactory answers, if, indeed, it offers any at all.

2. Conditions of the Apportionment. — We usually feel obliged to content ourselves with saying that the amount of money which is used by a community depends on its population, the amount and character of its business, the general range of prices, the degree of perfection of its credit machinery, and the extent to which credit is used. Just what relations exist between the quantity of money needed and each of the other factors mentioned, we cannot say. In many popular discussions, and in some scientific ones, the relation seems to be regarded as one of simple proportion. It is often taken for granted that twice or thrice as many people will require twice or thrice as much money, "other things remaining the same"; that a community with twice or thrice as much business as another will use a proportionally larger amount of money. Such, however, is not the way of life. Increase in population and growth in volume of business imply a more intense economic activity, and not merely a quantitative increase of the economic organs. If the quantity of money changes, other things cannot remain the same. Even in a purely monetary milieu, one from which credit and its complexity of consequences were absent, the simple solution offered could hardly apply; and if it did, there would be no way of making the necessary allowances for the introduction of a system of credit. For we have to do with a complex of forces, whose operations are so interdependent that we cannot detect and trace the course of any one of them singly. The conditions of the problem make it impossible to get at the exact relation between population or volume of business and the quantity of medium of exchange; but it is possible, perhaps, to describe the character of that relation somewhat more specifically than is done in the general statements commonly made about it.

3. An Increased Volume of Exchanges requires Larger or More Efficient Medium of Exchange, but not necessarily More Money. — An increase in the volume of business necessitates an increase in the volume of the medium of exchange, or a greater efficiency in the system of exchange. While, in the long run, this usually implies, as we shall see, an increase in the quantity of money available, it does not necessitate such an increase at once, nor, possibly, for a considerable period of time, because there are several ways of effecting an enhanced volume of exchanges other than by increasing the amount of money in use. It may be done by changing the price level, or by an extension of barter, or by an improvement of the credit system either through its extension or its refinement, or by a higher efficiency, commonly called rapidity of circulation, of money, due to improved means of communication or transportation.

When there exist several ways of meeting an increase in the demand for means of exchange, that one will be chosen which is, for the time and under the circumstances, the least costly. Some important consequences follow from this general principle. In the first place, if the volume of exchanges to be effected increases, the business will be done and the changes made with the existing volume of money, on a lower level of prices, if the difficulties of barter or the expense of extending the credit system be too great to warrant resort to either of these means of effecting exchanges; or if the difficulties in the way of improving transportation and communication make it, for the time, impracticable to increase the efficiency of the existing supply of money. Since a new supply of metallic money can always be had at some price, the fact that the community does not seek or get this supply is the best of evidence that it is less costly to do the business on a lower level of prices, and suffer whatever loss that change entails, than to incur the expense of adding to the supply of metallic money. The periods of falling prices, from 1848 to 1860, and 1873 to 1896, are really to be explained in this way. There never was any good evidence that the supply of gold commercially available was exhausted. The real meaning of the situation was that the cost of getting gold, under the conditions of mining which then prevailed, was greater than the loss entailed for the world by falling price levels. When this loss became great enough to make the extension of gold mining under the old conditions once more profitable, and, still more, to make it profitable to seek new processes of extracting the metal, capital was turned from other uses to gold production, and the supply of that metal has, in consequence, rapidly increased.

If the expense of getting new gold is very large, and if the credit system is not sufficiently expansible, a resort to direct barter may be less costly to the community than a falling price level. It is somewhat difficult to give historical illustrations of the enlarged use of barter in a community which has become accustomed to the use of money; yet there is reason for thinking that under a régime of fiat paper, issued in excess, some communities have preferred to enlarge the amount of their exchanges performed in this way, rather than run the risk of further loss by depreciation. It is difficult, too, to offer direct evidence of an increase in what is usually called the rapidity of circulation of money. Yet we know that in monetary stringencies and crises money is hoarded, or circulates less rapidly than usual, especially in rural communities; whereas, when business is good and prices are rising, money payments are much easier and more frequent, and a given quantity of money performs a larger volume of payments, while at the same time the volume of credit enlarges. It is difficult to trace any one of these movements separately, because in the complex system of exchange of a modern community more than one of these means of meeting an increased demand for means of payment are likely to be resorted to at the same time. The total result, however, is to give the community, through the play of competition, the least expensive mode of meeting the demand which the conditions for the time permit. Consequently, an additional quantity of money may not be brought into use by the demand for an increased means of payment, and the relation between the quantity of money and the volume of business is, therefore, by no means one of simple proportion.

4. The Amount of Metallic Money in a Country tends to a Minimum. — A second important consequence of the general principle that the community will make its payments by the method which is for the time the least expensive, is the tendency of a country to reduce its holdings of metallic money to a minimum. It is not, as a rule, advantageous, but wasteful, for a community to accumulate metallic money beyond the amount brought to it by the ordinary operations of business. For it is usually more expensive to increase the supply of gold than to meet the additional payments by some other means, because, in order to increase this supply, real capital must ordinarily be diverted from some other use. Hence, no commercial community will incur for long the expense of keeping more gold than is necessary to perform its direct money payments and to sustain its credit system. The truth of this statement is most evident in the case of a new country. The people of a new community always try to get on without metallic money. This is the explanation of the attempts in our own country, in the early days, to circulate a large volume of paper money. It was an effort on the part of the community to do its business without turning any of its real capital to the production of metallic money, because its real capital was employed, or was thought to be employed, in more profitable ways. Under a system of purely metallic money, this tendency of each country to reduce its holdings to a profitable minimum would show itself in the physical transfer of its surplus. Such transfers do not cease, of course, under the modern system of credit exchange, but they are, perhaps, less frequent than they would be in the absence of credit. What is transferred now is usually not the money, but the claims to money. The transfer, therefore, is not a physical one, but a transfer of paper evidences of ownership.

5. Readjustments in the Exchange System caused by a Demand for More Medium of Exchange. — A demand for a more adequate means of exchange usually is met first by an adjustment of the mechanism of credit, and a study of some phases of credit, especially of the proportions in which it enters into payments for different population groups and volumes of business, will throw a good deal of light on the amount of money used as population and business grow. If credit is well developed in a community, if a good credit system is in existence, so that the people have what may be called the credit habit, they will resort readily and easily to an extension of credit to meet the changed demand for means to effect exchanges. They will increase and improve their credit machinery through considerable periods of time, if necessary, to avoid the expense of adding more metallic money to their circulation. For the credit system, in the last analysis, is a labor-saving device. Like new machinery or improved processes, it can be used profitably only when the operations of business are large enough to furnish a sufficient demand for its product. Within limits, the extension of the credit system is less expensive than the devotion of real capital to the production of an increased supply of gold. Accordingly, as an increased portion of business calls for a larger medium of exchange, the first effort will be to use the existing mechanism to its fullest capacity. The bank which served three thousand people, and did the business they furnished, will be made to serve six or ten thousand people, without increasing its real capital. Banks will establish branches to avoid the necessity of duplicating capital. They will consolidate to avoid such duplication, to economize in administration in order to withstand shocks, and in other ways try to bring the exchange efficiency of the money which constitutes their real capital to its maximum. This country in recent years has been passing through such an experience. No other significance can be attached to the increase in the number of national banks from 3590, in 1899, to 4756, in 1903; and to the rapid multiplication of such banks with the minimum capital allowed by law, in rural communities where banking facilities did not exist before; to say nothing of the increase of banking institutions under other than national charters. Nor can there be any other economic meaning to the tremendous consolidations of great banking houses which the past few years have seen. All these phenomena mean only that credit is playing for the time a larger rôle; that the portion of the volume of business effected by credit is for the time larger than before, and the amount of money smaller in proportion to the total volume of transactions. It is impossible, of course, to find direct evidence of this. No one knows the exact amount of metallic money in a country or in the world, nor is it possible to tell either the number of exchanges or the total volume of business at any time or through any period. The volume of metallic money undoubtedly has grown rapidly in the past few years. There are signs, however, that it has not grown so rapidly as has the total volume of business.

While growing population and increase of business make necessary a resort to a larger use of credit, both relatively and absolutely, they at the same time furnish certain social conditions which make the use of credit easier. Increasing population implies greater density, greater complexity of business relations, more extended economic interdependence — conditions all of which may be described briefly as greater economic solidarity. These changes broaden and deepen that mutual knowledge and confidence which form the basis of all credit transactions, and so stimulate the growth of credit, while at the same time improved means of communication and transportation facilitate its use.

We conclude from all the circumstances that, where credit is freely used, where a well-developed credit system exists, the proportion of credit payments to the whole volume of business increases, on the whole, as population and business grow, and that the amount of metallic money actually needed becomes less in proportion to the total volume of payments.

6. The Extension of Credit Exchange slower as the Volume of Exchanges Increases. — The extension and refinement of the credit economy cannot be carried on indefinitely, however. There is some point beyond which the extension cannot be carried profitably. There is some density of population, some volume of business, whose demands cannot be completely satisfied in this way. Beyond this point an extension of the credit means of payment must be retarded, and the amount of money put into use as compared with the whole volume of business must become larger. There are several reasons for holding this view. The first argument to prove this slowing up of the increasing use of credit in making payments rests upon the necessities of arithmetic. For not all exchanges are effected by credit. The percentage of credit paper in the medium of payment cannot exceed 100. If, for any volume of business, the percentage of payments made by means of credit is 60, this percentage cannot multiply proportionally with the increase in the volume of payments. If the volume of payments multiplies ten times, the total amount paid by means of credit paper may also multiply ten times, but the percentage of credit payments cannot do so. To speak algebraically, the value of the ordinate, Y, cannot exceed 100, while that of the abscissa, X, may be indefinitely large. After a time the curve showing the percentage of credit payments to all payments must, under these conditions, tend to become parallel to the axis of X.

The second reason for thinking that there is a point beyond which the extension of credit goes on more slowly than before is found in the conditions of the increase of business. If we assume that at any time the exchanges of a country are effected by means of a certain proportion of credit paper and a certain proportion of metallic money, and that the credit system is extended to its point of maximum efficiency, new increments of business are likely to be carried on outside of the credit system, that is, by means of direct money payments. There is, so to say, a unit of operation in the credit mechanism, a certain portion of the credit machinery, a certain group of operations which must be put in motion if the machinery of credit is used at all to effect a given transaction. If a new increment of exchanges is less than this unit will perform, it cannot profitably be done by credit. The railroads of the country of late years have been increasing the size of their locomotives, until now it is a question whether the point of decrease of profitableness in size and hauling capacity has not been reached. It certainly is not profitable to increase the power of locomotives beyond what is necessary to do the amount of hauling which they will ordinarily be called upon to do. Similarly the credit machinery, when it has become vast and intricate, is not applicable to small exchanges. They must be cared for by an additional supply of money. Proof of this statement is found in the way whereby clearing-house balances are settled in different places. In New York, for example, money is used to a larger extent for this purpose than in many smaller cities. Some years ago, when statistics were collected concerning the proportion of credit paper in bank deposits, the statistics of clearing-house operations were asked for, including the method of settling balances. The returns showed that a larger proportion of the balance was paid in money in New York City than in most of the smaller cities.[1] New York used $2,971,000 in United States notes, and $3,950,000 in United States currency certificates

[1] Cf. Report of the Comptroller of the Currency, 1896, p. 98.

to settle her balance of $6,921,000 on the day in question. Atlanta, Georgia, Denver, Colorado, Louisville, Kentucky, and many other places paid their clearing-house balances entirely by manager's checks. Yet it is in New York City that credit machinery is most delicate and extended, and where, therefore, one would expect at first thought to find the use of money for this purpose most completely eliminated. The explanation is very simple, and is found in the fact that the more complex and delicate the credit machinery, the larger the minimum debt which it will pay to discharge by its means; the larger, that is, will be the balance of payments made with money. In a small place, with a single bank, whose bookkeeping is simple and whose office expenses are small, it may pay to handle checks for so small an amount as a dollar, or even fifty cents. There is no clearing-house process to go through, no duplication of transfers and other records. The case is quite different in the great credit centres. The credit machinery of New York is too costly to use on sums so small. It is easier and less expensive to make such payments in money. Similarly, as the business of a community becomes larger, there is a considerable portion of it whose settlement is more cheaply made with ready money than by the costly credit mechanism. For, as population grows, an increasing proportion of it is made up of people of small means—people who have small incomes and make small purchases. These small purchases are more likely to be made with ready money. Neither the income nor the ordinary expenditures of individuals in this group of population admit of the profitable use of the credit machinery. Small and frequent purchases for ready money become more common and form a larger total. The increase in the number of small stores, as a community grows in population, is evidence of this new demand for ready money. The ease with which they enable the individual to buy at a moment's notice just as much of any goods as he needs, promotes small and frequent purchases and stimulates ready money payments. Under these circumstances people need not buy their household necessaries so far ahead, and therefore need not buy so largely at a time. In the ordinary family in this country, for example, the buying of necessaries is, without doubt, done less from month to month and more from week to week, or even from day to day, than used to be the case. The changed conditions call for a larger amount of ready money.

7. Other Conditions which retard the Growth of Credit Exchanges. — There is, too, a growing tendency to shorten the period of payment of wages and salaries. Hence the recipients get smaller sums at a time and the disbursement of money is less difficult. Many who bought on credit when the wage or salary period was a quarter year or a month will buy for cash when the period is only a week; and since the payments are smaller, money is more convenient than checks. This greater use of money as incomes become smaller or more frequently paid is a matter concerning which it is very difficult to get any direct evidence. From one source, however, we get a little light. The smaller purchases and payments must make necessary a greater use of money of the lower denominations. Now there is some evidence that the proportion of the lower denominations in circulation grows as population increases. Mr. J. B. Martin, writing of the circulation of the Bank of England notes between 1844 and 1878, remarks: "There is no material alteration in the demand for bank notes of intermediate values, but in the case of those of the highest and lowest denominations the change is very remarkable. The circulation of five-pound notes here is seen to have doubled itself in actual volume and to have risen 12 per cent. in its ratio to the total circulation, while the circulation of one-thousand-pound notes has diminished by more than one-half in actual volume, and 12 per cent. in its ratio to the total circulation. . . . There can be but little doubt that the increase of banking facilities has tended to the settlement of all but very small accounts by cheque; but the increase of population, the greater amount of business done, and, I hope we may add, the greater prosperity of the masses, have caused a still more rapidly increasing number of these small accounts to demand their settlement by bank notes."[1]

The increase in the proportion of small change

[1] *Journal of the Institute of Bankers*, Vol. I., p. 288.

has occurred in our own currency also. Some evidence of this is found in the fact that while between July, 1896, and March, 1903, the total outstanding paper currency of the country increased about 33 per cent., the one-dollar notes increased in number 71 per cent.; the twos, 61 per cent.; the fives, 30 per cent.; the tens, 48 per cent.; and the twenties, 64 per cent.[1]

Another bit of evidence of the increase in the proportion of money used under the conditions discussed is found, possibly, in the fluctuation of the percentage of credit paper in bank deposits for the United States since 1881. The writer has criticised[2] the opinion that this falling off means a diminution in the use of credit mechanism. We probably find the true explanation in the thesis we are now discussing. We may have been passing through a period of relatively increasing use of money.

8. Periodic Character of the Growth of Money and Credit Payments. — Since, under certain conditions, the proportion of payments made by means of credit increases, while under others that made by ready money becomes larger, there is a periodicity or, at least, an alternation[3] in the use of credit machinery and ready money to make the payments

[1] Computed from data in the *United States Treasury Monthly Summary of Commerce and Finance.*

[2] See *Journal of Political Economy*, March, 1897, p. 173.

[3] If the credit mechanism is at its limit of application, the amount of money may not increase at once, even though business is expanding. It may be less costly to let prices fall.

called for by new business. To bring out this fact more clearly, let us suppose the case of a community of given size and volume of business. It uses a certain amount of ready money for direct payments, a certain amount as a basis for the emission of credit paper, and it effects a certain amount of its payments by cancellation through credit paper. Population and business may increase for a time without making necessary an increase in the amount of money used directly, or to support the credit system. The existing money basis may be made to serve as basis for an extended credit by using a more refined credit system, a more complex and delicate credit machinery. But there comes a time when the expense of making payments with credit paper between the centre and the outskirts of the community is as great as it was between the two separate neighborhoods before the population became large and dense enough to admit of a highly developed credit system; and the expense of such a credit system in the thinly settled portions of the community is too great to justify its maintenance. It is cheaper to use more ready money. There comes a time, too, as we have seen, when a rise occurs in the minimum amount for which it pays to use the existing credit machinery. This minimum can be reduced again only by an extension of the credit machinery in a simpler form through the investment of new capital; that is, by lowering the marginal unit of operation of the credit system.

But before this is done, a period elapses during which it is cheaper to use more ready money. The money can be obtained in just the amount needed, while the minimum amount of capital that it would pay to invest in credit machinery would produce a larger extension of the system than the situation demanded. When the amount of a certain kind of work is small, we do it by hand labor; when it is large, we use machinery. When our need for goods is small, we buy at retail; when it is large, we buy at wholesale. So when our need for more paying medium is small, we buy it as we need it — in the shape of ready money; when our need is large, we supply it, and anticipate further needs by new investment of capital in extending the credit system.

The process of development, when demand for medium of payment presses on supply, is, then: first, the refinement of the existing credit machinery to its maximum efficiency; then a period during which it is less costly to supply the new demand by means of ready money; and, third, the expansion of the credit machinery by the investment of new capital. Of course these stages of growth are not in fact distinct. Doubtless the money supply may increase, and the credit machinery be both refined and enlarged simultaneously.

There must, then, be a fluctuation, an alternate expansion of the circulating money part, and the credit part, of the medium of exchange. And this alternation is not simple. It is a complex movement of several series of fluctuations, of different sweep or amplitude. Each community which uses credit is, in a measure, independent of others in supplying itself with a medium of payment. As its need increases, it refines its credit system. When the point is reached where no further expansion is feasible on the basis of its internal means, it draws on the neighboring communities with which it forms an intermediate group, so to say, in the interdependent national trade organization. The undulatory movement is felt in time by this whole group. It, in turn, relies at first on itself to supply new needs, but in time must press on similar groups in the world's exchange area. Thus we should expect a series of undulations, one included within another. The period between the points when it will be necessary either to get more money or to make a new investment in credit machinery will, therefore, be longer where the credit machinery is extensive and complex.

What has been said thus far about the method of adjustment of the medium of exchange to demand has had reference to the conditions of an increasing demand. When business is decreasing and the demand for means of exchange is falling off, the same general principle controls the situation. A community will use the least expensive mode of payment. It will, therefore, discard first its most expensive mode of payment, or it will discard portions of one or more modes of payment until the expensiveness of the marginal unit of each kind of payment is just met by the new demand. In other words, if a community finds that it can contract its credit machinery as business falls off, with less loss than it can diminish its holdings of metallic money, it will do so. If, on the contrary, it is less expensive to devote some of the metal now in the form of money to use in the arts, that may be done. Still again, if the situation does not justify either of these proceedings, the efficiency of money will fall off, and the money will pass more slowly in circulation. All this, however, will occur, provided it is to the interest of a community to maintain the prevailing price level. If business will suffer less from a falling level of prices, even from a contraction of the medium of exchange in any of the ways mentioned, then prices will be allowed to fall.

The method of adjustment of the supply of medium of exchange to changed demand is not affected, if there is a sudden and unexpected increase in the supply of money. The process of adjustment, as it has been described, is for the moment arrested, but at once begins again on the basis of the new conditions caused by the increased supply. That is, if the increase in the supply is not continuous, the price level, or the credit machinery, or the rapidity of circulation will, one or all, change, in order to accommodate the new supply of money. Business will be stimulated, the demand for medium of exchange increased, and a new equilibrium will be established among the factors mentioned.

It may serve to bring out more clearly the theory which this chapter is endeavoring to establish if we recapitulate the points in the argument. As population and business grow, creating a demand for an increased quantity of medium of exchange, a community will endeavor to retain the prevailing level of prices by extending the credit system to meet the new demand. This process of extension will go on until it is no longer profitable. The community will then seek to add to its holdings of metallic money, provided the expensiveness of securing the necessary additions will not entail a greater loss than would be suffered by permitting the price level to fall. Thus there will be an alternate extension of the proportion of payments made by the credit mechanism and by money, respectively. There will also be a slow increase, through long periods, of the proportion of payments made by money.

9. Relation of the Theory of this Chapter to the Amount of Money needed by a Country. — But of what practical value is all this? Does it throw any new light on the money question? It certainly does not tell us anything about the absolute amount of money that a community uses or needs. But it does throw some light upon the relative amounts used by communities of different size. To bring out its practical bearings, let us imagine a community with a fixed amount of money, a credit system well established, and a growing population and business. We neglect, as before, the demand for currency for wholesale trade. We may call the money needed for actual circulation, A; that used as a reserve for bank credits, B, which furnishes the amount of credit-paying medium that we will call C. Then $A+C$ will represent the total volume of payments. In other words, C represents the bank deposits; or, more properly, that portion of the deposits which at the time in question is in active use. As business grows, a larger amount of payments medium is, of course, needed. In a modern community the demand falls first on the credit machinery. We go to the banks when we need money. The result will be a stretching, or refinement, of the credit system, on the basis of the same reserve. In other words, the amount of money used for a reserve will be made to do the largest possible service. But by and by it will not suffice. Then, perhaps, the community takes some money hitherto used in making actual payments. B becomes larger at the expense of A, and the new volume of payments, which we will call $A'+C'$, will be greater than $A+C$. But there is a limit to this process. Money cannot be taken indefinitely from the amount which is ordinarily used in making direct payments. Soon the community must face a condition of stationary business and falling prices, with all the evils and loss incidental thereto. It is possible that a supply of new money is available at a price; but this price may be so high that there is less social loss in permitting the price level to fall for a time than in paying the price for a new supply of money. There comes a turning-point, however, when the reverse will be true. Then the community will purchase more money; there will be a comparatively sudden rise in the relative proportion of money payments as compared with credit payments.

The supply of money would not, therefore, be steady, even apart from the vicissitudes of mining. If gold and silver mining were of a character such that a steady supply could be relied upon to meet the varying demands, we still would find periods of relatively sudden increase and sudden decrease of the volume of metallic money, as against the volume of credit payments. We appear at present to be passing through a period of relative increase of metallic money. The past twenty-five or thirty years has been a period of relative increase of the use of credit payment. But the credit machinery has apparently been strained beyond the point where the existing amount of metallic money constitutes an adequate reserve. The world, therefore, was confronted with a régime of falling prices. That this fallen price level has been a great hardship to many, there can, of course, be no denying. But if our reasoning is correct, it must be true that the world has suffered less from the fallen price level than it would have suffered by changing its policy and increasing the volume of metallic money. Otherwise it would have done so.

10. Artificial Increase of the Money Supply Inexpedient. — If these conclusions are correct, they suggest certain matters of importance. It would appear (1) that the world will get a new money supply when it really needs it. It would seem (2) that an artificial increase of the supply of money by such devices as bimetallism would only be a temporary expedient. It would not change the law of the growth of the relative volumes of credit payments and specie payments. It would simply substitute a higher price level for the existing price level for a time. It would seem (3) that an artificial stimulus of the credit machinery is also undesirable, because it hastens the time when the community will need a larger amount of metallic money in order to avoid the evils of falling prices.

It is clear from what has been said, that the ratio of the increase of money is by no means one of simple proportion. Indeed, the amount of money on hand may relatively decrease, for a time, with population and business growing. This, of course, is a well-known fact. But in no case does it appear that expanding business calls for a steady and proportionate increase in metallic money. The amount may be less or more than proportionate, and is never steady in its growth.

CHAPTER VIII

THE VALUE OF MONEY

REFERENCES: Del Mar, A., Science of Money, Ch. 15; Farrer, Lord, The Quantitative Theory of Money and Prices, Gold Standard Defence Association, No. 29; Hardy, S. M., The Quantity of Money and Prices, 1860–1891, Journ. Pol. Econ., March, 1895; Laughlin, J. L., The Principles of Money, Ch. 8; Mill, J. S., Political Economy, Bk. III., Chs. 8–9; Mitchell, W. C., The Quantity Theory of the Value of Money, Journ. Pol. Econ., March, 1896; Nicholson, J. S., Money and Monetary Problems, 5th ed., Pt. I., Ch. 5, Pt. II., Ch. 5; Pareto, V., Cours d'Économie Politique, Vol. I., § 290 ff.; Ricardo, D., Works (McCulloch's ed.), Ch. 27; Scott, W. A., The Quantity Theory, Annals Amer. Acad., March, 1897; Money and Banking, Chs. 3–4; Walras, L., Théorie de la Monnaie, Ch. 2; Elements d'Économie Politique Pure, 3d ed., p. 383; White, H., Money and Banking, 1st ed., pp. 419–426.

1. Difficulty of the Subject. — The most complex and difficult subject in the theory of money is the determination of its value. The popular treatment of the subject is simple enough, and receives considerable support from the usual scientific exposition. Since it is obvious that the value of money must have some relation to its quantity, it is usually said that the value of money varies with its quantity; that an increase in the amount of money will cause a fall in its value and a rise in prices; and that conversely a decrease in the quantity of money will cause a rise in its value or a fall in prices, in each case in proportion to the change in quantity. This view of the matter is far from being complete or accurate, and the subject requires careful analysis if we are to arrive at a conclusion which is definite, to say nothing of being correct.

2. The Price Level distinguished from Relative Prices. — The value, or general purchasing power, of money is indicated by the amount of goods which one standard unit of it will buy. This amount is the typical, or composite, unit of commodity, which may be described as composed of a quantity of every article in the market, the value of each article in the unit being the same proportion of the value of the whole unit as that of the whole amount of the article is to the total value of all the goods on sale. The value of money is a question of the relation between goods and money, and not between one kind of goods and another. In asking what is the value of money, we ask not why one article costs $1 and another $2 but why the articles cost $1 and $2 respectively, rather than some other amounts, as $5 and $10. The question why one article costs $1 and another $2 is a question of relative prices, a question of the relation of goods to one another. The other question is an inquiry of the relation of goods to money. What we are seeking to determine is the value which will attach to the money article, as money, in consequence of being actually exchanged for goods at a given moment.

3. Conditions assumed to simplify the Problem. — The problem is one of considerable complexity, because there are so many factors of which the value of money is a resultant. An equilibrium must be determined, in the first place, between the value of the money article for monetary purposes and its value for use in the arts; then between this value and that of the goods for which it exchanges. Finally, when these equilibria have been determined, they are modified by the introduction of credit and by the retention of exchange by barter. For the solution of a problem so complex it is necessary that we should isolate certain of the factors, as well as we can, and seek to determine their action when regarded as operating by themselves. Accordingly we assume, first, that the money article is used for no purpose but to effect exchanges. It facilitates exchange and serves as a measure of value, but it is of no use for direct consumption. It is assumed, further, that there is on hand, and actually offered in exchange, a given quantity of such money, and a definite amount of goods; and that money passes at each sale, no commodity being exchanged by barter or sold on credit. Under these conditions, what determines the value of money?

4. The Value of Money a Social Fact. — The value of money which we are seeking is, we must remember, a social phenomenon. It is not the purchasing power set upon money by any individual. It may be that, of the indefinite number of people who participate in its determination, no two agree, and that not one individual valuation is the same as that which finally emerges from the competitive struggle. The value in question depends primarily upon the service which it renders, as a medium of exchange, to society as a whole. The nature and amount of that service is found in the addition which money exchange makes to the utilities at the disposal of society, and this addition marks the upper limit of the value of the money at the disposal of society.

5. Advantage of replacing Barter with Money Exchange. — Let us assume a society composed of people unacquainted with exchange, who by the bounty of nature possess ten thousand million units of goods. Each member of the community consumes what he himself produces and exchanges with no one else. All the people together consume directly five thousand million units and are entirely contented with that amount of consumption, so that no further satisfaction can be obtained from the rest of the goods. The remainder of their possessions, therefore, have no utility and no value for them. Suppose, now, that one thousand million units of goods are bartered, and thereby get into the hands of people who want them. The result will be an increase in utilities to the community, and the amount of increase in utility will represent the advantage of simple barter, or direct exchange. If, in accomplishing this amount of exchanges, the community used any quantity of goods up to one thousand million units, it would gain. Hence it could afford to consume any quantity up to that amount, in performing the exchanges necessary to carry off the additional one thousand million units of goods. As a result of the inability of the members of the community to get together at the right times and places, with the right amounts and kinds of goods, the other four thousand million units of goods cannot be exchanged, and their value would therefore be lost.

Suppose that money is now suddenly introduced. The community all at once finds that some article possesses the quality of universal marketability, so that each individual is willing to give it for goods he wants and does not have, or take it for goods he has and does not want. By means of this money the people are enabled, we will suppose, to exchange at one moment all the remaining four million units of goods, actually paying out a piece of money in each exchange for a unit of goods. The consequence of this change is an increase of utilities to the community, and the amount of this increase represents the advantages of a complex barter, or money exchange. In order to secure these additional utilities, the society can afford to expend any amount up to their total value.

6. The Maximum Value of the Money Supply which a Society can afford to Have. — If the means, the machinery, created for performing the exchanges, lasted through more than one period of exchanges, the society could afford to provide it, if, within its life, it returned its original cost at the current profitableness of production. That is, the upper value of the means of exchange to society will be that of an investment of capital, whose product is equal to the expense of barter thus saved. In other words, let us suppose that the cost of exchanging goods by barter is represented to a community by the consumption of A units of utility, in one set of exchanges, or in one period of exchange. Let Y represent the quantity of money introduced; and B its cost, in units of utility consumed in its production. If Y, the money, lasts only through one set of exchanges and then perishes, society will save in performing the exchanges A units of utility and will expend B units, thus saving by the exchange $A-B$ units. If the money lasts through two exchanges, the saving in each is $A-B/2$; if through three exchanges, $A-B/3$. If there are X exchanges, the saving in each is $A-B/X$. If X is indefinite, that is, if the money lasts through an indefinite period, as is practically the case with gold, then the fraction B/X approaches zero, and, to use a mathematical phrase, the saving would approach A. At this point, society can afford to invest a value which, at the current profitableness of production, will yield A units of utility within the period of duration of one complete set of exchanges. This is true whatever the physical character of money. If the money is paper and lasts only for one or two exchanges, the cost of production, B, grows smaller, and the number of exchanges through which it lasts grows smaller too. In other words, the fraction B/X approaches zero, as in the case of commodity money. However, B/X will always be larger for paper money than for gold money. At the limit of profitableness of its use, therefore, the cost of production has no effect on the value of money. The maximum amount of money which a community can afford to acquire will depend, therefore, upon the current profitableness of its industry, and will have a value such as, at that rate, will yield, within the period necessary to complete one set of exchanges, a return equal, at the maximum, to the expense of making the exchange by barter. In other words, if it be assumed that the amount and nature of money as an instrument is such as will enable exchanges with it to be so extended that the greatest possible amount of utilities derivable from exchange will be secured, then this greatest possible amount of utilities derivable from exchange will set the upper limit to the total value of money.

7. The Minimum Value of the Money Supply to a Society. — The total value of money to society also has a lower limit. It is often said that any sum of money, however small, would suffice to perform the exchanges; that the only difference that would be caused by using a larger or a smaller quantity would be in the terms in which prices were expressed. In other words, it is said that to reduce, or to multiply, the amount of money in use ten times, would simply change the money valuation of all articles and scale prices according to the change in the quantity of money. This statement has an element of truth, but needs to be carefully made in order not to mislead. If the money in use were non-material, the statement would be true; but the money article is material. In order to serve its purpose it must be divided and distributed among many people, over large areas. This physical division and distribution cannot take place unless there is a certain quantity. There must be enough to work with, else the physical difficulties of barter would simply be replaced with the physical difficulties of money exchange. When this working minimum of money, whatever it is, is obtained, an actual ratio of exchange between money and goods emerges. This minimum just removes the expense of the most expensive portion of barter exchange. The total value of money may, therefore, fluctuate between this minimum and the greatest possible amount of utilities derivable from exchange, but will always be determined by the utilities which it creates or saves. The total value of money being determined, the value of the unit of money will be proportionate to the number of units.

8. The Unreality of the Above Conditions and the Actual Limits of the Money Supply. — But no society, no community, no country, ever acquires this maximum; for in none does that state of affairs ever obtain wherein a piece of money actually changes hands for one, and only one, unit of goods within the period of a single set of exchanges. Each piece performs its service many times within each period. Moreover, in a society which makes its exchanges entirely without the use of credit, the money exchange would never wholly supplant the barter exchange. Nor would any society remain content with the minimum supply. In the absence of credit, and under the conditions which were assumed as to the character and services of the money article, each society will push its acquisition of money to the point where the investment of further labor and capital for the exchange of an additional unit of goods would yield no utility over exchanging the goods by barter.

The application of successive units of money to effect exchanges is attended by results of varying importance. Each unit applied adds a less proportionate value than the last preceding one, up to the point where the social cost of making another exchange will be the same whether made by barter or by money exchange. Any addition of money beyond the quantity necessary to bring this about will lower its marginal utility below the point of profitableness. The value of the unit of money would under these conditions be lessened. The total value of the money would not change, however, because nothing has been added to the utilities afforded by money exchange. Hence the decrease in marginal utility, or the value of the monetary unit, must be, beyond this point, inversely proportional to its quantity. The use of money beyond this point would involve a social loss.[1] Subtractions from the amount of money, when it is in excess, take nothing from the total utilities its use confers on society and will not affect its total value while the excess remains; but the value of the unit will increase in proportion to the change in quantity.

If the amount of money available is less than sufficient to substitute money exchange for barter, down to the point of equilibrium of advantage from the two methods of exchange, additions to its amount will add something to the utilities derivable from exchange by means of money, and will increase its total value. For, although the value of the unit will decrease, since each succeeding unit applied in effecting exchanges adds a less proportionate value than the preceding one, the decrease will not be in proportion to the increase in the number of units. Subtractions from its amount will take something from the utilities derivable from money exchange, and will therefore reduce its total value, but not in proportion to the decrease in the amount, because the value of the unit will increase, since the last unit now used in effecting exchanges has a greater value than any of the units dropped from use.

[1] Under certain conditions an addition to the quantity would add less than nothing to the utilities derivable from exchange, and would lower the value of the unit in greater rate than the increase in the number of units. This would occur, for example, if confidence in government paper were shaken when it was the only money in use.

9. Limitation upon the Freedom of Choice between Barter and Money Exchange. — Two hypotheses underlying this discussion are so vital to its logical consistency, and to the conformity of the theory with actual conditions, that it is important to consider how far they are realized. One of these hypotheses is that in the effort to secure the cheapest means of exchange at any time, society is able to resort, without loss, to barter or to money exchange, indifferently. This is, however, far from being possible. The use of money develops an amount of business to which barter could not possibly be applied; and, moreover, even in the cases in which it was formerly used, when it has once been abandoned, it cannot be again resorted to to any large extent. For not only will the money-using habit have been established, but the money is a tool which, once produced, must be used. It cannot be put aside without loss. It represents to society a fixed investment which will prove a loss if its use is abandoned. It would seem, therefore, that a quantity of money once produced in excess of the amount which will make the marginal exchange profitable, may be used with less social loss than its abandonment would occasion. It would seem, therefore, that the effect of a change in the quantity of money on its value could not be readily and effectually checked through resort to a larger or smaller use of barter, and would therefore be more violent than the discussion above would indicate.

The restriction on the resort to barter after the money exchange has become established is of less importance, however, than the above remarks of themselves would justify us in believing. For, in the first place, although resort to direct barter is not available, society can vary its exchanges through credit, and will do so until the marginal utility of money for effecting exchanges directly is equal to its marginal utility for effecting them through the credit machinery.

Again, the unavailability of a resort to barter to check the effect of changes in the quantity of money is offset in a measure by the fact that a change in the quantity of money induces, immediately or soon, a change in the amount of goods to be exchanged. Society has, therefore, an economic escape in at least two ways from changes in the value of money due to sudden changes in its amount.

10. The Relation of the Quantity of Goods to their Marginal Utilities. — The second important hypothesis which underlies our theory of the value of money is that the marginal utilities of goods are not proportional to their quantities. This seems so obvious as scarcely to need mention, yet it seems not infrequently to be ignored in discussions of the value of money. We have seen that under certain conditions the value of money is proportional to its quantity — a point which we shall soon establish in another way. Too often, however, the modifying conditions are omitted from the statement. It holds true, as we shall see later, only when the quantity of goods for which this money is exchanged is assumed *to remain constant*, so that their marginal utility does not change, although the quantity of money does change. Under these circumstances the marginal utility of the money article, if it has no other use, must be constant, and the size of the marginal unit will depend entirely on the total quantity. That is, as the mathematicians say, the marginal unit whose utility remains unchanged is a magnitude of a different order from the marginal unit before the change.

11. The Value of Money at any Moment determined by Demand and Supply. — If, then, money is available at a cost, society will gradually extend its use down to the point where its marginal service equals in value that of other means of exchange. It will do so through the competition of individuals who are seeking to exchange their products. That is, the value of the money in use at any time will be fixed by competition for it; and, socially speaking, it will be the capitalized value of the service rendered in the marginal exchange. Each exchanger of goods will be willing to give for it the capitalized value of an amount that equals the utility of money exchange over barter, as applied in the exchange of the last unit of goods he sells. For this, to him, is the marginal cost of exchange. These costs, and the utilities equivalent to them, which are created by the use of money, differ for different producers. Hence they compete for the money, offering amounts which represent the capitalized value of its service to them. As a result of this competition, the value of the money unit at any moment will be that imputed to the last unit of money demanded, as measured by the utility of the last unit of goods offered in exchange for the money. In other words, the value of the money will be the value of its marginal unit offered and accepted in exchange, and will be equal to the utility of the last unit of goods necessary to bring into use the whole amount of money demanded.

In order to make this clear, let us illustrate the method of procedure by which the ratio of exchange between two articles is fixed. Suppose there are five men who wish to sell wheat and five who have money to offer for it. Let us suppose that—

A offers one bushel of wheat for $0.97.
B offers one bushel of wheat for $0.98.
C offers one bushel of wheat for $1.02.
D offers one bushel of wheat for $1.03.
E offers one bushel of wheat for $1.00.

That is to say, each one of these men estimates the value of a bushel of wheat to himself as equivalent to that of the amount of money represented by 97 cents, 98 cents, etc., respectively.

Now, the owners of money who want to buy wheat do not know, any more than do the holders of wheat, what is the price that must obtain in order to carry off the entire product in exchange for all the money which they offer. Therefore they will offer different amounts of money per bushel. To continue our illustration, let us suppose that —

A′ is willing to give for a bushel of wheat $1.00.
B′ is willing to give for a bushel of wheat $1.05.
C′ is willing to give for a bushel of wheat $0.95.
D′ is willing to give for a bushel of wheat $0.98.
E′ is willing to give for a bushel of wheat $0.99.

Each would-be buyer wishes, of course, to get his wheat as cheaply as possible, and is not likely to offer his maximum price. The man who is willing to give $1.00 rather than go without, will wait to see whether somebody else does not get wheat at a lower price. If so, he will not give $1.00. Let us suppose that the offers begin at 90 cents and rise gradually. At 90 cents per bushel any one of the holders of money would buy, but no one of the owners of wheat would sell. This state of affairs would continue until the price offered reached 97 cents, the lowest figure which any seller is willing to take.

When the price was at 97 cents four would be willing to buy and one to sell.
At 98 cents four would be willing to buy and two to sell.
At 98½ cents three would be willing to buy and two to sell.
At 99 cents three would be willing to buy and two to sell.

At 99½ cents two would be willing to buy and two to sell.

At 99¾ cents two would be willing to buy and two to sell.

At $1.00 two would be willing to buy and three to sell.

At $1.05 one would be willing to buy and five to sell.

It is obvious that the sales would take place at a point between a little over 99 cents and a little less than $1.00.[1]

If there is an increase in the supply of wheat, its marginal utility will fall and more of it will be offered for the same amount of money. If there is a decrease in the supply of wheat offered, the opposite state of affairs will be true. As a result of the competitive forces in the case under consideration, we find, then, that the value of money is fixed at a point where approximately $1 will exchange for one bushel of wheat. If, instead of wheat, we use our composite unit of commodity, there will be no difference in the illustration. The effect of offering two articles instead of one for money, at the same time, is simply to offer a composite commodity unit of the kind we have described, composed of two articles, each entering in to form the unit in the ratio determined by its relative value. If we add three or more, the same

[1] Just where the fluctuation would stop and the exact price emerge, is still an uncertain question.

thing is true. Instead of one bushel of wheat we have now a composite unit of three or more articles. If the amount of money is increased, each additional increment brings out for exchange an additional quantity of goods, which, at the former price, was kept out of the market. That is, as money is added the price rises to the value which the next marginal seller must get for each unit of goods that he is willing to sell.

It is obvious, therefore, as was already said, that the value of money is fixed in precisely the same way as the value of other articles. It is equal always to the marginal utility of the last unit of goods necessary to absorb, or put into use, all the units of money wanted, and the number wanted will be fixed by society at the point where the advantage of money exchange will be in equilibrium with that of other means of exchange. It may happen, when the value of money has been for the moment fixed, that there are owners who impute a higher value to their goods than is contained in the amount of money which they could get for them. In that case they will either consume the goods themselves, or exchange them by barter, or suffer loss.

12. The Quantity of Money and its Value.—If the amount of goods remained the same through several sets of exchanges, while the quantity of money changed, the marginal utility of the goods would be constant, the amount of money which the marginal unit would command would change, but the marginal utility of this changing amount would remain the same, since it is but the borrowed, or reflected, utility of the marginal unit of goods. In this case the value of the money would vary inversely as its quantity. This is the same conclusion at which we arrived when considering the value of money from the point of view of a social investment. To bring this point out clearly, let us suppose that there are one thousand units of goods, and that the marginal utility of the goods is three units of utility. Then one unit of goods will exchange for $\frac{1}{1000}$ of the money, and the marginal utility of the money also will be three. In other words, the whole quantity of money will be divided into one thousand pieces, each piece will exchange for one unit of goods and the marginal utility of each piece will be that of a unit of goods. Supposing now the quantity of money is arbitrarily doubled, what will be the effect on its value? Obviously, under our assumption, one unit of goods will exchange still for $\frac{1}{1000}$ of all the money. The new unit of money will be twice the quantity of the old unit, but its marginal utility will be the same, for its marginal utility will be that of the goods it buys. Obviously, therefore, the marginal utility of money has sunk one-half. The value of the present quantity of money which is equal to that in the former marginal unit will be $1\frac{1}{2}$. In other words, the value of money has changed inversely as its quantity. The same conclusion holds for diminution of the quantity of money.

The relation between the quantity of money and its value, *under the conditions we have assumed*, is, therefore, purely quantitative. The value is proportional to the quantity in an inverse ratio. The reason for this is, as has been pointed out, that the money has no marginal utility of its own. It is of no use, *under our hypothesis*, excepting for exchange. Once on hand, it must be used in exchange unless, indeed, it becomes so voluminous as to check the confidence of the community in its stability of value, and so to cause it to be abandoned.

13. The Relation of Quantity and Value in the Case of Commodity Money. — The quantitative relation just described can exist, however, with only one kind of money, — inconvertible paper. The fact is that the money article has always had direct utility, a marginal utility derived from the fact that it was in demand for other purposes than exchange. The effect of the existence of a marginal utility due to other uses than exchange is to render ineffective the relation between the quantity of money and its value. To prove this, let us refer to our former illustration. According to that, one thousand units of goods with a marginal utility of three were exchanged for one thousand units of money, and the marginal utility of the money was also three. When we doubled the quantity of money, we found that each unit of goods exchanged for just double the former quantity of money, and that the value of the money was halved. But according to our present supposition, the value of the money is the result of an independent force. The demand for it for direct consumption fixes a marginal utility upon it as a commodity, irrespective of its use as money. Now the marginal utility of a commodity does not vary inversely as its quantity. If we double the quantity of wheat, we may not thereby halve its value; or, on the other hand, we may reduce it by more than half. Similarly, doubling the quantity of a money article of direct utility may not reduce its value one-half. Suppose the increase of quantity reduces the value one-third, so that the utility of the amount of money in the old marginal unit is 2. The amount of money which has this marginal utility is one-half that of the new marginal unit, whose utility is, therefore, 4. The marginal utility of the goods is still 3. Hence we will give, not 2 units of the old size, but 1½, for a unit of goods. For 1½ units, with a marginal utility of 2 per unit, will give us 3 units of utility, which is the value of a unit of goods. Thus the former proportion between the quantity of money and its value no longer holds.

A slight modification of the above reasoning is necessary in order to be true to facts. We assumed that the marginal utility of money was fixed independently of its use as money, by the demand for it for direct consumption. This is not wholly correct. The marginal utility of the money is a resultant of the demand for money for purposes of exchange and the demand for the money article for other uses. Therefore the marginal utility which emerged would, perhaps, not be 2, as we assumed, but it could hardly, under any circumstances, be $1\frac{1}{2}$. We see, then, that the value of commodity money cannot be in the inverse ratio of its quantity; but that this relation may hold, under the conditions assumed, in the case of inconvertible paper money. But one of the assumed conditions, the constancy of the volume of goods exchanged, can never be realized, so that even with this kind of money the proportional relation between value and quantity fails. For if the volume of goods changes, their marginal utility does not change in the same ratio. But the value of the money is but the reflected marginal utility of the goods.

The importance of the conclusion just drawn, both in theory and practice, cannot be overemphasized. It shows us that while it is true that the value of money has some relation to the quantity, it is not proportional to the quantity, excepting in the case of inconvertible paper; and even here we may later have to note a limitation. Even under a purely monetary régime, such as we have assumed, an increase or decrease in the quantity of money would affect prices in a much less degree than the change in the quantity might lead us to expect. For the additional supply in the one case, and the amount withdrawn in the other, would include a portion devoted to other than monetary purposes. We shall see later that under some circumstances the value of money may fall with a decrease of its quantity.

14. The Establishment of Equilibrium among the Various Demands for the Money Commodity. — The fixing of the marginal utility and the value of money, by the establishment of an equilibrium between its marginal utilities for the two classes of uses, is important enough to justify a somewhat more careful and detailed examination of the process. The demand for gold for either of the two classes of purposes, arts or money, is not simple. Gold is called for in the fine arts, in dentistry, for personal adornment, and for many other uses. Clearly, the same amount of gold used in any one of these ways must afford an amount of satisfaction equal to what would be obtained from its use in any other. The value of the money commodity as fixed by the demand for it for use in the arts is a resultant of the rates of exchange established for all of these purposes; but we need only consider the method by which its value is established for a single one of them.

Let the cost of successive equal portions of the money material, which we may assume to be gold, be 1, 1.1, 1.2, 1.3, 1.5, etc., of our composite units of goods. Let the number of composite commodity units which the holders of goods are willing to offer for successive units of gold for use in the arts be 2, 1.8, 1.6, 1.3, etc. Then the value of gold as a commodity will be fixed at the point where the amount of satisfaction derived from the possession of gold, as measured in terms of the commodity unit, will equal the cost of getting the gold in terms of the commodity unit. The amount of gold offered at this rate will equal the amount demanded at the same rate. An equilibrium will be established between demand and supply, and the relative values of the money commodity and other commodities will be thus fixed.

The demand for gold for use as money, like the demand for it for the arts, is not of a simple character. Gold is used in making direct payments, and for a reserve to insure solvency. An equilibrium is established between the marginal utility of gold for these two purposes, and then between this equilibrium and the marginal utility of goods.

The value of money as it emerges from any set of exchanges is, therefore, the resultant of a complex group of forces. To produce this resultant, equilibrium must be established (*a*) between the cost of the money article and its value; (*b*) between its marginal utility for making exchanges and for other purposes; (*c*) between its marginal utility for direct payments and for reserves; (*d*) between its marginal utility to society in making exchanges and that of other means of making the exchanges; (*e*) between its marginal utility and that of the goods it exchanges for; and (*f*) between the cost of the goods and their marginal utility. The mere enumeration of these interdependent factors shows how futile is the attempt to establish a relation of simple proportion between the quantity of money and its value.

15. The Volume of Business and the Value of Money. — What has been said does not prove that no relation between the quantity of money and prices exists, but that the relation is not one of inverse proportion, and that it is remote and indirect rather than immediate and direct. Somewhere in the vast volume of exchanges is a demand for money, standard money, for payment, which, in conjunction with the demand for it for other purposes, determines its value. For it is not true that the demand for standard money for use has an insignificant effect on its value, and that its value is fixed entirely by other than monetary demand. The actual use is considerable notwithstanding, and, indeed, because of, the vast volume of credit exchanges; for the growth of the total volume of credit exchanges is likely to leave a growing balance calling for the direct use of money. At any moment the value of the standard money is fixed by the interplay of competition between buyers and sellers of gold; but it is a competition to buy and sell, not gold in general, but a definite amount, a definite supply. The demand is not for an amount sufficient to settle all exchanges, but sufficient only for the settlement of the balance of exchanges. Now, the same balance may represent very different total volumes of exchanges, at different times, on the same price level. That is to say, the demand for money for immediate payment may remain the same for very different volumes of business, or it may be larger, or smaller, for the same volume of business at different times. The total volume of exchanges, therefore, is not a safe index of the demand for money for actual payment, and a changing volume does not imply need for a changing supply of money to keep the same price level. The demand for money for direct payment, added to the demand for money for reserve, constitutes the total demand for monetary purposes. Now, the amount of the money demand is fixed at any moment at the point where the marginal utility of money for direct payment and for reserves equals its marginal utility for other uses. If the volume of exchanges is increased, the amount settled by direct payment may grow smaller, or larger, or remain the same. If it grows smaller, money may pass from use for direct payments to reserves just fast enough to absorb the amount set free from direct use. In that case, the marginal utility of the money article for exchange purposes may not change. That is, the price level will remain the same, despite the change of the total volume of business. If the reserve money does not increase so fast as that, the ratio of exchange will change in favor of the goods offered for direct payment, and prices will rise, as is evidenced both by the fact that a smaller balance of goods is offered for the amount used for direct payments, and that there is a larger demand for money for indirect payments.

The price level, or the value of money is, therefore, not the ratio of exchange between all the money and the total volume of goods; nor between the amount of money directly used in payments and the total volume of goods; but between this last amount of money and the balance of exchanges not settled by other means.

The only way in which a changing total volume of business can affect the price level is by varying the balances to be settled by direct payment. But the relation between these balances and the total volume of business which gives rise to them is by no means constant, so that the total volume of business, and therefore the goods offered for sale, bears no direct relation to the quantity of money available, and cannot exercise a direct influence on the price level.

In all this discussion it has been assumed that the quantity of standard money, that is, the amount of the money commodity used for direct payments and for reserves, is constant. We must remember, however, that a change in the value of the money commodity at any point causes a new distribution of the money; therefore, a change in prices in any direction will be less than if there were no non-money uses for the money commodity. If we suppose a change in the supply of money, the effect on prices will depend upon the readjustment produced in the distribution of money between direct and indirect payments. All of the additional supply may remain in the service of direct money exchanges; or part of it may so remain, while the rest becomes the basis of the extension of credit exchanges. If the former happens, and if there is no change in the total volume of exchanges, the other means of settlement, that is by reserves, must decrease to the point where a new equilibrium is established between the marginal utility of the new balance of goods and the new supply of money used in direct payments.

On the other hand, the new supply of money may go mostly to facilitate exchanges by indirect payments, that is, for use as reserves. Then the volume of exchanges performed by the indirect method will increase, and the balance remaining for direct money exchange will be less, but not in proportion to the total increase of money, nor in proportion to the addition devoted to direct exchange.

CHAPTER IX

STABILITY OF THE VALUE OF MONEY

REFERENCES: see references for preceding chapter; Marshall, A., Principles of Economics, 3d ed., pp. 185, 208, 319 note, 432 note, 424, and 673–674, note; Mill, J. S., Principles of Political Economy, Bk. III., Chs. 8, 9; Nicholson, J. S., Money and Monetary Problems, 5th ed., pp. 63–64, 68–71; Pareto, V., Cours d'Économie Politique, § 306; Philippovich, E. von, Grundriss der Politischen Oekonomie, 4te Aufl., Erster Band, § 94.

1. Nature of the Price Level. — The value of money, as we have thus far considered it, results from the competition of buyers and sellers acting together at one time. That is to say, it is the value which emerges from a single set of exchanges. It is important to determine how, if at all, our conclusions must be modified to adapt them to conditions of business activity which last long enough to allow for the occurrence of the ordinary vicissitudes of trade. If, for the sake of example, we think of the work of a season, or period, of production as finished, and all the products brought together to be exchanged in one group of transactions, we will have what is here meant by a single set of exchanges. Two or more such sets of exchanges will form a series. A value of money emerges from a single set of exchanges; the recurrence of that value from each succeeding set of exchanges furnishes the continuous level of prices which is of interest to business men. The price level, thus regarded, is not so much the result of lapse of time as of a succession of groups of exchanges. The value of money through such a series of exchanges is not the arithmetical average of the values that emerge from the single sets of exchanges. Rather, as has been well said, it is a mean "such that had it been a constant price during a period, the amounts bought and sold would have been just what they actually are."[1] The condition of the maintenance of this level, of the continuity of this mean, are the conditions of steady prices. What these conditions are, under what circumstances the value that emerges from a single set of exchanges may keep steady, is a question of great practical, as well as theoretical, importance.

2. Rapidity of Circulation. — In order to make the problem clear, let us assume that all the conditions of the determination of the value of money, thus far considered, are constant. It might seem that if the quantity of goods and the quantity of money remain the same, in two successive sets of exchanges, the value of money would not change. This, however, does not follow. In order to complete or effect the first set of exchanges, the money changes hands, or circulates a certain number of

[1] Fisher, I., "Mathematical Investigations into the Theory of Prices," *Trans. Conn. Acad.*, Vol. IX., July, 1892, p. 21.

times. If, in performing the second set of exchanges whose total volume is the same, the same amount of money changes hands a different number of times from what it did before, the resulting value of money will be different. The number of times which the money changes hands in order to do a given volume of business is known as its rapidity of circulation. This is an expression which needs some explanation. The word "rapidity" suggests to the mind the thought of time; and the common explanation of the phrase is, that it is the number of times which money changes hands in a given time. This, however, is hardly correct. It is conceivable that money should change hands twice as often in one year as in another, without any change at all in the rapidity of circulation, using that phrase in its proper sense. If the price level in the second year is one-half what it was in the previous year, the volume of business done will be the same in the two years, and the true rapidity of circulation will be the same, although the money has changed hands twice as often in the one case as in the other. On the other hand, if the volume of business doubles, without any change in the quantity of money, or in the price level, the rapidity of circulation is doubled; but it does not follow that the money has changed hands twice all around, instead of only once.

Again, if in two communities the same volume of business is done in a year, and if the amount of money is the same in each, while its value in one place is double its value in the other, and if the business of one locality is done with only half the number of transactions that occur in the other, the rapidity of circulation is the same in both, although the money changes hands twice as often in the one place as in the other, in the same period of time. In short, the rapidity of the passage of money from hand to hand must vary, not with the time, but inversely as the price level, if the volume of business is constant and the amount of money used is to remain unchanged. The idea which the expression conveys is the amount of exchange work which a unit of money does in a given total of business, and is analogous to the thought conveyed by the word activity, or power, in mechanics. It is the proportion of a given total amount of work which a given unit of force is capable of doing. It takes the same amount of work to raise a ton of coal vertically ten feet, whether the work be done in a year or in ten minutes; by a boy with a bucket, or by a scoop which lifts the coal all at once. If, as Mill suggests, we could find another phrase, such as efficiency of money, activity of money, or power of money, something might be gained in clearness.

The desirability of a clear understanding of this factor of the price level is great enough to justify further explanation of it, even at the risk of tediousness. To illustrate it, let us suppose that there are ten people, one of whom has one hundred units of money or dollars, while each of the other nine has an amount of goods that will exchange for one of these units of money or dollars. Now, suppose further that A, who has the $100 gives it to B in exchange for his goods; B gives it to C in exchange for his goods; C to D; and so on to the end of the series. When all the exchanges are completed, each quantity of goods has changed hands, and the money is in the hands of the tenth man instead of those of the first. Each has received $100 for his goods. The price level is, therefore, one hundred. Let us suppose, however, that instead of giving all his money directly to B, A wishes to purchase at the same moment from each one of the men who has goods. In order to do so, he will need as many times $100 as there are individuals ready to sell, if the price level is to be the same. He will need, therefore, $900. One hundred of this he gives to B, one hundred to C, and so on. The price level is $100 as before, but the quantity of money used in effecting the exchanges is nine times as much. The difference is due to the different rapidity of circulation in the two cases. It will be noticed that nothing has been said, and that nothing needs to be said, about the time required to perform the series of exchanges. Whether the time be a day or a year, whether the time required be the same in the two cases or not, makes no difference. In order to perform this volume of business in one way we need $100 and in order to perform it in the other way we need $900.

3. Influence of the Rapidity of Circulation on the Price Level. — It is clear from what has been said that if in any way we can increase the rapidity of circulation, the quantity of money needed to do a given volume of business will be smaller; and that if for any reason the rapidity of circulation diminishes, the quantity of money needed to do the same volume of business must be larger, provided the value of money remain the same in each case. This fact constitutes an important modification of whatever relation exists between the quantity of money and its value, or the price level. Money moves most rapidly — that is, a given amount performs a larger volume of business — in an industrial and commercial community that is highly organized, where competition is active and economic opportunities are made the most of. This is, however, the kind of community in which an increasing amount of money is constantly needed, because business is constantly expanding. The very activity that creates the demand for an enlarged supply at the same time creates influences which make necessary a smaller supply than would otherwise be the case. The need for a larger performance of monetary service is met with an increase of intensity rather than of quantity.

It will thus be seen that the rapidity of circulation of money is a factor in the maintenance of the price level, rather than in its establishment. The value of money is fixed, or may be regarded as fixed, through the action of a single group of exchanges coming at one time, rather than through a period. If, however, we are to have the same value from a second set of exchanges in which the quantities of money and goods are respectively the same as in the first set, we must have also the same rapidity of circulation. At least one writer[1] has made the mistake of thinking that because the rapidity of circulation is not an element in determining what we have called the momentary value of money, it has therefore no effect on the price level. Its importance is in the maintenance of a value once fixed by the conditions present in a particular set of exchanges.

4. Factors which affect the Rapidity of Circulation. — The causes which increase the efficiency or activity of money are its relative scarcity, density of population, improvement in means of communication and transportation, a coinage well adapted to the scale of prices and incomes, and general prosperity. Of course, if money is relatively scarce, men try to make each piece do more work. In such a condition, hoarding is likely to be less, unless, of course, the hoarding is due to panic. The influence of improved means of communication and transportation, in connection with density of population, is evident enough. Money, or its representatives, actually circulates in the physical sense more easily, safely, and rapidly under such circumstances. As to the influence of coinage, obviously, if the coins put out

[1] Mr. Carlile. See his "Evolution of Modern Money," p. 163.

for common use are not adapted to make payments in the amounts usual with the mass of people, the coins will not be used. The last influence mentioned, prosperity, lends greater facility to money transactions by inducing a feeling of confidence among the people, and therefore they spend their earnings.

The causes which reduce the rapidity of circulation of money are fear of panic and a low state of business activity. In an undeveloped country, or in an agricultural district, the amount of money and its rapidity of circulation might be small, while, of course, its purchasing power, or the price level, might be the same as in a centre of great industrial activity, because the volume of business would be correspondingly small. Ordinarily, the intensity is greatest in industrial centres. In any case, however, when the volume of exchanges of a community varies, the community in its effort to keep its price level steady will change either the amount of money it uses, or the intensity of circulation, or both, so that, having regard to their relative costs, the marginal advantage of the two methods of attaining its purpose will be the same.

Rapidity of circulation is a factor in credit, as well as in money, exchange. When applying the term to credit payments, it is perhaps better to speak of it as the mobility of balances. The easier it is to transfer the balances in the accounts of individuals, the larger the amount of business which can be done on the basis of the same reserve. It is evident, however, that the facility of payments afforded by the use of credit must vary considerably in different countries. It depends mainly on the development of banking machinery, and is greater in the United States and England than elsewhere. Its effect on the purchasing power of money is similar in character to the influence of the rapidity of circulation of money itself.

5. Reciprocal Action of Demand and Supply on the Value of Money. — The second important condition of the maintenance of the value of money which has been fixed by a single set of exchanges lies in the influence which a change in the quantity of money has upon a change in the supply of goods. Up to this point we have supposed that the supply of goods remained unchanged, and have accounted for changes in the value of money by supposing changes in its supply, or *vice versa.* In other words, we have supposed that only one of these two factors changes at a time. The fact is, that a change in the one induces a change in the other. If the supply of money changes, the supply of goods will for that reason necessarily change. The goods offered at any moment on the market for money are not all the goods that may be offered; they constitute the supply rather than the stock. There are others in reserve whose cost of production is such that it will not pay to offer them for money at the prevailing rate. Let the value of money fall, and some of this supply will come out; let it rise, and some of the supply already on the market will withdraw. It is contrary to the facts of life to believe that all the goods must remain on the market and be exchanged for all the money. In order to illustrate the effect of this fact, let us suppose that the supply of money decreases. We regard the changes now taking place from the point of view of society as a whole. We recall that, according to our theory, successive units of money were added to society's stock for effecting exchanges, so that the marginal difficulty of barter continually balanced the marginal utility of the last unit of money added. Now the units of money that are withdrawn when the supply decreases are those which replace the barter exchanges that represent the smallest cost of all the barter exchanges which were replaced with money exchange. A diminution in the supply of money, therefore, leaves the last unit used with a higher marginal utility. That is, the value of money has risen because of its diminution. Now, the common assumption is that the same quantity of goods will still be offered, and that the value of money will therefore vary inversely as its quantity, or in some fixed proportion to its quantity. Part of the effect of a variation in the quantity of money will be felt, of course, in changing its value; but, theoretically, the change would spend itself in several ways. Since the marginal utility of money has risen, there would be, in theory, less loss now in using barter as a means of exchange for those units of goods whose marginal utility is less than the marginal utility of money. Suppose that the cost of exchange of a marginal unit of a given amount of goods was one unit by barter and .9 of a unit by money exchange. When the money supply diminishes, and the value of a marginal unit of money rises, the cost of exchange of this same quantity of goods by money exchange might become 1.1 unit. Then it would be cheaper to resort to barter, and the supply of goods offered for money would be less. That is to say, a diminution in the supply of money has directly induced a corresponding diminution in the supply of goods, so that the demand for money has fallen off. Hence, its value cannot rise in proportion to the diminution in its quantity.

6. Effect of Possible Resort to Barter or Credit Exchange on the Value of Money. — This consideration, however, is purely theoretical, and can hardly ever be realized. For the expense of resorting to barter, when barter has once been abandoned, is so great, that only a catastrophic change in the quantity of money would cause it. The investment that society has made in the money means of exchange is such that it will cause a smaller loss to society to continue the money exchange at a loss, than to throw away a considerable portion of its investment.

There is, however, another method of performing exchanges, to which society may resort as cheaply as by increasing the money exchange. The credit exchanges may be increased as the value of money rises. That is to say, there may be a relative increase in the amount of credit paper used in payments. For the increase in the value of money makes possible a larger business on the same reserve. Doubtless a rise in the value of money would cause some diminution of the amount used as a reserve, and the remainder so used would support a volume of credit larger in proportion to the whole volume of payments. The volume of exchanges performed through credit may, under such circumstances, decrease absolutely, but yet form the larger proportion of the total volume of payments.

For the reason already mentioned, practically no change in the way of increasing exchange by barter can be effected. The sphere of credit exchange, however, is very flexible, and the play between direct and indirect money exchange is easy. If the amount of money available is not sufficient to effect the exchanges of society directly without a considerable rise in its value, part of it may be made to effect a larger volume of payments through indirect exchange, and the rise in its value thus be checked. If the quantity increase, so that it becomes less expensive to use money than to maintain a credit machinery to effect certain payments, the proportion of credit payments may be diminished. For there is some minimum of payment for the discharge of which it just pays to use the machinery of credit. It is here that the marginal utility of the credit mechanism is equal to its cost of service, and is equal also to the marginal utility of direct money exchange. Of course if the quantity of money increases, effects the opposite of those described would ensue.

From these considerations it would seem that, under some conditions, the quantity of money, as well as the volume of business, might remain constant, and yet a change in the value of money might be brought about by a change in the relation between the different methods of exchange. Society may exchange goods by barter, or by means of credit, or by money. Here, as elsewhere, when society has a choice of means of accomplishing its purpose, it will use the most profitable; that is, the one which offers the largest net return, if there is a difference among them. Society, therefore, will make its exchanges by barter, by money, or by credit mechanism, and the extent of the net gain from the use of each will be the same; that is, their marginal utilities in serving society must be in equilibrium.

7. Effect of a Change in the Quantity of Money on Production. — Besides the influence which a change in the quantity of money may have in changing the offerings of goods actually on hand, it is likely, also, to influence production, so that in another period of exchange more or less goods will be offered according to the direction of the change in prices. This influence, however, especially when money is rising in value and prices of goods are falling, is likely to be lessened by the retarding influence of invested capital in preventing a rapid diminution of product. With a large fixed capital, it is better to continue producing at some loss than not to produce at all. For a time, therefore, the supply of goods would not diminish as rapidly as falling prices might justify us in expecting. It is possible, moreover, that the falling price level might stimulate producers to improvements that would lead to a lessened cost of producing goods. In that case, a given supply of goods would soon be produced at a cost which would offset the increased value of money, so that the equilibrium between the cost of goods and the value of money would not vary much from what it was before the quantity of money and its marginal utility changed.

8. The Cost of Production of the Money Article and its Value. — We cannot leave the question of the influence of the quantity of money on its value without further consideration of the effect of its cost on prices. We have found reason for thinking that the cost has no effect; that the value at any moment is independent of the cost, being fixed altogether by the play of supply and demand at a point determined by the subjective valuations of the buyers and sellers. If money were very perishable, so that it could perform only a few exchanges, its cost of production, if considerable, would very materially affect its value; but the fact that it performs its services through an indefinite number of exchanges, completely alters the situation, and prevents the cost from having any effect on its present value. These conclusions can best be tested by considering the effect which the annual production of gold and its cost have upon its purchasing power.

The normal market price of goods ordinarily has a definite relation to their cost of production. Unless the price received for them is, in the long run, sufficient to warrant the expense of production, they will, of course, cease to be made. This is not so, however, in the case of gold. For several reasons there has been, in the past, no relation between the cost of gold and its value. In the first place, until a very recent time, the production of gold has not been, properly speaking, economic. That is, it has not been carried on as a business, for profit. From the earliest times gold has had for men a peculiar fascination, which has led them to endure and, indeed, to court all hardships and dangers in order to procure it. The fascination of prospecting for gold, the desire to get rich quickly, has been at the bottom of nearly all the uneconomic production of the metal from the earliest times. Men have seen and have been attracted by the gold accumulated by the few who have been successful in their search for it, and have constantly forgotten the losses, the hardships, and the sacrifices of life and property, suffered by the much larger number who have been unsuccessful. Where one has succeeded, probably hundreds have failed in their efforts to secure a sufficient amount of the precious metal to offset their labor in seeking for it. Considering the gold possessed by the world, as a whole, therefore, every ounce of it has cost many times its purchasing power.

The second reason for the lack of a definite relation between the cost of production of gold and its usual purchasing power is to be found in the relative smallness of the amount produced in a year, or in any short period of time, compared with the quantity in existence. The value, of course, is determined by the whole supply offered on the market, and not by the annual supply. The addition of a few hundreds of thousands, or even millions, of dollars in a year could have very little influence on the many millions which constitute the large accumulation of the centuries through which the world has used gold.

9. The Production of the Precious Metals. — Of course, as the stock of gold has been increased by new discoveries, a change in the purchasing power of the metal has occurred, manifested, perhaps, in more or less lengthy periodic changes in the general level of prices. This change, however, was due to the fact that the supply was larger and, irrespective of its cost of production, could not maintain its old purchasing power if other things remained the same. Economic history shows periods of variation in the supply of the world's metallic money. At the beginning of the Christian era, Mr. Jacob estimates that the amount of gold and silver money in existence was about 358,000,000 pounds sterling; that at the beginning of the ninth century, this amount was reduced to 33,674,256 pounds sterling; and that for seven hundred years afterward, the annual wear and tear just offset the annual production, so that there was no real addition to the world's supply. In 1545 the silver mines of Potosi were discovered, and the metal furnished from America increased the average annual supply to 2.25 million Pounds. This state of affairs lasted for something like fifty years.

Mr. Jacob estimates the stock of gold and silver available as money, in Europe, in the last years of the sixteenth century at 130,000,000 Pounds. During the next one hundred years the annual production of these metals became 3,375,000 Pounds, and at the end of the seventeenth century the stock of money had become 297,000,000 Pounds. During the following century the silver of Mexico was added to the supply, yielding a net stock of money for the world, estimated at 380,000,000 Pounds, by 1810. During the following quarter of a century there was a falling off in production, and the net stock available for monetary purposes, in 1829, was estimated at only 313,388,560 Pounds. Soon after this time gold-bearing sands were found in Siberia, and in 1848–1850 the world's supply was increased by the discoveries in California and Australia. These discoveries augmented the annual production of gold until about 1860, when there came a falling off which lasted until 1896, although the quantity of silver in the meantime had very largely increased.

In recent years the discoveries in Alaska and South Africa, as well as new treatment of old ores in Colorado and elsewhere, have added largely to the world's stock. "The 1899 product is nearly nine times larger than the production at the time of the California discoveries; it is greater than the combined production of gold and silver (at coining value) in 1891, when the world's production of silver reached its high-water mark, and greater also than the combined production of both metals in each of the subsequent three years (up to and including 1894)." [1]

10. The Influence of the Increased Production of Gold on its Value. — The question may fairly be asked whether, in view of the great increase in the annual production, the doctrine that the annual product of gold has no appreciable influence on its purchasing power must not be modified. The quantity now annually produced is a very much larger percentage of the total stock than was the case at any other time in the world's history. Moreover, gold mining is rapidly becoming reduced to the condition of a regular business, subject to capitalistic methods of production and management, and largely freed from the acciden-

[1] Director of the Mint: Report on Production of the Precious Metals, 1899, p. 45.

tal features that have characterized it throughout the world's history hitherto. A yearly addition amounting to twenty per cent. of the total existing stock must have considerable influence on the purchasing power of the metal, so that we must admit that the annual production to-day is a more disturbing factor than it has been in the past. Its cost has doubtless been less, and certainly has been more exactly ascertainable, and may have been low enough to depress the value of the whole to some degree. But, after all, it is the current value that determines the limits of profitable cost. It fixes the cost of production that the purchaser can afford to incur. Therefore, the more rapidly gold mining becomes a regular business, in which large capital is invested, the more sensitive will it be to changes in the purchasing power of the vast stock in the world's possession. When the cost of production is such as to offer only the usual margin of profit, a fall in the purchasing power of money will very quickly be reflected in a diminution of the output. Therefore, whatever the annual production, as soon as the industry has assumed the character of a settled business, the disturbing influence of the annual variations in production will be minimized.

There is still another reason for believing that the annual production, however large, cannot cause any great change in the purchasing power of the stock already on hand. The product, whatever it is, finds its way into the world's business through the banks. The first effect of an increased supply is to stimulate discounts and to cause an expansion of business done on credit. The result, of course, is to increase the supply of goods offered for gold, and therefore to raise the price of gold. This influence will in time counteract any influence due to an increase in the annual production. Whatever effect the recent great production may have had in raising prices is attributed to the fact that the increased quantity has been produced at a cost approximately equal to, or less than, the existing purchasing power of gold. An increased supply will soon lower this purchasing power, and diminish the profitableness of mining at the present cost of production. The result will be a temporary check to investment in gold mining, so far as it is carried on as a business by invested capital.

It is true, to be sure, that a diminution of the profit in gold mining will stimulate further improvements to produce it at a lower cost as its purchasing power falls. This influence will work against a rise in the purchasing power, as it does in the case of all other goods. We may therefore expect in the future that, as gold mining becomes more and more subjected to the influence of a capitalistic régime, we shall have a more regular periodicity in its production and value, and periods of great increase will be shorter, while its purchasing power will fluctuate less as mining becomes more and more a regular business.

There is no reason to expect any early diminution of the great supply of gold. The supply has increased because gold became scarce enough to raise its price to a point which justified a larger expense in producing it. "There is no reason to expect any cessation of this annual increase for some years to come. The Transvaal has not nearly reached its limit; Australia, particularly West Australia, is not yet half developed; Alaska and the Yukon have only fairly begun to produce, while the recent steady increase in Colorado and other Western states shows no signs of abating. The present output differs from that in the fifties, when the California placers yielded such enormous stores of gold, because these could be exhausted, more or less speedily, while the present yield comes from the working of low-grade ore, rendered profitable by improved modern methods of reduction, and is practically unlimited."[1]

From all the considerations which have been adduced, it is very obvious that the effects of changes in the quantity of money on its value are very complex and difficult to trace. An increase or decrease of the quantity may, or may not, be reflected in the price level at all, or not to a degree that has any correspondence whatever with the change in the quantity. For (1) contemporaneous with a change in the quantity of the money article may be a demand for it for other

[1] Director of the Mint: Report on Production of the Precious Metals for 1899, p. 45.

uses; (2) the intensity of circulation will be likely to change; (3) the supply of goods will almost certainly change, and produce an effect opposite to that of the supply of money; (4) the change may react on other methods of making payments, especially the use of credit paper, in such a way as to offset its own effect.

11. The Cost of its Money Supply to a Country. — Up to this point our discussion has concerned the general value of money, the value to the world as a whole, and for goods in general as typified by our ideal composite commodity unit. We have found that this value, or purchasing power, or price level, as it is variously called, depends, in the last analysis, on the service which money renders, and that the evident measure of this is what we must give to get money. But the general value of money is nowhere realized. Goods are not sold in composite lumps, and the relative prices of goods, as well as the general price level, are an important matter for consideration. The general value of money could be realized only if competition were perfect and intelligent, knowledge of economic conditions equal, and the distribution of money costless. As in the case of every other economic activity, none of these conditions is realizable. Hence, we must expect to find different values for money in different places, and to find that changes in its quantity affect its relative values differently in different places.

The local value of money depends on the value

of the things that must be given for it. Goods have different values to different people, so that some may get a given quantity of money for less than others. This law of the relative value of money for different places is not different from the law that fixes the general value of money. The marginal utility of the money secured must equal the marginal utility of the goods given. It follows that the bullion which a country requires "will always cost as much to that nation in services of all kinds as the production of the articles, in return for which the bullion is obtained."[1]

It follows that one country may get its supply at less cost than another. The one to which the cost is greater would probably be satisfied with a smaller quantity. If, now, the total volume of business, rapidity of circulation, and other conditions were the same in both, the price level would be different in the two. Obviously, then, the value of money in a country is influenced in a measure by the ratio of exchange, or relative costs of production, of goods between itself and the countries with which it trades.

12. Changes in Relative Prices consequent on Changes in General Prices. — Hence, a change in the price of its exports will change relative prices within a country. Suppose a country has two commodities, *A* and *B*, only *A* being exported. If one unit of *A* exchanges for $2 and also for 3 units of B within the country, then $2 will buy 3

[1] N. G. Pierson, "Principles of Economics," pp. 369–370.

units of *B* and the price of one unit of *B* will be .66⅔. Suppose, now, that the foreign demand for commodity *A* increases, and forces its price up to $3 for one unit of it. Then the marginal utility of *A* will rise, and one unit of it will exchange for more of commodity *B* than it did before. Instead of exchanging for 3 units of *B*, it will now exchange, let us say, for 3.5 units of *B*. But one unit of *A* now exchanges for $3; therefore 3.5 units of *B* will also be priced at $3, and one unit of *B* will sell for .81. The result is not only a rise in the price of both articles, but a change in their relative exchange values. A similar effect in changing the relative prices is caused by a curtailment in expenditure, brought about by a diminution of the quantity of money. For such a reduction in expenditure would cut off the demand for different goods in varying degrees. A change of ten per cent., for example, in the supply of wheat will cause a greater change in its price than a change of perhaps six per cent. will cause in the price of steel rails or woollen cloth. The elasticity of demand, as it is called, is not the same for all articles, and it is not constant for any one article throughout the whole course of its sale from a single unit to the point of saturation of demand. Consequently, a falling off in the supply of money would possibly cause a cessation of demand for some things, a greatly reduced demand for others, and scarcely any change in the demand for still others. The composition of our composite unit of commodity would change. Instead of 1.5 *X*,

2 *Y*, 3 *Z*, and 3.5 *U* going to make up our typical unit, we might have 1.5 *Y*, 2 *Z*, 2.5 *U*. This would imply a change both in the price level and in relative prices. A change in relative prices would also be caused, of course, by an increase in the supply of money, if it raised prices so as to expand the demand for goods of different kinds. For the enlarged demand would expend itself on different goods with varying intensity. No matter in what way relative prices changed, however, the individual money holder would, of course, always spend his money so that the marginal utilities of the last units of the goods which he purchases with the same quantity of money would be proportional to their prices. For, as Professor Irving Fisher had pointed out, the theory of marginal utility in relation to prices "is not, as sometimes stated, 'the marginal utilities to the same individual of all articles are equal,' much less is it 'the marginal utilities of the same article to all consumers are equal'; but the marginal utilities of all articles consumed by a given individual are proportional to the marginal utilities of the same series of articles for each other consumer, and this uniform continuous ratio is the scale of prices of those articles."[1]

In other words, let us, for the sake of simplicity, imagine all the goods in each country fused into our typical or composite units. The utility of

[1] "Mathematical Investigations in the Theory of Value and Prices," *Trans. Conn. Acad.*, Vol. IX, July, 1892, p. 37.

the marginal unit may be regarded as the resultant of the marginal utilities of the component parts, and will equal the marginal utility of the money. But the marginal utility of the composite unit of goods differs for different countries. In still other words, we may say that the last unit of commodity bought has a utility equal to that of the money given; but the marginal utility of different commodities is different for different countries; hence, so, too, is the value of money.

CHAPTER X

THE SIGNIFICANCE AND CAUSES OF CHANGES IN THE VALUE OF MONEY

REFERENCES: Denis, La dépression Économique et Sociale et l'histoire des Prix, Ixelles-Bruxelles, 1895; Edgeworth, F. Y., Thoughts on Monetary Reform, Econ. Journ., Vol. V., pp. 434–451; Ettinger, Einfluss der Goldwährung auf das Einkommen der Bevölkerungsklassen und des Staates; Farnam, H. W., Some Effects of Falling Prices, Yale Review, August, 1895, pp. 183–201; Giffen, R., Prices and Income Compared, Journ. of Royal Statistical Society, Vol. 51, p. 713; Laughlin, J. L., Principles of Money, pp. 388 ff.; Nicholson, J. S., Money and Monetary Problems, 5th ed., Pt. I., Chs. 5, 7, Pt. II., Chs. 4, 6; Philippovich, E. von, Grundriss der Politischen Oekonomie, 4te Aufl., Erster Band, § 98; Pierson, N. G., Index Numbers and Appreciation, Econ. Journ., Vol. V., pp. 239 ff.; Principles of Economics, Ch. 7, § 8; Price, L. L., Money in its Relations to Prices, Ch. 2; Smart, W., Studies in Economics, Chs. 6, 7, pp. 208 ff.; Walker, F., Money, Ch. 4.

1. Questions to be discussed in this Chapter.— There are three questions of importance involved in the discussion of changes in the value of money. These are: First, in what direction and to what extent has the value of money varied? Second, are the changes in its value to be attributed to the money or to goods? Third, how do the variations affect social welfare? The first of these three questions is discussed at length in the twelfth chapter. The question is one of quantitative change, a determination of the total result. To answer this question it is not important to know whether, as has been remarked, it is "the pence that are few or the eggs that are many"; and it is a matter of indifference, from this point of view, whether the change is a consequence of variations in the prices of many articles or of few. Further, it does not make any difference what the effect is on any or all individuals.

2. Different Meanings of Appreciation and Depreciation.—The discussion of the twelfth chapter will show us, however, that the terms "appreciation" and "depreciation," of themselves, tell us nothing of the real character of the changes in the price level, the causes of these changes, or their import to social welfare. But the answer to the second question, relating to the cause of change in the value of money, involves a determination of the meaning of appreciation and depreciation. Appreciation, of course, means simply a change to a higher value; depreciation, a change to a lower value. But the value referred to may be a subjective value or an exchange value. Much of the discussion concerning the real nature of appreciation has been due to confusion of the two kinds of value. A change in the subjective value does not necessarily imply a change in the purchasing power, or exchange value, of money. To illustrate this, let us suppose that we are using a commodity money, like gold. If the supply decreases through wear, for example, no new supply coming to replenish the loss; and if at the same time the goods offered in exchange for gold decrease to a sufficient degree, it is entirely possible that the purchasing power of gold will remain unchanged, notwithstanding the diminution of its quantity. Yet in one sense gold will have appreciated, for it is scarcer than it was, and its scarcity raises its marginal utility. But as, according to our supposition, the marginal utility of the goods offered for it has changed in the same degree, no difference appears in the amount of goods secured for one unit of gold. That is, the purchasing power of gold has not changed. For example, suppose we have one thousand units of gold and one thousand of our composite units of goods. Call the marginal utility of each unit of gold and of each unit of goods one. If now the amount of gold is reduced to nine hundred units and the volume of goods is correspondingly reduced, a unit of gold will command the same quantity of goods and the marginal utility of the unit of gold and that of the unit of goods will be, perhaps, $1\frac{1}{2}$, or 2, or some other number larger than 1. The same amount of gold buys the same quantity of goods as before, but this quantity of goods yields a less amount of satisfaction. Similarly, there may be depreciation of gold not shown in changed purchasing power. It is possible that the cost of production of gold may diminish and that gold may increase in quantity; but if these changes are accompanied by corresponding changes in the cost of production of goods, there may be no change in prices. Goods would be more abundant, indeed; but, as Mr. Giffen has remarked, the "abundance would make itself felt in a rise of money wages, salaries, rents, and profits, and not in lower prices." This kind of appreciation and depreciation is sometimes spoken of as absolute appreciation. It is not of importance in the discussion of changes in the general price level, although it has considerable significance in relation to social welfare.

3. Different Manifestations of Appreciation and Depreciation. — It is conceivable, moreover, that the quantity of gold might increase, or decrease, without causing any change in prices, and without any accompanying change in the volume of commodities. For the change in the quantity of gold might be accompanied by a change, in the opposite direction, in the volume of other means of payment, there being, of course, no change in the standard of value. For example, if a bank of issue is established in a community whose people have been making all their payments with gold, a certain amount of the gold may be sent out of the place without altering prices. The community gets the benefit of a less expensive means of payment. Prices remain the same, not because the amount of exchange medium, now paper and gold, is unchanged, but because gold is still easily obtainable for the paper, and for the balance of exchanges which do not offset one another. It is urged that the familiar use of the term "depreciation" associates it with an excess of issue of money; that, therefore, appreciation ought to imply a scarcity, or insufficiency, of money. It hardly seems important to urge this view. Appreciation and depreciation are effects of excess and shortage of money, respectively, relative to demand, and do not depend upon the cause of the excess or shortage. Excess and shortage, in other words, are relative terms. By excess we mean more than the demand, and that more may be produced either by increasing the quantity of money or decreasing the quantity of goods. It is the fact that there is more that causes depreciation. Similarly, we may reason of appreciation. The question whether the change in the price level is due to changes in the quantity of money or in the quantity of goods has an important bearing on the social welfare, but none whatever in determining the meaning of the terms "depreciation" and "appreciation."

4. Various Phases of Appreciation. — Ordinarily, then, we mean by appreciation a larger purchasing power of money, or falling prices of goods, whether due to diminution of the money supply or to an increase in the supply of commodities. In short, we mean that a given quantity of gold buys a larger number of our composite units of goods. This might happen either (1) because the volume of goods offered for sale is the same, while the money supply has diminished, all other factors being unchanged; or (2) because the volume of goods offered has increased, while the volume of money remains the same, all other factors being unchanged; or (3) because, although the volume of goods sold and the quantity of money are unchanged, other media of exchange have become less. All other cases are variations of these. Let us consider the effect of each of these changes from the point of view of the community as a whole.

According to the first supposition, the volume of goods offered for sale is the same, while the money supply is less, and all our other factors, including the other means of exchange, are unchanged. In this case the purchasing power of gold increases, its marginal utility increases, but the marginal utility of goods remains the same, and the total social satisfaction obtained from the goods remains unchanged, excepting, of course, so far as the change in the marginal utility of gold, in its use as a commodity, affects the marginal utility of all commodities.

In the second case, we assume that the volume of goods increases, while the amount of gold remains unchanged, and the volume of business done by other means of exchange is constant. Here the purchasing power of gold increases, while its marginal utility remains constant; the marginal utility of goods decreases, because of the increase in their supply; and the total satisfaction which the society derives from the consumption of these goods will, of course, increase. From the standpoint of society this change is an indication of prosperity.

In the third case we assume that the volume of

goods remains the same, and that the amount of gold is unchanged, while the volume of business done by other means of exchange decreases. This throws a heavier burden of exchange work upon gold, so that its purchasing power is bound to increase. The marginal utility of gold and that of goods remains the same, however, because the supply of neither changes, and the total satisfaction which society derives from the consumption of goods remains the same because the quantity of goods has not increased.

We have, in short, three classes of cases in which prices fall; but the effects, from a social standpoint, on the subjective value of gold and of goods, and on the total satisfaction which society gets from consumption of the goods, are different. We may tabulate them thus: —

Case	Volume of goods	Amount of gold	Other means of exchange	Purch'g power of gold	Marg. util. of gold	Marg. util. of goods	Total social util. of goods
1	same	Dec.	same	Inc.	Inc.	same	same
2	Inc.	same	same	Inc.	same	Dec.	Inc.
3	same	same	Dec.	Inc.	same	same	same

5. Importance of the Distribution of the Effects of Appreciation and Depreciation. — The standpoint of the direct effect on society as a whole is not, however, a good one from which to view the change on welfare produced by a fall of prices. For a fall of prices, of itself, tells us absolutely nothing about its effects on welfare; it is, of itself, no indication either of prosperity or of economic loss. Whether or not it imports one or the other, depends on its cause and on the distribution of its effects. It may indicate merely a change in the productive power of a community, or it may imply a rise or fall of wages or incomes, absolutely or per capita, or it may signify the burdening or oppression of one or several of the economic classes of a community, or possibly the burdening of the whole community. The net result depends altogether on where the change in prices strikes, and how it works itself out. If prices change, say from 100 to 110, it is obvious that the purchasing power of money has fallen in the ratio of 110 to 100. It does not follow, however, that the person whose income was 100 at a previous date could buy as many commodities and the same amount of labor as could the owner of 110 units of money at a later date. He could buy the same amount of goods only if the prices of all had changed in the same proportion. But a fall of prices does not take place in this regular way. Prices of articles change in different proportions, and the effects of the fall will be different according to the changes produced in wages, incomes, cost of production of goods, and population.

To begin with, a fall of prices may conceivably take place while relative wages and incomes remain as they were before, the only change being in the quantity of money. If the producing capacity of society, the cost of production of goods, and population remain unchanged, the fall of prices produced by a lessening of the quantity of money would have no other effect on the economic sharers of the product of industry than to make necessary the use of a new scale of prices. It could occur, conceivably, without affecting either the welfare of society as a whole, or the relative welfare of its different groups. Practically, however, such a proportionate distribution of the effects is impossible. The blow would fall on different classes, not at the same moment and in the same degree, but in time and degree dependent on the relative economic strength of the classes.

6. Different Effects of Appreciation under Different Conditions. — If the supply of goods increases, owing to the extension of production under the influence of improvements, while the money demand for them is the same, all other conditions remaining the same, prices will fall. Money wages and incomes being unchanged, the fall is a sign and measure of the greater producing capacity of society, and implies enlarged consumption for all classes. In this case the community is just as well off as if the volume of money had increased sufficiently to prevent the fall of prices. Indeed, it is better off, because it has saved the investment of capital and labor necessary to produce the additional money. It will continue to be better off with a falling price level, under the conditions named, until the fall is great enough to offset the gain from the lowered cost of production of goods. If the falling cost of production be due to an increase in the efficiency of labor, the real price of labor will rise, as compared with that of goods. But as the money demand for goods is the same, their price must fall in order to afford labor a higher real return. The fall in prices under these circumstances is merely the evidence of the increased productivity, and consequent higher real wages of labor. Producers and capitalists lose nothing. These results will follow, even if the only goods which fall in price are the goods consumed by laborers, and constituting their real wages; for their fall will lower the general price level, but the change will imply no loss to any class in society.

Again, a fall of prices may be accompanied with rising money wages and profits, if the fall be caused by decreased cost of production, population and other conditions being unchanged, provided the fall of prices be less rapid than the decrease of cost. The fall here is a sign of the increasing producing capacity of society and of increased labor efficiency. If, however, prices fall more rapidly than cost, owing, for example, to decreased demand caused by a depression, both laborers and entrepreneurs will lose.

7. The Effect of Appreciation transmitted from Class to Class. — In each of these illustrative cases of falling prices, we have assumed that, with changes in some of the conditions of price equilibrium, other conditions have remained the same. As a matter of fact, a change in one condition induces changes in the other conditions which determine the price level. If the quantity of money becomes less, prices fall, and other things cannot remain unchanged. Those on whom the burden of falling prices falls first, will naturally try to shift it. When prices fall, the advantage, whatever it is, accrues first to money owners at the expense, primarily, of producers. The owners of money, however, are not allowed long to keep their advantage, for the producers, finding their profits curtailed, diminish production in order to raise prices; or else they force down the rate of wages, or in some other way try to recoup themselves for their loss of profits. Now, if production be curtailed, part of the loss felt by producers is passed on to wage-earners and consumers. The laboring class will by and by receive less in total money wages and, unless the population falls away, in per capita wages also; while, as consumers, they will pay higher prices. Other consumers in the community will feel the change by having to pay higher prices for goods.

If the fall of prices resulted in reducing wages, the laboring class would for a time suffer most, or all, of the loss. In time, however, their diminished consumption would cause a diminution of production and a rise of prices, and other consumers would share the loss. In a stationary society, in which producing capacity, cost of production, and population remain the same from period to period, the final result of a fall of prices would be a distribution of the burden among the economic sharers of the product, with more or less equity. It might seem that if this could be done, the change of price level would be devoid of significance for the industrial welfare of the community. The psychological effect of this change, however, cannot be neglected, even if the economic relations of the different classes be unchanged; for a lower range of incomes, prices, and wages accustom people to small things and lower standards, and the habit of looking at things in a small way deadens enterprise, and is likely to act against a recovery from the conditions which produced it.

8. The Normal Case of Falling Prices. — The normal case of falling prices for a long period is that of a progressive community whose producing capacity is on the increase at a diminishing cost of production, and with a growing population. Money wages and incomes do not fall and may even rise, and the fall of the price level would import prosperity to the community. It would mean that the advantages of decreasing cost of production and growing producing capacity are distributed among the different classes in society. The distribution would be gradual, however. Some one group or class at first would get more than its share of the advantage, as is the case in all economic changes, whether in the direction of economic improvement or deterioration. The entrepreneur would gain first from diminished cost, then the capitalist, then the consumer as such, and finally the wage-earner. For a lessened cost of production brings unusual profit to the entrepreneur and stimulates enterprise until the unusual margin of profits tends to disappear. The stimulation of enterprise causes an increased demand for capital and forces up the rate of interest; and the competition of producers to sell their goods tends to lower prices and to give consumers an advantage, while at the same time their desire to extend their business leads them to offer higher wages. Under these conditions the community at first endeavors to do the extra work of distributing a larger volume of goods with the same means of exchange, because for a time there is a larger net gain in straining the existing means of exchange to do the additional work, than in sinking more capital to increase the volume of money. This condition will continue until the net gain disappears and society finds it more profitable to increase the volume of money. This is doubtless the explanation of the relative decrease in gold in such a period as the twenty-five years following 1873. Throughout all this period, despite crises and occasional apparent retrogression, the population of the industrial countries of the world increased, together with their producing capacity; while invention, discoveries, the adoption of better business organization, and the utilization of new and more fertile land, all tended to force down the cost of production of commodities. The profit from investing in the production of other kinds of commodities than gold was greater than could be had, under existing physical and economic conditions of its production, from investments in producing gold.

Under the conditions above described, prices will continue to fall, until the fall wipes out the differential gain from other investments to a sufficient degree to make it profitable to extend investments in the production of the money commodity; or else men will be stimulated to the discovery of a cheaper process of production of the money commodity, in order to secure from investments in this direction as large returns as from the production of other kinds of goods. This is what has happened in recent years. The production of gold fell away, not because of the physical exhaustion of gold, but because, under the old conditions, its cost of production was so high as to make the margin of profit from investing in its production less than could be obtained in other ways. New processes of reduction of the ore, however, lowered the cost of production, so that the margin of profit from producing the standard money commodity became greater. Since then its output has increased. Whether or not the increase in the output has been the chief cause of a higher price level is at least open to dispute. The effect of the increased output might, under proper conditions, manifest itself in this way, and after a time its lower value would again lessen the production. Under the conditions that prevail now, however, it is likely that the net result has been further to stimulate the production of other goods, and to extend the credit machinery, so that the increased output is profitable on the rising scale of prices.

9. The Effects of Appreciation on Debtors and Creditors. — In our discussion thus far, we have considered the effects of a changing price level on the sharers of the product, in the economic sense of the word "sharers." That is, we have inquired into the effects of the appreciation of gold on the entrepreneur, the capitalist, and the wage-earner. Another line of economic cleavage gives us, however, a different classification. We may divide the people most affected by the change in price level into creditor and debtor classes. It is important to determine how the debtor class as such is affected by the appreciation of money. It is commonly understood, of course, that such a change is always detrimental to them, and beneficial to the creditors. The question is an important one, because, nowadays, production is carried on so largely on borrowed capital, and the whole producing class is properly regarded as a debtor class. It is clear, from what has been said, that in all cases of appreciation of gold, or falling prices, in which the cost of production of goods does not decrease, and money wages and money interest do not fall, the debtor producers must lose, and their creditors must gain correspondingly. Now, in a normal case, in a progressive society, the fall of prices is accompanied by a decreased cost, and the debtor producers lose less the more nearly the cost of production and the price level fall in the same degree. It is supposable, indeed, that they may even gain, but this is so highly unlikely as not to be worth discussing. As a rule, the debtor loses under appreciation, whatever may be its cause, and the effect on the welfare of some social classes may be serious, or even disastrous. Much depends, of course, upon the period of the debt. The longer the period, the greater is the burden likely to be. The distribution of the income of society is changed, then, by the appreciation of money. In the case mentioned at the beginning of the chapter, in which increased production of goods is accompanied with proportionate increase of the amount of money, so that the price level does not change, the advantage of the increased production is distributed throughout the community, and the social welfare increases. This is not the case, however, when the increase of production is not accompanied with a due increase of gold. The welfare of society as a whole may be improved, but only at the expense, in part, of some classes.

10. Comparative Disadvantages of Appreciation and Depreciation. — There has been a good deal of discussion of the question whether appreciation or depreciation is more advantageous to society. The usual opinion is that contraction and falling prices are a greater evil than is appreciation of money, because, it is supposed, the gradual appreciation of money in terms of commodities stimulates production and expands industry. It is urged that the prospect of rising prices constantly urges the entrepreneur to increase his product, in order to anticipate further increases. This statement, however, cannot be made as a general truth; for, in the first place, if the cost of production falls faster than prices do, the producer will gain just as truly as he will if prices are slightly raising. It is a matter of indifference to him what the cause of his larger profits is — whether they are due simply to a rising price, or to a cost decreasing faster than a slowly falling price. In the second place, the result to the producer depends partly on the way in which the change takes place. If the fall of prices occurs for all industries at the same time, and in the same degree, then it would be true that depreciation would be more beneficial to the producer than would its opposite. This simultaneous and proportionate fall of prices, however, is not usual. Indeed, it may be doubted whether it ever can occur. A change in the purchasing power of money in terms of goods shows itself in a fall of the prices of some articles sooner than it does in those of others. The consequence is to lessen the expenses of production of all producers who use these articles in their business, so that each producer makes a gain, until the price of the articles which he himself makes also falls to the same degree as his cost of production has been diminished. Moreover, it is questionable whether any gain which the producers make from the gradual depreciation of money in terms of commodities yields any gain to society unless money wages and incomes increase in such a way as to distribute the benefit among the various producing classes.

11. Causes of Appreciation and Depreciation. — The causes of changes in the purchasing power of money in terms of goods are very numerous, and the movement of changing prices may begin at different points in the economic scale. They may be due, in the first place, to changes in the physical conditions of production of the exchange medium. Much has been said in the past twenty years about the exhaustion of the gold mines. Of course, the truth about the matter is, that under the economic conditions of mining which prevailed, it did not pay as well to invest capital in producing more gold as it did to invest capital in producing something else. There really has never been any reasonable ground for the belief that the supply of gold was near exhaustion. The output of gold, or the amount of gold which it is profitable to produce, depends more on economic considerations than on physical conditions. That this is the case is well shown by the recent change in the gold-mining industry. The exhaustion of placer deposits, and the consequent unprofitableness of gold production, stimulated invention and discovery, so that, by new processes of extraction and refinement, the cost of production of the precious metals has been very much reduced, and the profitableness of investment in their production correspondingly increased.

A second cause of change in the purchasing power of gold is found in changing economic conditions. As has been repeatedly pointed out, under some conditions there is more profit in other lines of investment. Moreover, the capitalistic production of gold now is greater than the accidental production, although the opposite was formerly the case. That is to say, gold was obtained as a result of accidental discovery, by prospective miners who had no capital, while now gold mining has become a more or less regular industry, with large investment of capital. Like other industries, it has its periods of depression or comparative unprofitableness; and if these continue long enough, the capital invested in gold mining is gradually withdrawn, or, at any rate, is not increased.

A second economic change which influences the price level is an extension of the use of gold, either by the demonetization of other things used previously as money, so throwing a heavier demand on gold, or by an extension of the gold standard to a new country. For example, it is a common belief that the demonetization of silver by Germany contributed not a little to the rise in the price of gold. While undoubtedly too much emphasis has been placed upon this historical event, it is doubtless true that the influence, so far as it went, was in the direction indicated. Of course, the adoption of the gold standard by countries which previously used silver, raises the price of gold only as the actual use of gold is increased thereby.

A third economic change affecting the price level is the resumption of specie payments by countries which, for a considerable time, have been on a depreciated paper basis. This was the case in the United States in 1879, and in the empire of Austria-Hungary in 1892. In such cases a fund of gold is usually accumulated, even if it is not brought into general circulation.

A third group of causes affecting the price of gold is found in political and social changes, as distinct from economic. War, for instance, may cause a cessation of the production of gold, as was the case during 1899–1902, the years of the Boer War in South Africa. Between 1898 and 1900 the gold production of Africa fell from 120,566 kilograms to 13,048. Aside, however, from the direct influence on gold production by war, the disturbance of industry which it causes may affect general prices. Production is likely to be changed in a measure from its ordinary channels, and a large amount of goods is unproductively consumed.

A social change which leads to a larger use of gold in the arts also has an effect on the price level, unless the production of gold is changing fast enough to offset the change in this demand. If fashion, for example, calls for more general use of gold for ornaments, or for artistic purposes, the result is to raise the marginal utility of the money commodity, and very likely, too, its purchasing power.

A change in the purchasing power may be caused by legislation which seeks to foster the private interests of the owners of gold and silver mines. The Bland and, later, the Allison law in the United States, each of which provided for the purchase of a certain amount of silver by the United States government, are instances of this kind. The avowed purpose, and for a time the actual result, was to raise the price of silver; although, of course, later, the higher price stimulated production, and resulted in a renewed fall. Although silver was not then the monetary standard in the United States, the result of silver legislation was to cause a great increase in the amount of silver in circulation as money, so that for some years there was a heavy export of gold in excess of our production, and an impairment of business confidence which led to depreciation and falling prices.

12. Effect of Changes in Production on the Value of Money. — On the other side of the shield must be mentioned economic changes in the supply of goods. Technical improvements in production, which reduce the cost and increase the output, will, other influences remaining the same, cause an appreciation of gold. So, too, may prolonged strikes, and a rise in money wages and incomes.

Closely allied with changes which come from

technical improvements is the growth of industry and commerce due to the opening of new countries or undeveloped markets. New sources of raw materials, and the opening up of cheaper routes of transportation, have effects similar in character to technical improvements in production. Some authorities, like Mr. Sauerbeck, emphasize, for example, the opening of the Suez Canal as an important factor in the fall of prices during the twenty-five years following 1873. Undoubtedly, the development of the railway systems of the United States, and the consequent opening up of new and more fertile lands, has been for many years an important factor in the falling prices of grain.

The extension or contraction of credit, moreover, irrespective of changes in the supply of money commodity, will have an effect precisely similar in character. The effect of a general extension of banking is to lessen the demand for gold for actual payments, and for a time, therefore, to make the supply greater than the existing demand at the old ratio of exchange. A temporary contraction of credit, from industrial and commercial depression, will, for a time, cause a greater demand for gold in order to make payments, because the credit part of the exchange medium is less, and so will produce a fall of prices.

Different in character from any of the cases which have thus far been mentioned as affecting the purchasing power of gold, is that attributed to the effect of the fall of the gold price of silver on the gold price of goods. It is urged that since some countries with large export trade use silver, if silver falls in terms of gold, while the prices of other things in silver countries remain steady, then the gold prices of other articles of export will fall. Undoubtedly this may happen for a while, but such an effect can hardly be either general or permanent.

CHAPTER XI

CREDIT AND PRICES

REFERENCES: Colwell, Stephen, The Ways and Means of Payment, Ch. 7; Hadley, A. T., Economics, Ch. 8, § 274; Jevons, W. S., Money and the Mechanism of Exchange, Ch. 26; Knies, K., Der Credit, Ch. 6; Laughlin, J. L., Principles of Money, Ch. 4, § 8; Macleod, H. D., Theory of Credit, Vol. II., Pt. I., Ch. 12; *Ibid.*, Report of the Royal Commission on Gold and Silver, 1888, pp. 234, 245; Mill, J. S., Principles of Political Economy, Vol. II., Bk. III., Ch. 12; Nicholson, J. S., Money and Monetary Problems, Pt. I., Ch. 6; Philippovich, E. von, Grundriss der Politischen Oekonomie, 4te Aufl., Erster Band, § 109; Willis, H. P., Credit Devices and the Quantity Theory, Journ. Pol. Econ., Vol. IV., p. 281.

1. Meaning of Credit. — By credit we mean the power which one person has to induce another to put economic goods at his disposal for a time, on promise of future payment. Credit is thus an attribute, or power, of the borrower. There can be no transfer of goods from one person to another for future payment unless that other has some power or influence that induces the transfer. This power is not merely a desire to borrow. To be of avail in the market, to become an economic force, the desire must be, like the demand, effective. Credit, or borrowing power, is usually, if not always, expressed in terms of money. This custom, however, does not imply that money loans, or deferred money payments, are the only kind of credit transactions. Indeed, as a rule, it is not money that is borrowed at all, but goods, or a credit of wider circulation than the credit of the borrower. If a person buys goods from a merchant on a promise of future payment, his credit demand is simply a demand for goods additional to the direct money demand, and not a demand for money. Or, the credit of an individual may be exchanged for that of a bank, because the credit of the bank is more widely accepted. In the last analysis this latter credit demand is also a demand for goods. But whether the credit exchange be one or the other of these two kinds, it appears as a claim to money.

Credit is to be distinguished from mere confidence, although confidence is an important element of credit. Indeed, the essence of credit is confidence on the part of the creditor in the borrower's power and willingness to pay the debt. That confidence may arise from the creditor's belief in the integrity of the borrower, or from the offering by the debtor of sufficient property as security. Both forms, personal and secured, or real credit, are very commonly employed. Secured credit, so far as concerns bank loans, is most commonly employed in call, or demand, loans; while loans on time, which are usually discounts of mercantile paper, are more generally unsecured by a deposit of collateral. For example, the total loans of the national banks of the United States on September 9, 1903, were $3,481,446,722. Of this aggregate, demand loans to the amount of $717,258,621, and time loans to the amount of $655,439,130, or a total of $1,372,697,751, were secured by the deposit of stocks, bonds, and other collateral. On the other hand, loans to the amount of $2,108,749,021 were unsecured. Of the unsecured loans, $283,108,946 were call, or demand, loans, while the balance was time loans.

2. Nature of Credit Transactions. — Credit, or the power of borrowing, manifests itself in credit transactions. It is the credit transaction which is evident, which pushes itself upon our attention and attracts our notice. A credit transaction is one kind of exchange. It is a present transfer of economic goods or services, or property, in consideration of a promise of a future return of equivalent value. The transfer may be physical or merely legal; that is, it may consist in the transfer of an actual thing, or in the transfer of the title to a thing. The essential features of a credit transaction are these: goods are given up by the creditor to the debtor; the creditor must have confidence that he will be paid; his action is voluntary; payment is expected after a definite period; the thing transferred is economic goods, or titles thereto; the debtor receives a legal property in these, and the creditor receives in exchange a corresponding legal property in the shape of a title to future goods.

3. Credit Documents. — Out of credit transactions arise various kinds of credit paper, or instruments. The most common of these are bills of exchange, promissory notes, checks, and drafts. These differ in the matter of their origin, as to whether created by debtor or creditor; in their power of circulation, and in certain details of form; but all are evidences of a debt on the one hand, and of a credit on the other, and all purport to be claims for money. Nevertheless, in the last analysis, all but the bank drafts are based upon goods rather than upon money. Each piece of credit paper represents the purchase, or sale, of a certain amount of goods, whose value is expressed in terms of money on the face of the instrument. Credit instruments, therefore, are simply a means of facilitating the exchange of goods, and the obligations created by these credit instruments are met, in the main, by the cancellation, or offsetting, of the instruments against each other.

4. Difficulty of determining the Effect of Credit on Prices. — Perhaps the most important question in the theory of credit is the effect of credit transactions upon the price level. We may approach the subject from either one of two points. We may regard credit purchases as additions to the demand for goods, and trace the effect of the increased demand for commodities on prices; or, we may take into consideration the increase in the supply of the medium of exchange, in the shape of credit paper, and trace the effects of this increased supply upon the level of prices. On the whole, it is simpler to take the former course.

We must distinguish the influence of credit upon relative prices from the part played by credit as one of the determinants of the price level. An increased demand for particular goods, due to credit purchases, will, of course, raise their prices. The tradesman feels that he must be insured against possible loss through bad debts, and must be remunerated for lying out of the use of his capital. How much insurance and how much remuneration depends on the length of the credit period, on the ordinary rate of interest, on the rapidity with which the merchant ordinarily turns over his capital, and on the estimated risk of loss. We are not concerned here, however, with changes in relative prices, which are caused partly by differences in the amount of credit demand for different classes of goods.

5. Different Theories of the Relation of Credit to Prices. — There are several possible views of the character of the influence exerted by credit on the price level. In the first place, the view may be taken that credit usually, or normally, has no effect on prices. This view is based upon the supposition that credit demand, taken as a whole, cancels itself; that the credit demand has existed from the beginning of exchange, side by side with money demand, and that therefore it is not pertinent to say that credit has any influence on prices.[1] At first sight this theory seems plausible. But if credit has no influence on prices because it is coexistent with the level of prices, similarly money can have no influence on prices. If it is reasoning in a circle to say that we do not have a price level without credit, and that credit is therefore not a determinant of the price level, the same remark is equally true of money. In order to determine the influence of one of the factors of the price level, we must do our best to find out what would be the state of affairs in the absence of that particular factor. It is not enough to say that this factor is always present, and, therefore, we need not try to decide what would be the situation if it were absent. If it is present, it must have some effect.

In the next place, the view is sometimes taken that an increased demand for goods due to credit is precisely similar in its effect to an increased demand due to money. Here emphasis is laid on the fact that there is an increase in demand, and the fact is overlooked that the increase in demand in a measure automatically cancels itself by a simultaneous increase of the supply of goods, so that the total credit demand does not play directly on prices. Hence it is not correct to say[2] that the price level is influenced by the whole mass of credit

[1] This seems to be Professor Laughlin's view. See his "Principles of Money."

[2] Cf. Macleod, Report Royal Commission on Gold and Silver, 1888, pp. 234 and 245.

instruments created. It is not true that the prices of commodities are determined directly by the total amount of all the different kinds of circulating medium, rather than by the demand for, and supply of, standard money, under given conditions of the exchange mechanism. Nor is it quite correct to say, with Walker, that the general level of prices is determined by the amount of, and demand for, the standard medium of exchange; that on the level of prices thus fixed credit transactions occur, which cancel one another without the use of money; and that the credit instruments on which these transactions are based disappear when the transactions are closed, without exercising any influence on the level of prices. The uncancelled balance of indebtedness based on credit does, indeed, create a demand for money and will have a certain influence on the price level; but the whole amount of this unsettled balance, or the credit instruments which represent it, does not, as a matter of fact, enter in, like so much standard money, to influence prices.

6. Credit One of the Determinants of the Price Level. — According to the theory advanced in this book, every community has a choice of methods of exchange and means of payment, including direct barter, money exchange, and cancellation, or credit exchange. Under fixed conditions of economic life a community which has such a choice will push the use of each method of exchange and payment to a point where its use for the exchange of an additional unit-volume of goods would cause a loss to the community. At this point, since prices are expressed in terms of money, the marginal utility of the available money supply would indicate the level of prices. But the marginal utility of this money supply depends, in part, upon the demand for money for use as a reserve, to settle the uncancelled balance of credit transactions. Credit is therefore properly called one of the determinants of the price level. If credit exchanges were wiped out, without causing any diminution in the demand for goods, money would take on a higher marginal utility than before; that is, its value would rise, and the price level would fall. With the introduction of credit payments, an equilibrium would be established between the marginal utility of money for reserve purposes and its marginal utility for direct payment. This would mean a change of the price level from that which obtained in the absence of credit sales. This equilibrium would emerge when credit exchanges and direct money exchanges had each been pushed down to the point where the expensiveness of exchange to society by each method is proportionate to the volume of exchanges performed by each method.

7. The Effect of Credit on Prices depends on the Completeness of the Cancellation of Indebtedness. — Let us suppose that the volume of transactions in a given community at a particular time be called ten, all of which are done by direct money payment. Let us suppose, further, that over-night, as it were, credit exchange is suddenly introduced, to such an extent as to effect exchanges to the extent of five of the ten units of transactions, on the basis of existing prices. If, of the five units of exchanges now performed by credit, exchanges to the amount of four units cancel one another, one unit is left to be settled by means of money, and the community must keep a reserve sufficient to do this on the old price level. The four unit-volumes of money formerly used have now been set free, and if it were destroyed, or sent out of the community, the price level would not be changed, because the work formerly done by this money is now done by means of cancellation, without any additional strain on the money which is left in use. This money, replaced with credit cancellation, is likely, in part at least, to remain in monetary use. It will, therefore, raise prices to a new level. The price level will not rise in proportion to the number of money units used for direct payments, but will settle at some point where there will be an equilibrium between the marginal utility of money for use in direct payments, and for use as reserve. Another effect, however, will be to make a larger reserve necessary for the same volume of transactions because of the higher level of prices. The money set free on the old level of prices will, therefore, distribute itself between the reserve money and direct payment money.

If we suppose the case of a country on an exclusively metallic basis, into which credit is suddenly introduced, the reserve necessary to settle the uncancelled balance of credit transactions may be furnished by the money which is set free from direct payment by the introduction of credit purchases. If this should happen, we would have a smaller amount of money to exchange for a smaller amount of goods by direct payment, but not a proportionally smaller amount of money. The amount of goods will be less, proportionally, than the amount of money, because the credit purchases may be two or three times the amount of the metallic basis.

Again, the introduction of a less expensive[1] medium of exchange lowers the marginal utility of the money medium in use, saves some of the cost of exchange to the community, and, therefore, again raises the price level. Now the extension, or refinement, of the credit mechanism does just this thing. Credit exchange is essentially a return to barter by representative transfers of goods rather than by physical transfers. Hence it saves some expense of transfer. In doing so it diminishes the volume of exchanges made with money, and thus causes an increase in the quantity of money relatively to the volume of work it has to do. Therefore it lowers the marginal utility of money, or, in other words, raises the level of prices.

8. Causes which Produce a Permanent Balance of Indebtedness which must be settled with Money. —

[1] Not necessarily cheaper to secure, but of larger net efficiency, or profit, to the community.

We have said that by means of credit we can make exchanges of goods for goods by simple cancellation of values. The goods sold on credit approximate in value those bought on credit; there is, therefore, a constant approximation to a complete cancellation. If this cancellation were complete, credit, as has been remarked, could never be in excess of the means of payment available to settle balances. The cancellation, however, is never complete, but always shows a balance of operations. This balance is caused by a variety of circumstances, of varying importance. In the first place, it is quite impossible in trade to prevent lack of coincidence in demand and supply, either in time or in volume. In order to effect a complete cancellation of all goods bought and sold on credit, it would be necessary that the whole amount bought at one moment, or in one period, should equal the whole amount sold in the same time. Now, many purchases on credit are purchases for deferred payment, and, therefore, at the time of purchase, offer no goods which can cancel the demand. The demand, in other words, is present; the supply which would cancel it is future. There must, therefore, be a balance in such cases. If all credit were based on goods already produced and offered for sale, and if in all cases the amount of credit based on these goods equalled their market value, then the credit demand for goods would cancel itself. In order to illustrate this most simply, let us suppose the case of a manufacturer of cotton goods and a planter of cotton. The manufacturer, having finished some goods, ships them to the cotton planter and draws on him for the purchase price. This draft he gets discounted at his bank. In the meantime the cotton planter ships the manufacturer an equivalent value in raw cotton, and draws on him in turn, and gets his draft discounted. Obviously the transactions balance, and the drafts coming together, we may suppose in some New York bank, will cancel each other. In actual trade, however, the operation is not so simple as this, nor can we usually secure an exact cancellation. Either the demand of the manufacturer or that of the planter will be in excess and will not cancel the other. It is this anticipatory credit demand which chiefly determines the magnitude of the uncancelled balance of credit and influences prices. If business is good, the demand for loans not based upon finished goods, but upon some security which does not immediately cancel the loan, is likely to increase. In other words, opportunities for investment increase, and loans may be paid for not with present but with future goods. Therefore the balance of credit indebtedness is likely to become larger, and the demand for standard money to settle the balance must therefore increase.

In the second place, exact cancellation is prevented by the disturbances or accidents of production and trade. Changes in demand for goods, mistakes in correctly forecasting the demand and calculating the supply, changes of fashion, mistakes of judgment in determining the proper proportions of fixed and of circulating capital in some industry, and a hundred and one incidents of business which are continually occurring, are likely to cause such a disturbance.

Moreover, an unsettled balance of credit demand may be caused by a breakdown of the credit machinery at some point, leaving a number of engagements unfulfilled. This uncancelled balance, too, calls for money to settle it, aside from that which is used for direct money exchanges. Against this uncancelled balance a reserve must be provided whose amount depends upon the state of trade, the business habits of the community, and many other factors. The need for money to settle this uncancelled balance of credit demand is increased, moreover, by the distress and fear that some people exhibit in business transactions, which make them unwilling to wait through the credit period for the fruition of enterprises in which they have sunk their money.

The more perfect the cancellation, however, as has been repeatedly remarked, the less the amount of money needed, and the less, therefore, the reserve that needs to be kept. As credit machinery becomes more perfect and more widely extended, we should therefore expect a reduction of the amount of what may be called the normal bank reserve; that is, in the amount which in ordinary times the banking institutions of the country find it necessary to keep on hand to meet the demands of their customers for ready money.

9. The Influence of Reserves of Money for Credit Transactions on its Value. — The conclusion of all that has been said is that the credit balance causes an extra demand for standard money, since credit exchange does not diminish the money exchange as much as it would do if the cancellation of credit purchases were complete. Now, it is through the demand for money to settle this uncancelled balance that credit influences the price level. The amount of money needed to settle this uncancelled balance at any moment is the reserve of money which a community needs to sustain its credit operations. With a given supply of money, a community will so adjust its credit exchanges, on the one hand, and its direct money exchanges, on the other, that the money supply will be divided between use as a reserve and use for direct payments, in such a way as to make the marginal utility of the money for the two uses the same. But an increase of the balance of indebtedness necessitates an increase in the reserve money at the expense of money used in direct payments, and will, therefore, raise the marginal utility of money and cause a fall in the price level. Now, the total volume of transactions which yield a particular balance may be large or small, for the same remainder may be obtained from minuends and subtrahends of very different amounts. In theory, therefore, the credit demand for goods may increase indefinitely, while the demand for money as a basis of credit transactions need not increase simultaneously, or not so rapidly, because the balance of the credit demand, the only part for which money is needed, may not increase. If, on two selected dates, the volume of transactions done on credit is the same, but the balance is less on the second occasion than on the first, then the demand for money will be less, its value will be lower, and prices will be higher for the same volume of business. For with a given supply of money, the demand available for direct payments under these conditions will be larger. On the other hand, prices may fall, without any change in the amount of money. If, apart from a check to business confidence, the balance of credit transactions becomes greater at one time than another, although the total volume of transactions has not increased, but may have diminished, the demand for money must become greater too. Hence its value will rise, and the value of goods will fall. Reserves must become larger in proportion to the total volume of credit, and a new equilibrium must be established between the marginal utility of money for reserves and its marginal utility for direct payment. It follows that the level of prices may rise or fall without any change in the volume of standard money, but only a change in its distribution for use as reserve and as a means of direct payment. These changes are due, in other words, to the inexactness of cancellation of credit transactions. Most of our credit transactions are based upon bank loans and discounts. The bank needs to keep on hand an amount of money sufficient to pay the balance of indebtedness which experience shows is likely to accrue from day to day. If, now, the balance of credit transactions increases, the need for money for settlement becomes greater. The banks, feeling the pressure of the demand, raise their rate of discount. This curtails credit operations and reduces the difference resulting from the offsetting of the credit claims against one another. In other words, it reduces the volume of business.

If, on the other hand, the balance of credit transactions decreases, money becomes more plentiful in the banks and the rate of discount falls. Borrowing becomes easier and credit transactions are thereby stimulated. A new balance is thereby established, and consequently a new equilibrium is fixed between credit balances and the money reserve.

10. Limits of the Influence of Credit on Prices. — Now this variation in the price level, due to a change in the amount of credit operations, is self-limiting. Let us consider a case where prices are rising, due to an increased demand based upon the extension of credit. As prices go higher, the periods of returns to investments in different lines are likely to vary more and more. The probability grows less that a given amount of debts will be offset by a given amount of other debts, as the total number of debts increases. Hence, the balance of indebtedness grows larger. Some borrowers find it difficult to meet their engagements, seek an extension of their debts, and thus again disturb the amount of cancellation of debts. Under such circumstances the uncancelled balance must become larger, and prices must fall. The maximum to which prices can rise under the influence of credit demand is, therefore, not a fixed amount, but it is that at which, under given conditions of trade, the balance of indebtedness begins to grow and the strain upon the money reserve is, therefore, greater.

On the other hand, the lowest point to which prices can fall, while business is done by means of credit, is the point at which the total credit operations have so far contracted that the balance of indebtedness grows smaller and smaller, requiring a smaller amount of money to settle it and thus enlarging the reserve. The easy money thus produced attracts borrowers and stimulates the credit demand for goods. Then the price level turns upward again.

11. Interaction of the Demand for Money for Reserves and for Direct Exchanges. — All that has been written is on the assumption that the transactions which are done on the ready-money basis have not changed. This, however, is, of course, contrary to fact. There is a constant flux, a constant intercommunication, between the amount of money and the volume of credit. Let us for a moment suppose that the total amount of money in a community is fixed, and let us further confine our attention to standard money. At any given time this money is divided in a certain proportion between the credit and the ready-money transactions. On a given price level, a certain volume of ready-money business is done, and a certain amount of money is needed to do it. At the same time a certain volume of credit business is done, and a certain amount of money is needed as a reserve, or basis, on which to do this. It has been pointed out that if there is a more complete cancellation of indebtedness and, therefore, a smaller balance, from the offsetting of credit instruments against one another, the amount of reserve needed will become less. A certain amount of ready money is, therefore, set free from supporting credit transactions. We have supposed that it will become the basis, or reserve, for an additional volume of credit operations; but if we take into account, as we are now doing, the presence of transactions in ready money, it may happen that the money set free from the support of credit business may all go into circulation in the sphere of the ready-money business. In that case the value of money, the supply being increased, will fall, and prices will rise, so far as they are dependent upon the quantity of money available for the unchanged amount of direct money payments, or, what is the same thing, upon ready-money demand for goods. This result is precisely what we arrived at when we supposed that the money set free would be used as a basis of new credit operations. Whichever way the freed money turns, therefore, it will give an upward fillip to prices. All the free money cannot go to the ready-money transactions, however, for it would thereby raise prices above the level produced by the credit demand. Practically, the price level will be a new equilibrium between the amount necessary as a reserve for the diminished balance of credit and the increased volume available for direct payments.

Similarly, if the existing equilibrium between the balance of indebtedness and the money reserve is disturbed by an increase in the balance of indebtedness, a strain is thrown upon the money used in the ready-money transactions. Its value rises, and prices, therefore, tend to fall. In a régime where there were no ready-money transactions, the result would be only a contraction of credit transactions, in order to diminish the credit balance; practically, both results would doubtless follow. Credit will contract far enough to produce a balance of indebtedness which, in conjunction with an increased demand for money in ready-money transactions, will produce a new price equilibrium.

It will be necessary to consider now what results will follow if the existing price equilibrium is disturbed primarily by a change in the amount of money used in ready-money transactions. It is not hard to trace these effects, after what has been said. If, for any reason, the demand for money in the ready-money part of business should increase, the necessary addition could be drawn only from the reserve on which credit transactions were based. Means would have to be taken to reduce the balance of indebtedness by a more complete cancellation, or the total volume of credit transactions must decrease, until a new balance was found which could rest upon the diminished money reserve. Under the pressure of these changes, the marginal utility of money would be greater, and the price equilibrium somewhat lower. Similarly, if the need for money in ready-money business should fall off, the reserve available for credit business would be larger, there would probably be a disturbance of the uncancelled balance, and the price level would be a new equilibrium between the marginal utilities of money for the two services, on a higher level of prices. The resulting price level would be found somewhere between the points at which it would settle from a change in the ready-money business, and from a change in the credit business, acting alone.

In order to make our discussion complete, we need now to consider the effect of an increase in the total volume of money. This has been so fully discussed in another connection that we need only refer to it here. The first effect would probably be to stimulate credit business, because new money finds its way into circulation generally through the banks. An increased credit demand for goods would raise their prices, and a higher price level would necessitate a larger amount of money in active circulation, in order to perform easily the ready-money portion of business. The additional money would be divided, therefore, between the reserve necessary for credit and the money necessary for ready-money business, in a proportion which would produce a marginal utility for reserve money identical with that of the money used in direct payments, and this would be a lower value, or a higher price level.

Professor Essars has shown[1] that the German banks, where checks are largely used, need a smaller balance in turning over a given amount of money than do the French banks with a smaller use of checks. This means that the more commonly payments are made by check into a bank, so that the smaller the difference, or balance, between its debts and credits, the less money is needed by the bank. This difference may be regarded, as has already been remarked, as a normal reserve, and doubtless tends to become smaller as cancellation becomes more perfect.

12. Influence of Different Kinds of Credit Transactions on Prices. — Credit transactions are to be distinguished according as they do, or do not, give rise to credit instruments which circulate, or perform payments by passing from hand to hand like money. A purchase on credit may be registered in a book, and cancelled at a later time by another similar entry. This is the simplest form of book credit, or registering of deferred payments. In this case, the credit granted

[1] "La Vitesse de la Circulation de la Monnaie," *Jour. de la Société de Statistique de Paris*, April, 1895.

is not used as a basis for new credit. On the other hand, a purchase or a loan may be evidenced by the issue of a piece of paper, whether note, check, or bill of exchange, that may be used to make more than one payment before it is retired. It is important to determine whether the former kind of credit transactions exert less or more influence on prices than do the latter. Not infrequently it is thought that the circulating character of certain credit instruments gives greater power over the price level to the class of transactions out of which they arise, than is imputable to ordinary book credit. This opinion doubtless is based, in part at least, upon the close resemblance of the service which these credit instruments perform to the work of money. It is plausible to think that since credit instruments discharge obligations as does money, they are simply an addition to the medium of exchange, with all the functions that money possesses. This, however, is hardly a correct view to take. Strictly speaking, these credit instruments do not give rise to a greater volume of credit; rather are they results of a greater volume of credit. They give greater mobility to the credit demand to which a given amount of goods gives rise. In the case of ordinary book credit, the volume of the credit demand remains unchanged and uncancelled until the expiration of the credit period. In the case of credit demand out of which credit instruments arise, the credit granted is immediately made the basis of a new credit, and this, in turn, of another, creating a series of transactions, only the last of which is likely to call for money. The credit instruments, then, are simply a means of giving greater mobility to the credit demand. The greater the duration of their circulation, the larger the total volume of credit cancellation which they will perform, but the larger is the uncancelled balance of credit demand for goods likely to be. For this reason, a given volume of credit transactions of the class that gives rise to circulating instruments of credit is likely to influence prices more than an equal volume of credit transactions which do not originate such instruments. The greater influence of this kind of credit transactions on prices is due, therefore, not to anything in the nature of the instruments of credit, but to the fact that, making possible, as they do, a greater volume of credit demand, the uncancelled balance is likely to be larger.

13. Deposit Currency. — Modern banking has developed a method of cancellation by means of book credit which is far more rapid and effective than can be attained by circulating instruments like bank notes. This bank-book credit is called deposit currency, and consists of the deposits to the credit of individuals on the books of the bank. It is these deposits against which checks are drawn, and which form the most common paying medium in highly developed commercial centres. Indeed, in such centres, deposit currency plays a far more important part than does note currency.

The latter is adapted more particularly to communities in which the population is more widely scattered, and access to banks is more difficult. Under such conditions the possibilities of cancellation are less, and a larger amount of currency is needed, of the kind which will pass from hand to hand indefinitely; whereas deposit currency, represented by checks, must, from its very nature, return quickly to the banks. The relative importance of the two kinds of medium of exchange may be seen from the fact that on September 9, 1903, the national banks of the United States held $3,156,333,499 individual deposits against which checks were drawn, and only $375,037,815 of notes outstanding. This deposit currency arises from discounts. When a merchant takes a bill of exchange, or a promissory note, to his bank, the bank gives him its face value minus the discount, and credits him with the amount as a deposit. Obviously, if all the merchants of a community did their business at the same bank, their checks coming into this bank would cancel one another, and the whole discharge of indebtedness between them could be performed by transfers of credits on the books of the bank. Of course there is usually more than one bank in a community, and not all the tradesmen of the same place do business at the same bank. Under these circumstances the cancellation is accomplished through an agency known as a clearing-house. This is simply an institution, or a place, where the banks in the community exchange the checks on one another, received from their patrons, and pay the balance against them in cash. Indeed, they do not always pay the balances in cash, but sometimes by drafts on the clearing-house, which are entered in the books of that institution to the credit of the banks in favor of which they are drawn. Cancellation is thus carried to its most profitable extent, and the amount of money necessary to settle a huge volume of transactions is reduced to a minimum.

It should be noticed that the influence of credit in raising prices is cumulative. If the credit demand for goods raises the price, the possessor of those goods can get larger credit at his bank, since he borrows on the new valuation. If business is good, and if confidence and buoyancy prevail, this process may repeat itself until prices are forced to a very high level. The amount of credit based upon goods at this high level of prices may be so great that the balance, after cancellation, may be greater than the reserve can carry. In that case the business community is face to face with a monetary stringency, if not a crisis. The credit must be contracted, or an increased amount of money must be obtained for a reserve. Herein lies the great danger of credit as a means of payment. Unless the granting of credit is carefully guarded, it may lead to an inflation of prices that will destroy confidence and cause great loss to the community by a sudden fall of the price level.

CHAPTER XII

THE MEASUREMENT OF VARIATIONS IN THE PURCHASING POWER OF MONEY

REFERENCES: Adams, T. S., Index Numbers and the Standard of Value, Journn. Pol. Econ., December, 1901, March, 1902; Commons, J. R., Quarterly Bulletin No. 2, Bureau of Economic Research, October, 1900; Edgeworth, F. Y., Report of the British Association for the Advance of Science, 1887, pp. 254–301, 1888, pp. 188–219, 1890, pp. 133–164; Econ. Journ., Vol. IV.; p. 159; Journ. Royal Statis. Soc., 1883 (Vol. XLVI.), p. 714, 1888 (Vol. LI.), p. 346; Falkner, R. P., United States Senate (Aldrich) Report on Wholesale Prices, 1893; Jevons, W. S., Investigations in Currency and Finance, pp. 13–159; Journ. Royal Statis. Soc., 1879, 1884, 1886, pp. 592, 648, 1893, pp. 220, 247, 1903, pp. 87, 616; Laspeyres, E., Die Berechnung einer mittleren Waarenpreissteigerung, Jahrb. für Nat. u. Stat., B. XVI., pp. 296–314; Laughlin, J. L., Principles of Money, Ch. 6; Nicholson, J. S., Money and Monetary Problems, 5th ed., pp. 312–342; Padan, R. S., Prices and Index Numbers, Journ. Pol. Econ., March, 1900; Pierson, N. G., Further Considerations on Index Numbers, Econ. Journ., March, 1896; Taussig, F. W., Results of Recent Investigations on Prices in the United States, Yale Rev., November, 1893; Walras, L., Elements d'Économie Politique Pure, pp. 431–437, 457–468; Theorie de la Monnaie, Pt. 3; Walsh, C. M., The Measurement of General Exchange Value.

1. On the Possibility of measuring Changes in the Value of Money. — Attempts have been made from time to time to measure in terms of goods the amount of change which the purchasing power of money undergoes. In such attempts, of course, no attention is paid to the causes of the changes. The inquiry has to do merely with the extent of the change. It makes no difference for this purpose whether "it is the pence that are few or the eggs that are many"; nor is it of importance to ask whether a change in value due to a change in the supply is, or is not, influenced by simultaneous changes in commodities. The sole question concerning the change is: Can we measure it? The possibility of doing so has been scouted by some, who insist that we cannot measure the variation of one thing in terms of another thing, if both vary at the same time, partly or wholly, from independent causes. But surely this position is not correct. Although our standard varies, if we can measure its variations, or can show that they are according to a certain law, it will serve the purpose of a standard as well as if it were absolutely fixed.

2. The Importance of Measurements of Price Changes. — Ability to measure variations in the purchasing power of money is of importance for several reasons. It is desirable, in the first place, in order to fix the value of deferred payments, especially those which run for a long time. We have seen that hardship may be caused by variations in the value of money. If we could measure these variations periodically, and correct them, we would attain the purpose of an invariable standard; for all that it would be necessary to do to prevent one person from gaining at the expense of another, on account of the variation, would be to compute its amount.

In the second place, the ability to measure such variations enables us to compare the relative values of wages and incomes in different places, and at different times. This is a matter of some moment to those who have expenditures to make in many places. The investor whose capital is placed in the enterprises of half a dozen countries is a much interested party in the comparative values of one ounce of gold in these different places. Nor is the academic reason for desiring to measure these variations altogether to be despised. It is of no little interest to be able to compare the purchasing power of money at different periods in history, for the inquiry throws much light upon the economic condition of the various social classes at different times, and affords a kind of measure of social progress.

3. Nature of the Problem. — What we are called on to do is to determine, in the first place, the relation of a certain property of one variable, *A*, which is subject to numerous, undetermined causes of variation, to a similar property possessed by a multitude of variables, of which *A* itself is one, similarly subject to numerous causes of variation, which are not fully known; in the second place, to do this for different times, so as to compare these ratios, although in the meantime new causes of variation may have come in and old ones may have dropped out, and the relative importance of the various causes may have greatly changed. If we might seek an illustration to enforce the idea of the complexity of the problem, we might say that we are to determine at a certain moment the ratio of the height of one wave of the sea to the average height of all the waves, including the one which is selected for comparison. The problem is theoretically solvable and the answer is some kind of an average. This average tells us nothing about the prices of individual goods. They may be higher or lower than the general level, in approximately equal numbers; or many may differ from it only a little, and a few a great deal. In comparing any average with an average computed at a previous date, if we find it higher we must not conclude that the price of every article has risen; nor when a fall in general prices or in the "price level" has occurred, that the price of every article has fallen. It is conceivable that all but one may have risen or fallen, but the average will not show this. The change may be due to the one, and not to the many. Our result will therefore be more or less valuable according to the extent of our knowledge of the factors which determine it, and according to the purpose for which we intend to use it. Different averages are suited to different purposes. Any intelligent use of an average of prices must have regard, therefore, to the purpose for which that average was prepared.

4. **Index Numbers.** — The usual method of measuring changes in the purchasing power of

money is by means of index numbers. An index number is a number which represents the price of a chosen commodity, or group of commodities, or the average of closely consecutive prices of those commodities, at a selected date, which is used as a standard wherewith we may compare the prices of the same article at later dates. Suppose, for example, that sugar is quoted at 20 pounds for $1 to-day, and at 16 pounds for $1 at some day next week. The price of 20 pounds on the latter date will be $1.25, and the latter price is to the former as 125 to 100, and the 100 may be called the index number. Instead of taking the price of a single article as a standard, it is better, however, to take the average, or the sum of the prices, of a number of different articles, either at a single selected date, or for a selected period. The price of each article on the selected date is called 100 and the number which expresses its price, in terms of this base, at another date, is in the ratio of the later price to the earlier. The sum of the later numbers divided by the number of the articles will give the average for the later date, and the difference of this average from the base, 100, will show the change in the purchasing power of money over the goods that are chosen to make up the table. The standard formed either of all vendibles, or of a selected list, whose prices are thus manipulated for the determination of the base for the price level, is called a tabular standard.

We may illustrate the formation of index numbers by the following table of prices of six selected commodities: —

	1880	1890	1900
	PRICE — BASE	PRICE — RED. TO BASE	PRICE — RED. TO BASE
Steel, per ton . . .	\$25.00–100	\$23.00– 92	\$26.00–104
Corn, per bu. . .	.50–100	.45– 90	.55–110
Wheat, per bu. . .	.90–100	.92–102	.95–105
Wool, per lb. . .	.30–100	.25– $83\frac{1}{3}$	.28– 90
Coal, per ton . . .	2.00–100	1.80– 90	2.10–105
Sugar, per bbl. . .	15.00–100	14.50– $96\frac{2}{3}$	14.00– 93
	100	6)554 $92\frac{1}{3}$	6)607 $101\frac{1}{6}$

In 1880, the first date selected, the price of each article is called 100. Hence the simple average of the prices, or the base, is 100. In 1890, the prices having changed as indicated, the average becomes $92\frac{1}{3}$; and in 1900, $101\frac{1}{6}$. That is, as compared with 1880 the average of prices, estimated in these goods, was $7\frac{2}{3}$ per cent. lower in 1890, and $1\frac{1}{6}$ per cent. higher in 1900.

Instead of regarding the price of each article in the basic year as 100, we might simply add the actual prices of each year and divide by the number of articles. The ratio of the average of each later year to that of 1880 would then show the courses of the averages. Thus, the averages would be 43.70, 40.90, and 43.88. Regarding the first as

100, the others are 93.6 and 100.4, respectively. The results are different, but the course is the same.

5. Limitations of Index Numbers. — The accuracy and serviceableness of such an index as has been described are open to criticism both on theoretical and practical grounds. Its value depends upon the kind of average used in computing the base, upon the number of articles selected, upon the amount of each article, upon the kind of prices used, whether wholesale or retail, upon the accuracy of the price observations, and upon the extent of territory within which the price observations may be regarded as applicable.

There are, then, many "if's" in the way of securing a satisfactory table of prices. If (1) we could be sure of getting an accurate and just mean for our base; if (2) all goods could be included in making a tabular standard; if (3) we could determine in what proportion the goods should be used in order to form a universally just measure; if (4) we had to do always and everywhere with the same goods in the same quantities and of the same qualities; if (5) their exact prices were ascertainable and universally applicable; and if, finally, sundry other conditions, which depend upon the specific purpose in hand, could be fulfilled, then we might, perhaps, frame an accurate measure of the variation of the purchasing power of money in terms of goods. In other words, we could measure changes in the price level so far as it is determined by the value of material things. But the value of money may vary with reference to other things than material goods, — as wages, rent, and incomes from other sources. The unit of measure in all these cases would be different from the one which we have hypothetically described.

6. The Kind of Average used in Computing Index Numbers. — The first thing necessary is to decide on the kind of average of prices which we are to use as a basis in making our comparisons. Different writers have used different averages, including the arithmetical, the geometric, the harmonic, and the median.

If we use the arithmetical average as the average, or mean, price of an article through a period, we simply add the terms of the series of prices and divide by their number. If we use the geometric average, we multiply the numbers in the series of prices in the period and take that root of the product indicated by the number of terms. If we use the harmonic average, we find the reciprocal of the arithmetical average of the series of prices. The median is that term of the series which has as many terms above it as below it.

To illustrate: Suppose the price of a pound of cotton for five successive days was 5, 6, 8, 9, and 11 cents, respectively. The arithmetical average price would be 7.8; the geometric, 7.5; the harmonic, 7.2; and the median, 8. The arithmetical average of a given set of numbers is larger than the geometric or the harmonic.

Apparently, the answer to the question how much prices have changed in a given period, will depend largely upon the particular average chosen. It might appear, therefore, a matter of some importance to decide which is the proper, or the best, mean to use. The arithmetical mean is simple and easily found, but it is much disturbed by violent fluctuations. That is, it gives emphasis to the large numbers. The geometric mean, on the other hand, increases the influence of the smaller numbers, but it is more tedious to calculate. It is appropriate in a problem where the "quæsitum is a real thing or at least a unique type (as the average stature of a nation), or if the errors or deviations from the true mean which the data present obey a certain law of dispersion, which there is some reason for expecting prices to fulfil."[1] Moreover, the geometric mean is "more likely than the arithmetic mean to correspond to the greatest ordinate of the unsymmetrical curve which the statistics of prices are apt to form."[2]

The median, like the arithmetical mean, is easily found, but it may vary much from type; that is, it may be far from any actual price. It is less disturbed, however, by sudden great changes than is the arithmetical mean. The harmonic mean is best to apply if there is a large number of low prices, and a small number of large ones, in the series.

[1] Edgeworth in *Econ. Journ.*, Vol. IV., p. 159.

[2] *Journ. Royal Stat. Soc.*, 1888, p. 356.

But the mathematical characteristics of the different means do not enable us to determine which one to use. No one of these means is to be chosen because it is mathematically the most exact. The basis of choice is the economic purpose in view. If we have a number of prices that vary but little from one another, and our purpose is to determine how much money must be given on two separate dates, assuming that the same number of units of goods are sold on the two dates, the arithmetical mean is best. If we want to determine changes in the purchasing power of money as measured by total mass of goods purchasable, irrespective of their proportions, the geometric mean will best serve our purpose. If, in the series of prices, there are a good many which changed but little, and a few which had changed very largely, the harmonic mean would be the best to use.

7. The Number of Articles necessary to Furnish Proper Averages. — The number of articles to be chosen for the table of prices is mainly a question of convenience, provided it is large enough to be fairly representative, and provided that the articles are those of the widest demand. Opinions differ, of course, as to what things should enter into the list, at least after a certain number have been named; but there are many on which all persons agree. The error due to a restriction of a number of vendibles cannot, then, be wholly eliminated; but the whole calculation is of so rough a character that we can afford to neglect the error due to this cause. Moreover, we must understand in the case of this source of error, as in the case of others, that if it is approximately constant, it cannot affect the correctness of the relationships indicated by the results. We may, therefore, conclude that a list of articles ordinarily chosen in such tables as those of Sauerbeck and Soetbeer are sufficiently numerous to serve the purpose.

8. Relative Proportions, or Weights, of Articles Used. — But after we have determined what articles shall enter into our table, we must also fix upon the relative proportions of these articles. Goods are not all of equal importance. A table which gave equal weight to wheat and pepper, for example, would be misleading. As to what constitutes, or determines, the importance of goods in this connection, opinions differ widely, so that various measures have been suggested. The relative importance of goods, economically speaking, may be estimated, for the purposes of index numbers, on the basis of the relative quantities produced, of the relative amounts exported or imported, of the proportions in which they enter into the consumption of the mass of the people, or in any one of half a dozen other ways. Mr. Inglis Palgrave has chosen to weight the articles in his computation according to their relative importance in exports and imports. Soetbeer and Sauerbeck weight the articles in their tables according to their relative annual consumption. Professor Falkner, in the United States Senate Report on Wages, Prices, and the Cost of Living, chose to list the articles in his tables in the proportions in which they enter into the budget of expenses of the average workingman; and Mr. Giffen, a good many years ago, proposed[1] to use as his index numbers the ratio whose numerators are the price of the whole amount of each article consumed in the standard year, taken at the prices of each later year; and whose denominators are the same quantities at the prices of the standard year. Here again we find that, whichever method is adopted, we may expect, on the whole, similar indications in the results. All that is necessary is that the calculation of the price level at successive dates shall be made in the same way, with data which show the same facts for different periods. Indeed, although on the face of the argument it would seem impossible to get correct indications from tables of unweighted index numbers, in reality the advantage of weighting is questionable. In the first place, it is exceedingly difficult to select proper weights, and impracticable to apply them to a long list of articles; and, in the next place, if the number of articles is large, the use of weighted prices has little influence on the result.

We must notice, however, that the relative quantities chosen, at the date when the table is first computed, may not represent the relative importance of the same group of goods at any subsequent date. Many articles are in great

[1] Report on Imports and Exports, 1885, Table V.

demand to-day and almost out of use to-morrow. Their vogue depends upon the whim of fashion. Consumption changes its character. With the exception of a few articles included among the necessaries of life, there is almost nothing the demand for which may not change very much, between two dates of computation. If the relative values of the commodities which enter in to make up the table change during the interim, the quantities exchanged will be different, and the proportions in which they should enter into the table of prices at subsequent dates should change.

9. Influence of New Commodities.—Still further, it may be urged with much force that the usefulness of the averages obtained from such tables of prices is impaired by the fact that new articles may come into use between the dates on which averages are struck. Such articles must, of course, be taken into account if the tables are to serve the purpose for which they are devised. This difficulty, however, may be overcome in a measure by making frequent revisions of the table. As Professor Marshall has pointed out, when a new article appears on the market no notice should be taken of it, in comparing the average of prices in the tabular standard, at the date of its first appearance. At the next subsequent date of making up the table, however, the article should be put in the list. The interim will allow its price to settle down to a normal condition.

10. Whether Wholesale or Retail Prices furnish the Better Comparison. — In the next place, it is important to know whether we should use wholesale or retail prices in making our index numbers. The choice depends on our purpose. If we wish to show simply and solely the change in the level of prices, there is no theoretical objection to the use of wholesale prices. If, however, we wish to discover the effect of changes in the price level on the economic condition of a certain social class, we should use retail prices, because these are the prices that the people pay. Wholesale prices are, however, more uniform and more easily gotten. They apply to a larger area, and they are more sensitive, more subject to the breath of competition.

11. The Different Purposes of Tables of Prices determine their Character. — There are certain other possible causes of error which need careful consideration before we can finally make up our minds concerning the usefulness of index numbers. A table may give the same average level of prices at two different times, although in the meantime there have been many and great variations in the price of the different articles, because the variations may have offset one another. To a person who is interested in but a few of the commodities in the table, it is of little interest or importance to know that the price level has remained constant, while the goods that he deals in have either fallen or risen. The importance of this objection depends, again, on the purpose of the tables of prices. If the aim is to show changes in the level of prices, the objection loses force; for it is not claimed that the index numbers tell us about relative prices, and it is obvious that the same average may be derived from many different values of the same series of articles. If, however, the tables are intended to show changes in relative welfare of different social classes, the objection is important.

Even if all the difficulties thus far mentioned could be overcome, the result would be more or less misleading, according to the area over which the chosen prices prevail. The prices which one is likely to obtain are not, of course, universal. They do not hold good in all the markets of the world. The mean price of the same article may, therefore, be very different in different places, for the same series of dates. Moreover, the mean may be seriously affected by extreme variations of prices in the same locality. Professor Marshall points out that if we take as an index number the mean price of strawberries in May, June, and July, we will have an average which is not representative. It is made up of prices to which equal arithmetical weight is given, although some of them do not apply to the bulk of the supply of the commodity. Strawberries are most plentiful in the middle period of the three months mentioned. At the beginning of the season we find them selling at a high price, soon there is a considerable and somewhat sudden drop to a price which varies but little until near the close of the season, when there is again a sudden and a large rise. If we strike an average giving equal weight to the mean price in May, June, and July, we will get a result that is too large. The price in the middle of the season may apply to a thousand times more berries than the price of early May, or of late July. To get a correct mean, therefore, in a case like this, we must weight the price for the middle of the season. In general, in forming our tables, we must give less weight to articles whose prices vary very frequently.

Whether or not wages and rent in the ordinary sense, will be included in deriving the index numbers, depends altogether upon the use to which the numbers are to be put. If they are for the simple purpose of indicating the changes in the general purchasing power of money, wages and rent need not be included, because they are already counted in the prices of goods. If, however, we are seeking light upon the condition of wage receivers and income receivers, we must include both of these items in our table.

12. The Services of Tables of Prices. — After all these things have been attended to, all causes of error eliminated, or corrected as far as possible, and the table constructed in the way best suited to the purpose, of what value is the result? It certainly cannot be regarded as very accurate. Yet it serves very well the purpose of students of economic history to show changes through long periods, in the general purchasing power of money, and in economic conditions at different times. The more numerous the commodities represented in the table, the more closely, as has already been remarked, will the index numbers do this, provided the other conditions necessary remain the same. The result, however, will be of little importance to any individual or, perhaps, to any class. Like the ready-made suit of clothes, it may fit the average man, but the average man is nowhere to be found. It becomes of more importance to an individual, or class, in proportion as the list of things included conforms to a list which the individual or the class buys or sells. It has been remarked several times that the selection of articles for a table of prices, and the method of using the data for deriving a set of index numbers, should be determined by the purpose in view. Hence, as Professor Edgeworth remarks, "there are therefore many methods — not one method — of measuring and ascertaining variations in the value of money. The path which we have to investigate has many bifurcations. To decide at each turn which is the right direction is either impossible or at least presumptuous. It is impossible when both ways are right, directed to different, but equally legitimate, ends."[1] The purpose may be (1) to find for the use of the student of economic history a rough measure of changes in welfare from time

[1] Report of the Brit. Assoc. for Adv. of Sci., 1887, p. 259.

to time, as shown by changes in the value of money; (2) to furnish a standard to keep general prices steady in order to keep trade stable; (3) to furnish a basis for the equitable discharge of long-time debts; and (4) to supply a means for measuring the purchasing power of wages and incomes in different places or people. We can form tables which will serve very well each one of these purposes, with much more ease, and much more accuracy, than we can form a table that will serve them all at once. As Professor Taussig puts it, "Proceeding from the social point of view, it might be possible from a given set of figures, to conclude that the expense of living for the workingman had risen; while yet from the simple monetary point of view, the same figures might make it clear that prices had fallen."[1]

For the first and second purposes enumerated, all vendibles ought properly to be included. As this is impossible, the tables should be as extensive as practicable, and should contain not only material goods, but wages of labor and incomes. For the third purpose, sufficient accuracy would be obtained by choosing for our list the articles common to the demand of both creditor and debtor. Perfect coincidence is of course unattainable, except in peculiar cases. For the fourth purpose, it would be best to select a "certain region of industry and get an index number from its products which indicates changes likely

[1] *Yale Rev.*, November, 1893, p. 235.

to become general."[1] We would need as many tables as there are classes who have money to spend. The more exactly the articles in the table are those consumed by a special social class, the more accurately, as has been said, does the result represent changes in the value of money for the members of that class. We might, therefore, construct a table of index numbers for each social class, according to the different kinds and amounts of wealth that its members consume. For the entrepreneurs, or employing class, such a table should include the price of labor. For wage-earners considered as consumers, the things they most largely consume should make up the table; while as producers the varying value of money for them should be measured by index numbers of wages. For the wealthier classes of society, the list selected should contain the necessaries of life, as before; but should include many things which are beyond the reach of the mass of the people, and should also include wages paid for personal services. Other forms of a table could be suggested, but these are sufficient to indicate the variety that is possible.

13. The Best Kind of Table for General Purposes. — For general purposes, however, changes in the value of money can be fairly shown by a table constructed of the prices of articles of general consumption. It is true, as Professor Foxwell has urged, that the "consumer is not every one";

[1] Report of the Brit. Assoc. for Adv. of Sci., 1887, p. 257.

but it is also true that every one is a consumer. In constructing a table on the basis of quantities consumed, raw materials should be excluded, excepting in those cases where we cannot get accurate prices of the finished products. The question of the choice between wholesale and retail prices is of great importance here. Consumers, as consumers, usually pay retail prices; on the other hand, these are subject to much friction, and show innumerable local variations. Wholesale prices, as has been pointed out, are easier to get and usually differ less as between different places; yet they may not be accurate, because the producer may be obtaining the same price for an article at two different times, although the lessened cost of transportation may make the quoted market price lower at the second date than it was at the preceding one. Now, it is market prices which are used in making up index numbers. On the whole, however, in this special table, as in a table of a more general character, we are likely to get into less trouble by using wholesale instead of retail prices. As to the relative weights to be assigned the different articles, the relative quantities produced at the given dates may well be used; or the relative quantities marketed or consumed at the given dates, either by consumers in general, or by the working classes as shown by their budget of expenses. If we use the latter method of weighting, we run across another source of error in the possible inaccuracy of the budgets.

In this consumption standard the table of wages of labor employed in producing commodities, as distinguished from the labor expended in personal services, should not be included. For the wages of the former have already been allowed for in the prices of the goods produced, and it is necessary in calculations of this kind that the various observations made, or statistics obtained, should be as far as possible independent of one another. Moreover, what we want to know from this table is the change in the power over goods due to changes in the value of money. We should defeat our purpose to a certain extent, so far as the inquiry relates to the laborer, if we included in our table records of the wages which he gets. Wages paid for personal services, however, are on a different footing. They are not represented in the prices of goods, and they represent expenditures by another social class. As to rent, in the economic sense, it should not be included in the tables. For it represents a differential advantage, and does not affect the prices of commodities. Rent in the common sense, such as house rent, as distinguished from rent of location, may, however, be included because it is one of the ordinary expenses of the people.

14. The Similarity of Results in Different Tables. — At first thought it seems a surprising fact that computations of price changes made in the crudest way yield results of the same general character as are yielded by calculations into which enters every refinement of mathematics for the correction of the various errors that have been described. They all show, for example, that the prices of goods, measured in gold, rose from the period of 1845–1850 to 1873, and fell from that date until within the past half-dozen years. The agreement is not so surprising, however, when we recall the large number of possible sources of error. As has been remarked already, to seek refinement of method with data that can never be accurate is useless labor.

15. The Table of the London "Economist." — Different tables of index numbers have been constructed, but the best-known examples are those of the London *Economist*, Jevons, Soetbeer, Sauerbeck, and Falkner. The method of the London *Economist* begun by Mr. Newmarch[1] is, perhaps, the simplest and crudest. It contains 22 articles, the simple average of whose prices for six years, from 1845 to 1850, constitutes the base. The price of each article was noted on January 1 and July 1. The mean of these was taken for the price at the starting-point, and called 100. As there are 22 articles, the index number for all is 2200. Each year thereafter the percentage of rise or fall of each article is added to, or taken from, the original 100. The sum is found, and according as this sum varies from the original 2200, so has the price level

[1] See the *Economist*, March, 1864. The articles are coffee, sugar, tea, tobacco, butchers' meat, wheat, cotton, wool, raw silk, flax and hemp, indigo, oils, timber, tallow, leather, cotton cloth, copper, iron, lead, tin, Pernambuco cotton, and cotton yarn.

varied. The *Economist's* table, with the figures for January 1 only, is as follows:—

THE "ECONOMIST'S" TABLE[1]

Year	Total of All Articles	Average for All Articles	Year	Total of All Articles	Average for All Articles
1845-50	2,200	100	1882	2,435	111
1851	2,293	104	1883	2,342	106
1858	2,612	119	1884	2,221	101
1861	2,727	124	1885	2,098	95
1862	2,878	131	1886	2,023	92
1863	3,492	159	1887	2,059	94
1864	3,787	172	1888	2,230	101
1865	3,575	163	1889	2,187	99
1866	3,564	162	1890	2,236	102
1867	3,024	137	1891	2,240	102
1868	2,682	122	1892	2,133	97
1869	2,666	121	1893	2,120	96
1870	2,689	122	1894	2,082	95
1871	2,590	118	1895	1,923	87
1872	2,835	129	1896	1,999	91
1873	2,947	134	1897	1,950	88
1874	2,891	131	1898	1,890	86
1875	2,778	126	1899	1,918	87
1876	2,711	123	1900	2,145	97
1877	2,715	123	1901	2,126	97
1878	2,529	115	1902	1,948	89
1879	2,225	101	1903	2,003	91
1880	2,538	115	1904	2,197	99
1881	2,376	108			

This table is crude, its list of articles is too short to be representative, and the small number gives undue weight to a change in the price of a single one, since the prices are not weighted. Moreover,

[1] The *Economist's* Monthly Supplements.

one article, cotton, appears too often; and the choice of the prices of two single days, January 1 and July 1, to represent the price of the year, is likely to cause large error.

16. The Work of Jevons on Index Numbers.— Professor Jevons it was who first attacked the study of price changes in a thoroughgoing and masterly manner. His first publication[1] on the subject, in which he used 39 articles, appeared in 1863. He found the arithmetical average of the prices of each of these for the six years from 1845 to 1850, and used this as the base. To get his yearly average price for each article, he took the arithmetical average of the mean monthly prices of the highest and lowest grade of each. He then divided this annual average by the basic average. The resulting percentages showed the price changes. He manipulated his data in other ways and used certain refinements of mathematical calculations, as the geometric mean and logarithms, but they do not really add anything to the value of the result.

17. Soetbeer's Tables.—Soetbeer chose 114 articles, the prices of 100 of which he took from the Hamburg market, and those of the other 14 from the English market.[2]

[1] "A Serious Fall in the Value of Gold ascertained and its Social Effects set Forth." See his "Investigations in Currency and Finance."

[2] See his "Materialen zur Erlaüterung und Beurtheilung der Wirthschaftlichen Edelmetallverhältnisse und der Währungsfrage," (transl. in "Bimetallism in Europe," United States Exec. Doc. No. 34, 50th Congress, 1st Sess., 1887).

SOETBEER'S TABLE OF RELATIVE PRICES[1]

1847–1850 = 100

YEAR	I AGRICULTURAL	II ANIMAL	III TROPICAL, ETC.	IV EAST INDIA GOODS, ETC.	V MINERAL
1847–1850	100.00	100.00	100.00	100.00	100.00
1851	99.00	110.38	90.00	99.94	95.70
1852	110.71	106.68	95.33	99.95	95.76
1853	128.18	114.94	124.78	115.28	109.24
1854	150.49	121.12	112.91	118.17	115.95
1855	158.82	123.54	142.03	121.02	119.10
1851–1855	129.99	114.79	110.43	110.97	107.03
1856	149.03	127.61	155.95	123.95	116.65
1857	138.11	140.18	169.32	140.32	124.58
1858	119.92	127.02	120.69	112.76	109.04
1859	119.48	130.69	113.40	115.74	108.57
1860	133.75	133.75	120.36	120.28	108.66
1856–1860	131.84	132.31	134.72	122.61	113.59
1861	131.46	124.79	122.08	117.19	102.40
1862	126.80	127.19	113.93	117.28	101.88
1863	120.12	124.12	114.97	116.87	102.92
1864	117.89	129.21	109.41	125.74	104.53
1865	126.48	135.23	114.01	146.11	98.93
1861–1865	124.46	128.24	114.13	118.64	102.11
1866	137.64	135.64	126.30	117.90	96.54
1867	146.38	132.68	126.44	114.35	93.28
1868	141.59	133.48	120.75	116.75	91.76
1869	132.40	143.25	115.58	122.10	96.33
1870	131.23	139.32	118.57	120.56	99.68
1866–1870	137.74	136.35	121.54	118.32	95.47
1871	144.76	144.14	122.99	120.22	101.85
1872	144.17	155.82	125.36	130.25	121.63
1873	146.21	156.72	132.15	134.32	140.60
1874	150.99	157.76	145.02	136.74	116.70
1875	138.16	158.59	131.35	132.11	107.49
1871–1875	144.90	154.57	131.50	130.72	116.90
1876	141.06	155.79	128.69	129.74	106.27
1877	145.34	152.51	140.55	130.29	98.87
1878	132.50	141.53	134.34	125.61	94.14
1879	132.92	137.60	139.10	123.34	84.28
1880	138.11	147.30	154.65	122.92	88.33
1876–1880	138.12	146.76	138.91	126.38	94.35
1881	137.50	151.21	146.57	122.60	84.87
1882	138.45	155.17	139.23	122.47	86.99
1883	143.33	156.40	142.38	120.17	82.93
1884	123.85	150.26	120.16	117.90	78.69
1885	110.75	140.45	123.78	116.39	74.23
1881–1885	130.77	150.65	134.41	119.91	81.55
1886	101.31	133.53	122.44	115.45	70.52
1887	96.28	129.93	121.81	116.59	72.50
1888	98.18	128.97	120.09	116.41	75.57
1889	102.06	130.95	127.57	118.82	78.55
1890	107.53	129.85	138.61	119.35	83.54
1886–1890	101.07	130.64	126.10	117.32	76.13
1891	119.88	131.66	139.99	113.56	84.72

[1] U. S. Sen. (Aldrich) Report on Wholesale Prices, Vol. I., p. 294.

MEASUREMENT OF CHANGES IN PRICES

SOETBEER'S TABLE OF RELATIVE PRICES[1]

1847–1850 = 100

Year	VI Textile Materials	VII Divers	VIII British Exports	I-VIII Total of 114 Articles
1847–1850	100.00	100.00	100.00	100.00
1851	104.39	103.98	97.98	100.21
1852	105.01	95.09	95.98	101.69
1853	101.43	105.17	100.61	113.69
1854	111.64	119.44	99.53	121.25
1855	103.58	109.63	98.27	124.23
1851–1855	105.20	106.65	98.47	112.22
1856	100.02	100.50	98.50	123.27
1857	112.18	108.01	101.25	130.11
1858	103.59	99.70	100.91	113.52
1859	104.69	115.57	105.77	116.34
1860	108.74	116.83	105.60	120.98
1856–1860	107.12	108.21	102.41	120.91
1861	110.85	119.65	105.84	118.10
1862	124.31	156.99	114.22	122.65
1863	151.84	161.36	133.45	125.49
1864	154.26	162.58	146.53	129.28
1865	117.80	121.06	137.80	122.63
1861–1865	131.83	144.33	127.56	123.59
1866	134.94	111.30	140.36	125.85
1867	130.31	108.13	133.91	124.44
1868	127.18	101.25	127.56	121.99
1869	130.52	98.17	128.15	123.38
1870	122.87	111.21	122.68	122.87
1866–1870	129.17	105.90	130.55	123.57
1871	119.23	117.48	122.64	127.03
1872	122.79	128.54	130.07	135.62
1873	119.58	119.14	128.52	138.28
1874	112.80	112.21	126.06	136.20
1875	111.47	98.74	124.96	129.85
1871–1875	117.17	114.98	126.44	133.29
1876	105.54	101.78	119.23	128.33
1877	108.33	99.80	114.04	127.70
1878	102.33	97.24	111.03	120.60
1879	98.76	90.21	105.93	117.10
1880	96.72	95.23	108.15	121.89
1876–1880	102.33	96.79	111.70	123.07
1881	99.29	94.89	103.03	121.07
1882	95.10	99.10	104.72	122.14
1883	95.93	95.38	104.72	122.24
1884	97.02	84.82	103.36	114.25
1885	95.89	81.35	100.48	108.72
1881–1885	96.65	91.11	103.28	117.68
1886	89.76	78.75	97.03	103.99
1887	81.42	77.30	95.98	102.02
1888	82.17	74.31	94.91	102.04
1889	89.05	86.41	96.60	106.13
1890	81.92	91.70	94.90	108.13
1886–1890	84.86	81.69	95.88	104.46
1891	80.40	85.06	95.11	109.19

[1] U. S. Sen. (Aldrich) Report on Wholesale Prices, Vol. I., p. 294.

His tables, which are probably the best we have, begin with 1847 and extend to 1888, the period for which data were collected by the Hamburg Bureau of Trade Statistics. Dr. Soetbeer continued his table from other sources, from 1886 to 1890.[1] He used the simple arithmetical average, taking as his base the average of the period 1847–1850. He grouped his articles into eight classes, according to their character: agricultural, animal, tropical and kindred products, East India goods, mineral, textiles, sundry, and British exports. His table is on pages 248, 249.

18. Sauerbeck's Tables. — Sauerbeck's table of English prices is, perhaps, the most generally quoted. He uses the unweighted arithmetical average and takes average prices for 1867–1877 as his base. Thirty-seven different articles are used, but several of them are introduced more than once in different grades, so that a total of fifty-six items appears. They are all raw materials. This last fact is, of course, a defect. So, too, are the small number of articles used, the absence of weights, the admitted inaccuracy of some of the price quotations, and the occasional use of actual single prices instead of averages. Sauerbeck's table is as follows:[2] —

[1] Jahrbuch für Nationaloekonomie und Statistik, III., F. B. III., pp. 588 ff.

[2] United States Senate (Aldrich) Report on Wholesale Prices, Vol. I., p. 247; *Journ. Royal Statis. Soc.*, 1886, 1893, 1903.

MEASUREMENT OF CHANGES IN PRICES

SAUERBECK'S INDEX NUMBERS

GROUPS OF ARTICLES AND TOTALS 1867–1877 = 100

YEAR	VEGETABLE FOOD (CORN, ETC.)	ANIMAL FOOD (MEAT, ETC.)	SUGAR, COFFEE, AND TEA	TOTAL FOOD	MINERALS	TEXTILES	SUNDRY MATERIALS	TOTAL MATERIALS	GRAND TOTAL
1846	106	81	98	95	92	77	86	85	89
1847	129	88	87	105	94	78	86	86	95
1848	92	83	69	84	78	64	77	73	78
1849	79	71	77	76	77	67	75	73	74
1850	74	67	87	75	77	78	80	78	77
1851	73	68	84	74	75	75	79	76	75
1852	80	69	75	75	80	78	84	81	78
1853	100	82	87	91	105	87	101	97	95
1854	120	87	85	101	115	88	109	104	102
1855	120	87	89	101	109	84	109	101	101
1856	109	88	97	99	110	89	109	102	101
1857	105	89	119	102	108	92	119	107	105
1858	87	83	97	88	96	84	102	94	91
1859	85	85	102	89	98	88	107	98	94
1860	99	91	107	98	97	90	111	100	99
1861	102	91	96	97	91	92	109	99	98
1862	98	86	98	94	91	123	106	107	101
1863	87	85	99	89	93	149	101	115	103
1864	79	89	106	88	96	162	98	119	105
1865	84	97	97	91	91	134	97	108	101
1866	95	96	94	95	91	130	99	107	102
1867	115	89	94	101	87	110	100	100	100
1868	113	88	96	100	85	106	102	99	99
1869	91	96	98	94	89	109	100	100	98
1870	88	98	95	93	89	106	99	99	96
1871	94	100	100	98	93	103	105	101	100
1872	101	101	104	102	127	114	108	115	109
1873	106	109	106	107	141	103	106	114	111
1874	105	103	105	104	116	92	96	100	102

SAUERBECK'S INDEX NUMBERS

Groups of Articles and Totals 1867–1877 = 100

Year	Vegetable Food (Corn, etc.)	Animal Food (Meat, etc.)	Sugar, Coffee, and Tea	Total Food	Minerals	Textiles	Sundry Materials	Total Materials	Grand Total
1875	93	108	100	100	101	88	92	93	96
1876	92	108	98	99	90	85	95	91	95
1877	100	101	103	101	84	85	94	89	94
1878	95	101	90	96	74	78	88	81	87
1879	87	94	87	90	73	74	85	78	83
1880	89	101	88	94	79	81	89	84	88
1881	84	101	84	91	77	77	86	80	85
1882	84	104	76	89	79	73	85	80	84
1883	82	103	77	89	76	70	84	77	82
1884	71	97	63	79	68	68	81	73	76
1885	68	88	63	74	66	65	76	70	72
1886	65	87	60	72	67	63	69	67	69
1887	64	79	67	70	69	65	67	67	68
1888	67	82	65	72	78	64	67	69	70
1889	65	86	75	75	75	70	68	70	72
1890	65	82	70	73	80	66	69	71	72
1891	75	81	71	77	76	59	69	68	72
1892	65	84	69	73	71	57	67	65	68
1893	59	85	75	72	68	59	68	65	68
1894	55	80	65	66	64	53	64	60	63
1895	54	78	62	64	62	52	65	60	62
1896	53	73	59	62	63	54	63	60	61
1897	60	79	52	65	66	51	62	59	62
1898	67	77	51	68	70	51	63	61	64
1899	60	79	53	65	92	58	65	70	68
1900	62	85	54	69	108	66	71	80	75
1901	62	85	46	67	89	60	71	72	70
1902	63	87	41	67	82	61	71	71	69

19. Falkner's Tables.—The table of prices and index numbers[1] which for extensiveness takes precedence of all others, is that compiled by Professor R. P. Falkner, formerly of the University of Pennsylvania. Professor Falkner gathered together continuous lists of prices for 90 articles for the 50 years preceding 1891; and for 223 articles for the 30 years preceding that date. Of the 223 quotations, 81 were for different varieties of the same article. The basic year is 1860, and its prices, on the first of January, are called 100. Many of the price quotations are not averages, but prices on selected dates. The index numbers were computed both from unweighted prices and from prices weighted according to the importance of the articles in the budgets of expenses of 2561 families of workingmen in the United States. Such a method of weighting is excellent for tables designed to show changes in the economic condition of the class whose expenditure the budgets represent; but the results can show changes in the command of money over goods in general only so far as the articles in the budgets enter into the expenditure of all classes, and that, too, in the proportions in which they are weighted. Budgets in whose accuracy and completeness confidence can be had are difficult to get, and introduce into index numbers errors peculiar to themselves. In Falkner's tables somewhat

[1] United States Senate (Aldrich) Report on Wholesale Prices, etc.

FALKNER'S RELATIVE PRICES, 1840–1891 — PRICES OF JANUARY, 1860 = 100

Year	All Articles Simply Averaged	All Articles Aver. Acc. to Importance, Certain Expend. Uniform	All Articles Aver. Acc. to Importance (68.6 per cent. of Total Expend.)	Year	All Articles Simply Averaged	All Articles Aver. Acc. to Importance, Certain Expend. Uniform	All Articles Aver. Acc. to Importance (68.6 per cent. of Total Expend.)
1840	116.8	98.5	97.7	1866	191.0	160.2	187.7
1841	115.8	98.7	98.1	1867	172.2	145.2	165.8
1842	107.8	93.2	90.1	1868	160.5	150.7	173.9
1843	101.5	89.3	84.3	1869	153.5	135.9	152.3
1844	101.9	89.8	85.0	1870	142.3	130.4	144.4
1845	102.8	92.1	88.2	1871	136.0	124.8	136.1
1846	106.4	96.7	95.2	1872	138.8	122.2	132.4
1847	106.5	96.7	95.2	1873	137.5	119.9	129.0
1848	101.4	92.0	88.3	1874	133.0	120.5	129.9
1849	98.7	88.9	83.5	1875	127.6	119.8	128.9
1850	102.3	92.6	89.2	1876	118.2	115.5	122.6
1851	105.9	99.1	98.6	1877	110.9	109.4	113.6
1852	102.7	98.5	97.9	1878	101.3	103.1	104.6
1853	109.1	103.4	105.0	1879	96.6	96.6	95.0
1854	112.9	103.4	105.0	1880	106.9	103.4	104.9
1855	113.1	106.3	109.2	1881	105.7	105.8	108.4
1856	113.2	108.5	112.3	1882	108.5	106.3	109.1
1857	112.5	109.6	114.0	1883	106.0	104.5	106.6
1858	101.8	109.1	113.2	1884	99.4	101.8	102.6
1859	100.2	102.0	102.9	1885	93.0	95.4	93.3
1860	100.0	100.0	100.0	1886	91.9	95.5	93.4
1861	100.6	95.9	94.1	1887	92.6	96.2	94.5
1862	117.8	102.8	104.1	1888	94.2	97.4	96.2
1863	148.6	122.1	132.2	1889	94.2	99.0	98.5
1864	190.5	149.4	172.1	1890	92.3	95.7	93.7
1865	216.8	190.7	232.2	1891	92.2	96.2	94.4

less than 70 per cent. of the total expenditure of the social class considered was represented. Of course the prices were for the United States, and tables were made both of retail and of wholesale prices. These tables carried the prices down to 1891. In 1900 Professor Falkner prepared a second table of wholesale prices from 1890 to 1900, which is substantially a continuation of his previous table, although in a somewhat different form and for a fewer number of articles. Ninety-nine series of prices were used in the second tables, and the base used was the average of nine quarterly prices from January 1, 1890, to January 1, 1892. Falkner's table is on page 254.

Professor Falkner's supplementary table gives average prices for each quarter, from January, 1890, to July, 1899. The January figures[2] are as follows: —

Year	All Articles	Year	All Articles
1890	102.0	1895.	84.7
1891	100.6	1896.	85.2
1892	96.5	1897.	82.0
1893	97.2	1898.	83.3
1894	89.6	1899.	86.5

A comparison of all these tables shows, what has been already urged, that the same general

[1] United States Senate (Aldrich) Report, etc., Vol. I.

[2] Bulletin of the United States Department of Labor, No. 27, March, 1900, p. 263.

conclusions are reached by all the methods allowed, so that the labor involved in mathematical niceties is hardly worth while.

20. Other Tables of Prices. — The tables mentioned are by no means the only ones that have been compiled. Among others which are worthy of mention are the English tables of Rice Vaughan, who compared the prices of 1650 with those of 1352; of Bishop Fleetwood in 1707; of R. H. I. Palgrave, and Mulhall; those of the German writers Laspeyres, 1831–1863, Paasche, 1863–1872, continuing the work of Laspeyres; and Conrad; the French table of De Foville, who compiled a table of French prices of imports and exports, 1847–1880; and the tables of the United States Department of Labor.[1]

21. Other Methods of Measuring Price Changes. — Other methods than the use of index numbers have been suggested for measuring variations in the value of money. Two or three of them are important enough to deserve mention. Dr. Drobrisch has suggested[2] a comparison of the values at different epochs of an average 100 weight of goods. Of course, there is no such thing as an average 100 weight of goods, so that the method is a purely fanciful one.

Professor Newcomb has proposed to measure changes in the value of gold by noting the change

[1] Bulletin of the United States Department of Labor, March, 1902.

[2] See Report of the Brit. Assoc. for Adv. of Sci., 1887, p. 265.

in the value of the product of an average individual worker per unit of time. It is easy to measure an electrical current, or a head of water, by noting changes in the amount of work done under fixed conditions; but we cannot fix the conditions of individual character. There is no average individual, and if there were, the value of his product would be one of the factors entering in to cause variations in the value of gold.

Professor Nicholson has suggested a somewhat elaborate method, which takes account theoretically of all things bought and sold. It is briefly as follows: let $p, p_1, p_2, \cdots p_n$, represent the price per unit of every commodity sold on a certain date. Let $q, q_1, q_2, \cdots q_n$ represent the total number of units of each article. Then $pq - p_1 q_1 - p_2q_2 - \cdots p_nq_n$ are equal to the total value exchanged, or $X. Hence the value of $1 will be $pq - p_1q_1 - p_2 q_2 - \cdots p_n q_n$ all divided by X. Now, if this process be repeated at any other date and the value of $1 deduced, we shall be able to determine the change in the price level. Obviously, however, we cannot construct a series of all the prices of all articles. To make the series manageable, and the scheme practicable, we must (1) group similar articles, and (2) omit the less important articles, so as thereby to reduce the number of terms; (3) we must allow for increase or decrease in old items and the addition of new items. By making all these allowances the series may be reduced, as Professor Nicholson reduces it, to very manageable shape.

Mr. Giffen and others have suggested as a measure of the changes in the value of money, variations in the amount of money as compared with those in the amount of goods imported and exported at different times. In other words, he seeks to compare the volume of money with the volume of foreign trade. Obviously, if all other things remain the same, an increase in the volume of trade would reveal an increase in the amount of money. If the amount of money has not increased *pari passu* with trade, its value must have fallen.

22. Professor Edgeworth's Presentation of the Solutions of the Problem of measuring Price Changes. — The various solutions of the problem of measuring the changes in the value of money have been admirably grouped by Professor Edgeworth in a table which, modified in form, is as follows:[1] —

We may have

A. A solution irrespective of any hypothesis as to the cause of the changes, the object being
- I. The consideration of a standard for deferred payments, the standard being required to be
  - 1. Constantly equivalent to the same quantity of valuables and its constituents being determined by
    - *a′* Items of national consumption.
    - *b′* On some other basis than national consumption.

[1] Report of the Brit. Assoc. for Adv. of Sci., 1887, p. 260.

2. Varying on the principle of a sliding scale to the constituents.
   - *a*′ Corresponding to the items of national consumption.
   - *b*′ Determined on some other basis than national consumption.

Such as

- *a*″ National incomes.
- *b*″ National capital.

II. Something else than consideration of the standard for deferred payments.

B. A solution being based upon some hypothesis as to the cause of changes and their

I. Being irrespective of the quantities of the commodities, or

II. Account being taken of the quantities of the commodities.

CHAPTER XIII

THE STANDARD OF DEFERRED PAYMENTS

REFERENCES: Clark, J. B., Ultimate Standard of Value, Yale Rev., November, 1892; Fetter, F., Total Utility Standard of Deferred Payments, Annals Amer. Acad., May, 1895; Jevons, W. S., Money and Mechanism of Exchange, Ch. 25; Jordan, W. Leighton, The Standard of Value, 6th ed.; Knies, K., Das Geld, pp. 396–431; Laughlin, J. L., Principles of Money, Ch. 3; Merriam, L. S., Theory of Final Utility in its Relation to Money and the Standard of Deferred Payments, Annals Amer. Acad., January, 1893, May, 1894; Nicholson, J. S., Money and Monetary Problems, 5th ed., pp. 19–28; Report of the Indianapolis Monetary Commission, 1898, pp. 92–112; Ross, E. A., Standard of Deferred Payments, Annals Amer. Acad., November, 1892, November, 1893; Scott, W. A., Money and Banking, Ch. 3; Walker, F. A., Money, Trade, and Industry, Ch. 3; White, H., Money and Banking, Ch. 6.

1. Definition of the Standard. — By the standard of value is meant, strictly speaking, the value of a definite quantity of the commodity chosen to measure value. We commonly say that this or that commodity, as gold, is the standard. But this is only a short way of saying that it is the value of a certain quantity of the selected commodity which is the unit of measure of value of all other things. A distinction is to be made between the mint standard and the standard of value. The mint standard is simply the quantity of the money material which the law requires to be put into a given unit, or denomination, of money. The value standard is the value, or purchasing power, of this legal quantity. But we cannot infer that the value of this quantity of gold is invariable like its weight. For example, the amount of fine gold in one dollar is 23.22 grains. This amount is invariable, as long as the law is not changed, but its value is not so.

Confusion sometimes arises from attempts to compare the unit of measure of value with the ordinary units of measure of length and weight. The essential difference between the two classes of units lies in the fact that the unit of measure of value changes with every change in the demand for it, while the unit of measure of length, or of weight, is not affected, however great or however small the demand for it may be.

2. Steadiness of the Standard Important for Deferred Payments. — The fact that the standard of value fluctuates is not of importance in the case of exchanges that are settled at once. If goods are sold and paid for at the moment, we may assume that neither party to the exchange gains or loses through any change in the value of the standard. Quite contrary is the case, however, if the sale is made at one time and the payment at a later time. During the interval between the sale and payment, or between the creation of the debt and its discharge, a change in the standard may occur, which will confer upon the amount of money given in settlement a greater or a less purchasing power than it had at the time the debt was created. The great majority of business transactions are done on credit. Purchases are made to be paid for in thirty, sixty, ninety days, or later. The longer the period between purchase and settlement, the greater the opportunity for loss on account of the variation in value. If, for example, a farmer should borrow $1000 at six per cent. for one year, when wheat is selling for $1 a bushel; and if, by the time of payment, the price of his wheat had fallen to 90 cents, it would be necessary for him to sell $1177\frac{7}{9}$ bushels to pay his debt. Measured in wheat, the rate of interest has become 11.8.

3. Assignment of the Gain or Loss due to a Change in Prices. — It is, then, the relation of debtor and creditor which gives importance to the standard of deferred payments. The standard should be such that the discharge of the debt shall preserve the equities of the exchange between creditor and debtor. It is difficult, indeed, to decide what constitutes equity in such cases. A change in the standard implies that the amount of money which the borrower will surrender at the time of the repayment of the debt will buy more or less goods than at the time of the creation of the debt. Should the benefit of appreciation go entirely to the creditor and the loss fall entirely on the debtor, or *vice versa?* Or shall the gain or loss go to neither, or shall it be shared between them? It is sometimes urged that a change in the price level is a social change, and that the gain is, to the one who gets it, an unearned increment, and the loss an unearned decrement. Those who insist that all unearned increment, all value due to social progress rather than to the efforts of individuals, justly belongs to society as a whole, urge that it is the community to which the gain should accrue, or on which the loss should fall. While a defence of this claim can be made, the impossibility of fixing on society the gain or loss in any case makes the proposal impracticable. Moreover, the loss, if it went to society, would be distributed among the members of the community, and this distribution could not fail to be as inequitable as the receipt of the gain by creditors, or debtors, or both, might be.

The welfare of society is best promoted by letting the gain or loss, due to the change in the standard, be shared by the parties to the contract. The social advantage of this course is a phase of the benefits of private property and freedom of contract. As against each other, the creditor and debtor each has an equitable claim to share whatever gain accrues. If the value of money rises, the debtor confers a benefit on the creditor by giving him the advantage of a sure investment, for a definite period, during which his money increases in value. It is true that if the creditor had his money, he could get the benefit of the change in prices by renewed investment. The point is, that he is freed from the necessity of reinvesting at a lower rate. The benefit, such as it is, comes to him for a definite period. He secures an additional advantage, moreover, in the enhanced value of the money which he receives as interest. On the other hand, the debtor gets a benefit from having command of the money for a definite period, for an element of uncertainty is thereby removed from his business.

4. Apportionment of Gain or Loss due to Change in Prices between Creditor and Debtor. — In a truly ethical sense, therefore, the creditor and debtor are partners, and they should share the gains and losses of their partnership. Now, how ought the gain or loss to be shared? Shall it be in a proportion determined by the social welfare, or in a proportion determined by some standard of justice between the individuals? We want to provide that the loss caused by a change in society's economic efficiency, or fashion, shall not be laid altogether upon the unoffending backs of one group of its members, and the gain on those of another. We are seeking to provide that the money owner and the money borrower shall reap where they have not sown, but that neither shall be permitted to take the whole crop to himself. Perhaps the usual opinion is that the welfare of society is promoted by giving the greater share of advantage to the debtor class. If this be true, and if we believe that the gain or loss from a change in the value of money during a period of debt should be so apportioned as to promote the social welfare, then we would assign the larger share of the gain and the smaller share of the loss to the debtor. But a truer statement would be, that the welfare of society is promoted by apportioning the gain or loss according to the economic efficiency of the parties in promoting the social welfare. This would usually, but not always, give the debtor the larger share. Undoubtedly, the debt should be so paid as to leave each in the same relative position in the scale of economic welfare as he would have been if no change in the value of money had taken place during the period of the debt; or, what amounts to the same thing, in the same relative position in the scale of economic welfare as each held at the time of the loan, provided, of course, that no other cause of change in the economic condition of either of the parties arises in the meantime, or disregarding such a change if it does occur. At the time of the loan the money of the lender had a certain value to him, estimated by the subjective value of the articles which it would buy; or it stood for a certain profit if he employed it for the purchase of articles for use in his business. The same is true of the debtor. Our aim should be to apportion the gain or loss, due to a change in the value of money, in such a way that, so far as the debt is concerned, creditors and debtors shall have the same relative purchasing efficiency as they had before. We shall examine later the exact meaning of this phrase and its significance for the question in hand.

5. The Standard of Deferred Payments a Social Concept, not a Corrective of Individual Fluctuations. — Before considering the method whereby it is proposed to establish equity in the payment of debts, we must distinguish between a standard which is just[1] from the point of view of society as a whole, and one which is just between particular debtors and creditors. A standard could be just, both socially and in all individual cases, only if the prices of all goods had changed in the same degree. This, however, is impossible. For a change in the value of money, arising, for example, from a change in its quantity, causes disproportionate changes in the prices of goods, because changes in the marginal utility of commodities are not proportional to changes in their supply or in the demand for them. If the commodity of the debtor, wherewith he secures the standard commodity to pay his debt, has not changed with reference to the standard in the same degree as have other goods, he must give more or less of it than he otherwise would, in order to get the money which will buy a quantity of composite units of goods sufficient to discharge his debt. From the point of view of society, the debt is equitably discharged if the number of composite commodity units given in payment is to the

[1] This distinction must be made whatever ideal of justice between creditor and debtor is adopted.

number which the borrower received, in the inverse ratio of the values of these two quantities. If half the goods on sale go up in price and half go down, in such a way as to leave the price level unchanged, the return of the amount of money borrowed would be, from the social point of view, a just discharge of the debt, because this money commands at the two dates the same amount of goods in general. If, however, the goods of the debtor are among those that have fallen, while the goods consumed by the creditor are among those that have risen, neither debtor nor creditor escapes loss. Under other conditions the debtor may gain and the creditor lose, or *vice versa*. Suppose the debtor's commodity enters into the composite unit as $\frac{1}{1000}$ of the whole, while its exchange value has fallen $\frac{1}{2}$. Obviously, the value of the composite commodity unit, which is to be returned in payment of the debt, will be affected only in a very slight degree. The return of a given number of composite commodity units will, from the social point of view, be a just discharge of the debt; but the number of units of his own commodity which the debtor must now give, to get the money value of this number of composite commodity units, will be doubled. The failure of the general, or socially just, standard to apply to individual cases is similar to the failure of index numbers, which show changes in the level of prices, to tell us anything about the prices of goods consumed by a particular social class.

It is clear, then, that we cannot find a standard which will distribute equitably the gain or loss that accrues from a change in the price of the commodity which a particular debtor produces. The most that can be expected is to find a standard which will distribute the effects of changes of general prices, or offset the variations in the price level. It is disturbances of social, not individual, valuations that a general standard of deferred payments will prevent or correct, if it can be found; yet it is the variation of individual valuations that is important to particular creditors or debtors. The best that can be done is to find a general standard, if possible, and then to adapt it to particular cases, as the circumstances necessitate or justify.

6. An Invariable Standard Undesirable and Impossible. — Some people think that the hardships attendant upon a changing price level would be cured by the adoption of an invariable standard of value. By an invariable standard is meant one of which a given weight would always purchase the same quantity of goods. Such a standard, however, is impossible of realization. For, in the first place, the demand for a standard commodity for use in making payments is one of the causes of its value, and this demand is constantly changing. If there were no actual use of the standard in making payments, so that its value were independent of the demand for means of payment, its fluctuations would be less; but, even then, they could not disappear altogether; for a demand of some kind, whether for monetary purposes or not, is necessary to value, and a demand, although non-monetary, would be bound to fluctuate.

In the second place, a standard which was invariable, in the sense that it would measure and correct changes in the price level, could not, as we have seen, do the same for changes in the prices of particular articles, since the price level may change without any change in the prices of particular commodities; but it is in these latter that the interest of individual debtors and creditors centres.

Moreover, an invariable standard is undesirable, even if possible, because it would throw the benefit of industrial progress into the hands of the owners and producers of goods; whereas a perfect standard should distribute these benefits among the different classes of society. It should purchase more goods and less labor as time passes and progress is made; because, as Professor J. B. Clark has pointed out, industrial progress implies that a larger amount of goods shall be obtained for the same expenditure of labor; hence the purchasing power of the standard should rise as man's command over nature increases. A change of this kind will not remove the inequalities of distribution, but it will bring to the different classes of society some of the benefit to which they are entitled.

7. The Incompatibility of Returns of Equal Value, Equal Utility, etc. — We must search, then, not for an invariable standard, but for one whose variations correspond with changes of economic conditions, in such a way as to effect an equitable division of the benefits of these changes. By what one of the various returns which the debtor can make can this purpose be accomplished? Of course the debtor always returns either money or goods, but the character and the quantity returned depend on the standard of payment adopted. He may pay his debt in terms of units of goods, in terms of total utility, or in terms of marginal utility, or value. It is, perhaps, superfluous to point out that the return of the same consumption commodity, or the same quantity and quality of consumption commodities, does not imply a return of the same utility or value. The utility and the value of goods depend on their physical and psychical efficiency; that is, on their capacity to satisfy physical and psychical wants. We may bring out the difference between returning the same articles, the same utility, and the same value, by the following tables. At the time of borrowing, successive units of the article borrowed show utility, cost, and value as follows:—

No. of Units	Physical Efficiency	Psychical Efficiency	Utility	Cost in Days' Labor[1]
1	4.00	3.00	7.00	3. or 3.00 or 3.00
2	3.80	2.75	6.55	3. or 2.90 or 3.01
3	3.60	2.50	6.10	3. or 2.80 or 3.02
4	3.40	2.00	5.40	3. or 2.75 or 3.03
5	3.20	1.90	5.10	3. or 2.70 or 3.04

[1] See foot-note, p. 271.

At the time of payment the conditions are these: —

No. of Units	Physical Efficiency	Psychical Efficiency	Utility	Cost in Days' Labor[1]
1	4.00	2.00	6.00	Same as before, or less, or more.
2	3.80	1.80	5.60	
3	3.65	1.50	5.15	
4	3.45	0.90	4.35	
5	3.25	0.70	3.95	
6	3.05	0.35	3.40	
7	2.75	0.20	2.95	
8	2.70	0.00	2.70	
9	2.65	0.75	1.90	
10	2.60	1.00	1.60	

Suppose that four units of the commodity are borrowed. According to the first part of the table, we find that the borrower gets 25.05 units of total utility, 21.6 units of value, and a number of days' labor which varies according as the article is produced under conditions of constant, increasing, or decreasing returns. If, now, the conditions change, so that the value of the article in question falls as indicated in the second part of the table, it will be necessary to return five units in order to give back the same total utility. To restore the same value, eight units of the commodity must be given; and to restore the same labor cost either the same number of units of commodity, or more or less, must be given, according to the conditions of production of the article. Hence,

[1] According as the article is one of constant, of increasing, or of decreasing returns.

if we return the same number of units of the same commodity, we may or may not return the same physical efficiency, but we will certainly return less psychical efficiency, less total utility, and, probably, less cost. If we seek to return the same cost, we will very likely give back more goods, less value, and less total utility. If we would restore the same total utility, we would give back a larger amount of goods, a smaller value, and probably a different cost. According, then, as we choose one or another of these units, — commodity, cost, utility, value, — we have a different standard and return a different thing.

8. Classification of Standards of Deferred Payments. — Corresponding to the choice we make of the thing to be returned we have the following standards: —

1. The commodity standard. According to this the debtor returns the same quantity and quality of goods.

2. The labor standard. This standard requires the return of the goods produced in the same labor time as the articles borrowed.

3. The disutility of labor standard. By this standard the debtor is required to return goods in amount such that the disutility of the labor involved in the production of the last unit is just equal to the marginal utility of the quantity of goods borrowed.

4. The total utility standard. According to this standard an amount of commodities is returned

whose utility is somewhat greater than the absolute utility borrowed, by an amount dependent on the degree of change in the price level.

5. The marginal utility, or value standard. The debtor, under this standard, is expected to return commodities embodying the same value that he borrowed.

6. What may be called the purchaser's surplus standard. By this standard the debtor will return to the lender an amount of goods which will leave each in the same position relatively to the marginal purchaser as he was before; that is, will afford the same proportionate purchaser's surplus as the amount of money borrowed yielded each at the time of the loan. We proceed to the discussion of these standards in order.

9. The Single Commodity Standard. — The assumption underlying the commodity standard is that the return of the same quantity and quality of goods as were borrowed will constitute an equitable discharge of the debt. This is only another way of saying that the return of the same absolute utility is equitable. The debtor may make this return, according to circumstances, either by giving back the same quantity of the same commodity, or the same utility embodied in different articles. But the return of consumption goods, the same in quality and quantity as were borrowed, usually means, as we have seen, a return of a different value, a different utility, and a different cost. If the price level has changed at all, whether from a change in the article borrowed or in others, the return of the same article will fail to distribute the benefit of the change between creditor and debtor.

The only important instance of the discharge of debts by the return of the article loaned is that of money debts. This, of course, is the form in which debts are now usually contracted and paid. Money, however, embodies purchasing power in a general form, so that its utility and value do not depend on the physical and psychical efficiency of a single article. Therefore, it is on an entirely different footing from all other goods, and is not to be considered in this connection. It is easy to prove that no single consumption good can be a good standard of deferred payments; but the reasoning which proves this will fail in many respects when applied to money.

Wheat has been urged by some writers as a suitable single article for standard purposes, for the reason that it has, or is thought to have, great steadiness of value through long periods of time. Before the development of modern transportation the price of wheat was remarkably steady. Adam Smith remarked that "Corn . . . is, in all the different stages of wealth and improvement, a more accurate measure of value than any other commodity or set of commodities."[1] What Smith had in mind, however, in this statement, as an

[1] "Wealth of Nations," Bk. I., Ch. 11. (Rogers ed., I., 1, p. 198.)

ultimate standard, was really labor. He used wheat merely as a convenient means of measuring labor against gold and silver, because he believed that for long periods a given amount of wheat was more nearly a product of the same quantity of labor than was the case with any other article.

An interesting historical application of the wheat standard is the so-called Fiars' Price in Scotland. "Fiars' prices in the law of Scotland are the average price of each of the different sorts of grain grown in each county, as fixed annually by the sheriff, usually after a verdict of the jury; and they serve as a rule for ascertaining the value of the grain due to feudal superiors and to the clergy or to law proprietors of teinds, to landlords as a part or whole of their rents, and in all cases where the price of grain has not been fixed by the parties."[1]

A sufficient answer to the advocacy of the wheat standard, however, is the course of the price of wheat in the last ten or fifteen years. The opening up of fertile lands in the West, and the development of the transportation system of the world, have put wheat among the articles whose price varies in a marked degree.

10. The Nature of the Tabular, or Multiple Commodity, Standard. — Of greater importance, because of the support it has received from economists and publicists, as well as because of its more scientific character, is the proposal to establish

[1] "Encyclopædia Britannica," 9th ed.

a standard based on the prices of a number of articles. This is the Tabular Standard. The unit of measure under this standard is the aggregate price at a given time of a long list of articles, a definite quantity and quality of each being chosen, just as is done in making a table of index numbers. A table of the prices of these articles is made when the debt is created, and again when it is to be paid. If we call the sum of the prices of the articles at the creation of the debt 100, then the amount of money to be paid is to the amount borrowed as the sum of the prices at the time of payment is to 100. That is, the debt is really regarded as consisting of as many units of the Tabular Standard as the money loaned would buy at the time the debt was incurred. The amount of money which will buy these units when the debt is due is what the debtor pays. For example: if, on the first of January, A borrows $1000 payable in one year, he finds the number of units of the tabular standard which $1000 will buy on January first. Suppose this number is ten. He then gives his creditor a note for ten units of the tabular standard, and on the first of the following January reference is made to the price list then existing, to determine how much money ten units of the tabular standard will then command. He may find that $990 will buy the same quantity of the goods used in making up the table as $1000 would buy the year before. In that case the debt is settled by the payment of $990.

11. The Equity of the Multiple Standard. — Of course it would be necessary to have some means of insuring the accuracy of the prices quoted in making up the tabular standard. This would be done by creating an official commission, whose duty it would be to publish at stated periods, say weekly or monthly, changes which have taken place in the prices of the commodities entering into the table. With these prices in hand, it would be an easy matter for an individual to find out what his debt was worth in money, at any date. If the tables included all articles sold at the time, in the proportion in which they are offered for sale, and if the amount of each article in the table were scaled down so that the price of the whole should become that of a unit of money, the tabular unit would become what we have called the composite commodity unit. The aim of the tabular standard of deferred payments is, therefore, to return at the time of payment as many such composite commodity units as the money borrowed enabled the borrower to secure at the time the loan was made. The debtor, by this method, would return the same income in goods as he received. On the face of it, this seems just. What could seem fairer than that the creditor should get back as a payment an amount of consumable goods equivalent in quantity to that which he had loaned?

The plan, however, is really not so equitable as it seems. If throughout the debt period the scale of production and consumption remained constant;

if, in other words, the marginal utility of goods neither fell nor rose, so that the marginal utility of our composite commodity unit remained not only a constant quantity, but a constant derived from the same relative values, the proportion of the articles entering in to make up the unit being unchanged, then the tabular standard would be equitable. But changes in the price level are nearly always, perhaps always, accompanied by changes in values, changes in the marginal utility of goods. Instead of correcting these, the tabular standard gives the benefit of them to only one party to the contract. If goods become twice as abundant as they were, so that the scale of living has risen considerably during the debt period, the lender who receives in payment of a debt a quantity of goods equal to the quantity which he loaned the year before is thereby put lower in the scale of social welfare than he would be if he received an amount of goods increased in sufficient measure to give him his share of the increase in social prosperity. For we have seen that the same quantity of goods does not always represent the same quantity of value, or imply the same degree of welfare. By returning the same amount of goods, the benefit of a rise in prices is given wholly to the creditor, and the benefit of a fall wholly to the debtor. Each receives, in his respective goods, a value to which he is not entitled. But it is precisely this result that the tabular standard and all similar devices aim to prevent.

12. Theoretical and Practical Objections to the Multiple Standard. — As Mr. L. S. Merriam has pointed out,[1] the tabular standard aims to restore the same absolute utility as was loaned. Yet it ignores one of the elements of utility and of value. We have seen that utility is derived from the physical efficiency and the psychical efficiency of commodities; that is, their power to satisfy physical and psychical needs. If the latter were altogether removed, so that physical efficiency alone constituted want-satisfying capacity, then the tabular standard would be just enough. Its advocates seem to have been misled by concentrating their attention on the utility of such goods as wheat, and other necessaries of life, which have little or no psychical efficiency. Their utility depends exclusively, or mainly, upon their physical efficiency — their capacity to satisfy physical wants. The bicycle, however, is an example of another kind of goods. The loan of a bicycle fresh from the shop in 1895 could not be repaid in 1904 by the return of an exactly similar bicycle, made at the same shop and at the same expense, because fashion in bicycles has changed, and the element of psychical efficiency in their utility and value has largely disappeared. The physical efficiency of a bicycle is as great as ever; its total utility, or want-satisfying power, is less, because of the change in fashion, and its value is less. Its possession would now put the owner in a lower

[1] *Annals of Amer. Acad. of Pol. and Soc. Sci.*, III., 101.

position in the scale of social welfare than the possession of the bicycle he loaned would have done ten years ago. There are many other cases of this kind, and the tabular standard is not applicable to them. It is, after all, but a rough-and-ready method of returning the same amount of physical efficiency. It returns neither the same total utility nor the same value, nor a utility and value proportionate to changes in general prices.

The tabular standard is not suitable for ordinary business debts, for these are usually for short periods, so that the price fluctuations are not ordinarily great enough to require a corrective. Moreover, as Professor Laughlin has pointed out,[1] merchants' accounts could not be made to balance under the tabular standard, since it does not entirely replace money, and the business man would therefore be obliged to keep his accounts in both standards. He could not strike a balance between receipts and expenditures, partly in tabular standard units and partly in money. A third source of trouble would come from a lack of balance between notes due about the same time. A note for a certain number of units of the tabular standard would not have a fixed price, and could not well be discounted. A note which the business man had to pay in three months might not be met by the proceeds of another due him a week before, although both were made at the same time, represented a transfer of the same amount of money,

[1] "Principles of Money," p. 51.

and the same number of units of the tabular standard.

The tabular standard would be serviceable in cases where certainty in the amount of income in ordinary consumable goods was desirable. For the certainty of income in articles of consumption would in many cases offset any loss that might come from a change in the scale of values, accompanied, as that change would be, with uncertainty as to the amount of goods which a given amount of money would from time to time command.

13. The Labor-time Standard. — Labor has been advocated at various times as a standard of deferred payments. The labor standard appears under three forms. The first makes mere labor time the unit of measure; the second, labor cost; and the third, the disutility of marginal labor. The labor-time theory is based on the socialistic idea that labor is the sole cause of value, and that the return of goods produced by labor expended through equal amounts of time would be just. Different kinds of labor, however, produce unequal results in the same time, and there is no way of converting one kind into terms of another. Moreover, the efficiency of labor changes with progress, and the return of the same amount of labor time would not keep debtors and creditors in the same relative positions in a progressive society.

14. The Labor-cost Standard. — The labor-cost theory is based on the idea that equity is maintained by the return of equivalent costs of production. "We aim," says an advocate of this theory "not at the redelivery of article by article, but at the repayment of labor by labor, or of sacrifice by sacrifice."[1] Adam Smith suggested that "a day's work of an unskilled laborer does not vary much from generation to generation, and that it, therefore, may fairly be used as a unit of measure of value." "He, of course, did not mean that the same quantity of labor would always have the same exchange value, relatively to other things, but that the inconvenience or negative utility of a given amount of exertion might be regarded as constant. If all human beings at different periods were similarly constituted, and if all work could be expressed in accurate physical formulæ, then Adam Smith's contention would be sound. But neither supposition accords with the facts. We cannot reduce all labor to raising foot-pounds, nor can we suppose that the mental strain corresponding to the physical unit of work is constant. Still, for remote periods, in which the kinds of wealth differ very much, unskilled labor is perhaps the best measure of value."[2]

There is a certain amount of truth in Smith's idea, and it is one that has always had believers; but the cost involved in such a day's labor is difficult to estimate, and the constancy of its value is much less certain in these days of machinery than it was

[1] Leonard Courtney, *Nineteenth Cent.*, April, 1893.

[2] J. Shields Nicholson, note on Bk. I., Ch. 4, of the "Wealth of Nations," Nicholson's ed., p. 409.

in the time of Adam Smith. Labor cost would serve well in a state of society in which each one must draw "direct from nature the articles which supply his wants," but comparison of such a day's labor in a capitalistic régime with a day's labor in another economic régime is out of the question. So, too, is the comparison of labor of different kinds in the same economic régime.

15. The Disutility of Labor Standard. — Closely connected with the labor-cost standard is the disutility of labor standard proposed by Professor J. B. Clark. The disutility of labor in production is a different thing in an advanced society from what it is in a primitive economy. In the latter it is the pain, toil, and sacrifice caused by direct labor; in an advanced society it is, in a large measure, the indirect disutility caused by the fact that, while personal toil is less in amount and less intense in character, the producer is kept from enjoyment of the increasing good things of life throughout the period of production.

The marginal disutility of labor standard requires the return of goods whose marginal utility is equal to the direct and indirect disutility of further production. All disutility of marginal labor, both direct and indirect, decreases with improvements; hence this standard gives an increasing amount of commodities for a constant amount of disutility of labor. It certainly does, therefore, distribute the benefits of man's increasing command over nature. "If the creditor, in making the loan, gave to the debtor the power to get a hundred commodities, representing a hundred hours of labor; and if the debtor at the end of fifty years pays to his creditor money that will buy a hundred and ten similar commodities, but was earned by ninety hours of labor, the gains from progress are shared in a way that is practically even."[1]

This standard is applicable where the creditor and debtor are members of the same economic group, in the sense that the social utility and the disutility of labor are the same. It is not applicable, however, between societies in which this is not the case. It would not be an equitable standard for the discharge of a debt by an American if the debt were due to a Chinaman in China. Moreover, it ignores the element of psychical efficiency in value. A change of taste or fashion may change the effectiveness of goods in putting creditor and debtor in the same relative position in the scale of social welfare, even though the disutility of production of those goods is unchanged.

16. The Marginal Utility Standard. — The marginal utility standard of deferred payments calls for a return of equal social values as measured by marginal utilities. This standard confronts us with several serious difficulties. The marginal utility referred to must mean that of the composite unit of goods — or the tabular standard unit — to society,

[1] John B. Clark, "The Gold Standard of Currency in the Light of Recent Theory," *Pol. Sci. Quar.*, 1895, Vol. X., p. 398.

or to the creditor, or to the debtor. If it mean the marginal utility of goods to society, this is indicated by the price level, or the amount of money which will buy the composite unit of goods; and the standard calls simply for the prevailing money value of the debt. This, however, is not at all what the standard is intended to accomplish. Moreover, by the same value can be meant only the absolute value of the amount loaned at the time of borrowing, and not what would be at the time of payment the same proportion of social values as the debt was at the time of its creation. Hence, this standard would not restore to the creditor a value that would place him in the same relative place in the scale of social welfare as did the value he loaned at the time of the loan. What is wanted is not a constant value, but a value proportionate to changing social values. If these increase, the debt should be discharged by an increased amount of value. Otherwise, either creditor or debtor will not share in the benefits of social progress.

17. The Total Utility Standard. — The total utility standard, as proposed by Professor Ross, is essentially the tabular standard with an amendment. According to this standard, "the debtor is not to return a value measured in *labor*, nor yet a value measured in *commodities*, but a value measured in *objective utility*. And with industrial progress this is secured by a slight excess of commodities."[1] This slight excess of commodities is given to en-

[1] E. A. Ross, *Annals of Amer. Acad.*, November, 1892, p. 49.

able the creditor to share in the benefits of progress, and is to be sufficiently ample "to compensate him for the depreciation of that portion of his wealth devoted to satisfying the needs of his social nature."[1]

Objection might be made to this standard, in the first place, on the ground that the proposed slight excess of commodities is not definite in amount, and that the standard therefore cannot be definite. The slight excess might be a very different amount in the judgment of different people. Waiving this point, however, an examination shows a close resemblance of the total utility standard to the commodity standard, as exemplified in the tabular standard. The tabular standard returns the absolute total utility borrowed, minus a quantity due to the depreciation of that portion of the goods devoted, as Professor Ross says, to the satisfaction of the social nature; that is, minus a certain amount of what we have called the psychical efficiency element of utility. This standard would return the utility borrowed without that diminution; that is, the same objective utility. By this can be meant only units of utility as estimated by society at large, independent of peculiarities in the subjective wants of individual creditors and debtors. In other words, the units of utility must be determined without reference to the wants of any individual. Professor Nicholson's objection to Adam Smith's labor standard might well be made here. It is as im-

[1] E. A. Ross, *Annals of Amer. Acad.*, November, 1892, p. 49.

possible to estimate utility in units corresponding to foot-pounds, as it is to estimate labor in such terms. A more important objection, however, may be made. The return of the same objective utility does not enable the creditor and the debtor to share the benefits of industrial progress. The slight excess allowed to balance the diminution of the psychical efficiency element of utility in the goods loaned simply enables the creditor to get back what he loaned. Suppose that the total volume of social utility increased during the period of the debt; increased, that is, as measured in some objective unit, analogous to foot-pounds. Such a unit might be the number of heat units in a pound of wheat. If, now, 100 pounds of wheat are loaned, the loan implies the transfer of $100x$ heat units. If the total social utility rise from one million to one million and a half, during the period of the debt, the return of $100x$ heat units to the creditor will not give him any share in the increase due to the additional half million. The same number of heat units, or foot-pounds, is a smaller proportion of the whole. In other words, there is a surplus to be shared between the creditor and the debtor, altogether irrespective of the amount allowed for the diminution in the psychical efficiency of the goods borrowed.

18. The Purchaser's Surplus Standard. — The purchaser's surplus standard is based upon the idea that the satisfaction obtained by the purchaser, over and above the sacrifice involved in his expenditure, gives the measure of his position in the scale of social welfare. The spenders of money may be arranged in rank, according to the amount of surplus satisfaction which they obtain from the expenditure of the same amount of money. The purchaser of goods who receives no such surplus is the marginal purchaser, and market price in a competitive market is fixed by him.[1] The least efficient buyer, in other words, secures no advantage from his purchase. He has no gain and no loss. Every other buyer of commodities in the same market, at the same time, secures a surplus of satisfaction, whose amount is dependent upon his competitive efficiency as a purchaser. He has, therefore, a certain position in what we may call the scale of purchasers, and his surplus satisfaction bears a definite ratio to that of every other purchaser in the market.

This surplus satisfaction from the expenditure of the same amount of money, for composite units of goods, may be taken as an index of the welfare of its owners, so far as due to this amount of money. Now, what we are aiming to do is to return to the creditor, at the time of payment, such an amount of wealth as will make his purchaser's surplus from the amount returned bear to that of the borrower a ratio equal to that borne by their respective surpluses when the loan was made,

[1] That is, by him alone of the purchasers. The influence of the sellers, being the same for all the purchasers, may be here taken as constant.

assuming that any change which has occurred in the value of the debt has not been caused by the creditor alone, nor by the debtor alone, but rather is a social change which is to be shared by both as members of society. We have to do only with the sum of money loaned. A change in the fortune either of creditor or of debtor we cannot take into account. Our supposition is that, so far as all factors of individual fortune are concerned, the creditor and debtor are in the same relative positions as before. The only change that has occurred is in the purchasing power of the amount loaned.

When the price level changes, the surplus of all purchasers changes. Each one has to give more or less for the same amount of goods. Now, to any individual purchaser, the scale of marginal utilities of all the goods he buys is proportional to the scale of their prices;[1] and a change in the scale of prices will induce a corresponding change in the scale of marginal utilities. Hence, under the conditions assumed, the buyer's surplus of any individual, after a change in the price level, will bear to his former surplus the ratio of the new price level to the old; and the new surplus of any buyer will bear the same ratio to the new surplus of any other buyer as the old surplus of the first did to that of the second.

Now a rise in the price of goods takes away

[1] Cf. I. Fisher, "Mathematical Investigations in the Theory of Value and Prices," p. 37.

from the surplus of each purchaser a certain amount, which is not the same for all individuals. It diminishes the surplus of some more rapidly than that of others. In the diagram, let *de, fg*, etc., represent the surplus which results to different purchasers from the expenditure of a given

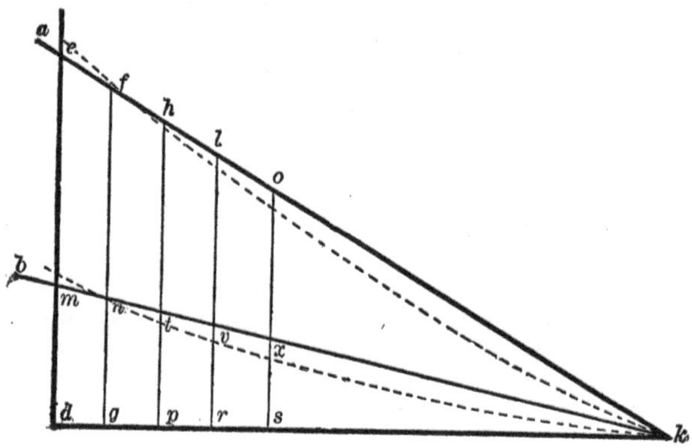

amount of money, say one dollar, on one scale of prices. The surplus utility of the goods bought with a dollar will be largest to the purchaser who has the largest amount of money, because to him a dollar has less value than it has to the others. A given rise of prices will cut off a larger portion of the surplus utility of some purchasers than it will of the others. Let it cut off *dm, gn*, etc., for the successive purchasers. The surplus utility for the series is now represented by *me, nf*, etc., on the new price level.

For the sake of simplifying the problem, let us assume for the moment that the utility curves, represented by *bk* and *ak*, are straight lines. Of course this cannot be true of actual cases, and the assumption represents the problem at what the mathematicians would call the limit of variation. Under this assumption, the line *bk* cuts the parallels representing the surplus of utilities of purchasers proportionally; so that *ed* is to *fg* as *em* to *fn*; that is, the surplus utilities from the amount of expenditure in question would have the same ratio on the two scales of prices, and the debt would be fairly discharged with an amount of money which was to the amount borrowed, in the ratio of the price levels. But, as we have remarked, the utility curves *ak* and *bk* cannot be straight lines. They are more correctly represented by the dotted lines. Hence the ratios are not quite equal, and the amount of money to be paid to discharge a debt will change in a ratio greater or less than the ratio of the prices. The amount of money which should be returned is, therefore, the new price, with an addition or subtraction sufficient to allow for this variation. As a matter of fact, the arrangements existing under a metallic standard are such that this amendment is largely automatic. It is brought about, as we shall see, by a fall in the rate of interest, a gradual shortening of the credit period, and the diminution of price oscillations through a refinement of speculation.

CHAPTER XIV

BIMETALLISM

REFERENCES: Barbour, D., The Theory of Bimetallism; Cernuschi, H., La Monnaie Bimetallique; Darwin, L., Bimetallism; Giffen, R., The Case against Bimetallism; Jevons, W. S., Money and the Mechanism of Exchange, Ch. 12; Laughlin, J. L., History of Bimetallism in the United States; Laveleye, E. de, La Monnaie et le Bimetallisme International; Nicholson, J. S., Money and Monetary Problems, Pt. I., Ch. 8, Essays 7, 8, 9; Scott, W. A., Money and Banking, Chs. 14, 15; Walker, F. A., International Bimetallism; White, H., Money and Banking, Ch. 7; Willis, H. P., History of the Latin Monetary Union.

1. The Nature of Bimetallism. — Besides the efforts to find a suitable standard of deferred payments by means of which to correct the harm done by the changing value of money, proposals have also been made which aim to make such a standard unnecessary by obviating or minimizing changes in the price level; attempts, not to repair the supposed mischief which such things cause, but to prevent it. One of the methods suggested for doing this, bimetallism, is of great historical and theoretical importance. It is important, historically, because it has been practised more or less extensively at different times, and undoubtedly has succeeded in a measure in preventing the monetary evils that would in its absence have arisen. It is important, theoretically, because the system is supported by arguments which are weighty, and, on some points, convincing.

Bimetallism, as its name implies, is a monetary system in which the principal, or standard, money is composed of gold and silver together, instead of either alone. According to this system, free coinage of both metals is established at a fixed ratio of exchange. Each metal is to be unlimited legal tender, so that people who have debts to pay may have the option of paying in either metal. Consequently, if either metal fall in value, in terms of the other, debtors will be free to take the bullion of the cheaper metal to the mints and have it coined at a legal ratio, which, it will be remembered, is higher than the market ratio, and with the coins thus obtained to pay their debts. This privilege would give the debtor the advantage of paying in a cheaper metal, and would seem to be against the interest of the creditor. It is urged, however, by the advocates of bimetallism, that the creditor would be protected by the fact that both metals are to be used concurrently, or at any rate alternately. It is further urged that if the ratio be properly chosen, and the system established over a sufficiently wide area, changes in the ratio would either be very small or would disappear altogether, so that, in either case, the creditor would be likely to lose little or nothing.

2. The Advantages claimed for Bimetallism. — The advocates of bimetallism insist that it would obviate many of the evils which attach to a monometallic monetary system. In the first place, they urge, the system would enlarge the stock of standard money and thereby lessen fluctuations of the price level. For the larger the stock of money, they say, the smaller will be the proportionate changes in its value, caused by additions to it, or by new demands for it.

It is also urged in behalf of bimetallism, that the use of both metals would cause a more rapid increase in the total money stock than could come from the use of one metal; and that the increase in the amount of money would cause its value to depreciate slowly, and thus furnish a gentle but constant stimulant to business. For, if money is depreciating, so that expected profits are constantly or frequently wiped out by the increase in the value of money, trade becomes depressed and the spirit of enterprise is deadened. While there is some truth in this contention, yet, as we have seen in another connection, there are counteracting forces which indicate that perhaps too much stress has been laid on the advantages of slow depreciation.

In the next place, the advocates of bimetallism bring forward historical instances of falling prices in order to show the economic evils to which contraction of the standard money subjects the community. They argue that in such periods as the twenty-five years following 1873, the great fall in prices was due to the use of gold alone; that the demand for that metal in the arts increased so fast that the annual production was not enough to maintain the old price level, and that the community was, therefore, subjected to all the evils of appreciation. They also emphasize the injustice of the single standard to debtors, insisting that the burden of debts is increased thereby.

The fourth important claim which the advocates of bimetallism put forth is, that the system would keep steady the par of exchange between countries which trade with one another. It is a well-known fact that a country which has a depreciated currency has to pay a higher price for its imports, in order to offset the depreciation that actually has taken place, and to insure the foreign importer against the risk attendant upon possible further depreciation. At present, if a merchant in a gold country sells a cargo of goods to one in a silver country, the silver price at which he sells them is determined by the rate of exchange between silver and gold on the date of the sale. He asks for as many silver dollars as will make his gold price. When the cargo arrives and the time comes for payment, however, the value of that silver dollar may have changed, so that the par of exchange between the two countries is not what it was on the day of the sale, and a loss will be incurred by one of the exchangers. The uncertainty attendant upon this fluctuating exchange is so great that it might seriously affect the foreign trade of the country. Competition is so keen that a very small margin of profit will decide whether or not certain goods will be brought from a particular country, or sent to a particular country. With a depreciated currency and a fluctuating par of exchange, a small margin of profit may be wiped out, or so seriously impaired that business men will not take the risk of exporting or importing goods. Therefore any means of keeping the par of exchange steady would be an advantage. The advocates of bimetallism claim that it would remove this element of risk from business.

3. The Maintenance of the Chosen Ratio of Exchange between Gold and Silver. — These are the principal advantages claimed for a bimetallic system. It is not within the scope of our work to examine the historical instances in which bimetallism has been applied, with more or less success. There is good reason for believing that for a considerable number of years much good was done by the maintenance of the bimetallic system in France. There are reasons for believing, however, that the good was more apparent than real, although the disadvantages caused were more elusive than the benefits. The first question that naturally occurs to one, in discussing the proposals of bimetallism, concerns the maintenance of the ratio. The most rational advocates of the system take the ground that the ratio adopted should be the market ratio prevailing at the time. It would be necessary to choose this ratio, or one very near it, because if a different one were chosen, the demand for the cheaper metal would have to be great enough not only to keep its price up in the face of a large increase in its production, but great enough also to overcome the difference between the market ratio and the ratio actually chosen. We must assume, in fairness, therefore, that the ratio chosen will be the market ratio. Even so, however, it would seem, at first thought, that the ratio could not be maintained against the influence of Gresham's law. We know that ordinarily, if an attempt is made to circulate two metals of different value side by side, people will export or melt down the dearer, and use the cheaper for monetary purposes. It would seem that this procedure would make bimetallism impossible. Undoubtedly, it would do so, if the bimetallic system prevailed in only one country. It is claimed, however, that if the system were applied over a sufficient area, if it were adopted by a sufficient number of commercially strong nations, Gresham's law would be neutralized, and the evils of constantly changing from one metal to another would be obviated. In support of this position, it is urged that as soon as one metal fell in value, or showed signs of falling, the demand for it would increase, the demand for the other metal would fall off, and the effect would be to check the separation of the values of the two. Suppose, for example, that the ratio of 16 : 1 were adopted. That is, for one ounce of gold we can get sixteen ounces of silver. If, now, the market value of silver falls, a given amount of gold will buy more silver in the form of bullion than in the form of coin. Instead of using the gold to pay debts and purchase goods, people will now buy silver bullion with it, and have this silver coined to make payments with. If this process went on long enough, it would seem that all the gold would go out of circulation. During the process the demand for gold to pay debts with is constantly growing less; hence, the value of gold would tend to fall. Meantime the demand for silver bullion, bought with the gold, tends to raise the market value of silver in terms of gold. That is, the increased demand for silver tends to check its fall in gold. In other words, the contraction of the money supply, caused by the withdrawal of the gold, will produce a fall of prices, or a rise in silver. We have, therefore, a cheapening of gold, the dearer metal, and an enhancing of the value of silver, the cheaper metal. The two movements, being in opposite directions, will tend to keep the metals from departing very far from their established ratio of exchange, and may, indeed, prevent any separation at all. The process which has just been described is known as the compensatory action of the double standard. There is some ground for the opinion that the oscillation, or alternation, of the standard would not occur, if bimetallism were universally adopted, but that the mere prospect of such a change would be discounted beforehand. For, the advocates of bimetallism insist, the larger the number of countries which adopt the system, the more powerful will be the forces at work tending to prevent a change of the relative values of the two metals. The claim is undoubtedly sound. If three countries have gold monometallism, the transfer of one gold monometallic country to the bimetallic group not only reduces the demand for the dearer metal, but at the same time increases the demand for the cheaper metal. Every addition of monometallic countries to the bimetallic group would strengthen that group much more than in the proportion of the number of countries added. In the last analysis, of course, the steadiness of the ratio between the two metals depends upon the rate of increase of the cheaper metal; but it is doubtful whether the rate of increase would ever be fast enough to outrun the increase in the demand for the metal whose value is falling. Hence, with bimetallism universal, or general, the ratio might be maintained.

4. Some Factors adverse to the Maintenance of the Ratio. — There are certain considerations, however, which modify the conclusion of the last paragraph. As societies grow stronger and richer, the scale of incomes and prices tends upward, and this fact has an important bearing on the steadiness of the ratio of exchange of the two metals under bimetallism. For a higher scale of prices and incomes calls for the use of a dearer metal as money, a metal with a higher monetary utility, with high value in small bulk. For this reason, as communities became richer, the demand for gold would doubtless increase. The monetary utility of silver, the cheaper metal, would decrease, and its serviceableness to richer communities would become less; hence the demand for it for general use would diminish. If, now, under a bimetallic system, the supply of gold, the dearer metal, should increase, as communities became richer, the effect would be to lower the value of the whole mass of the money material. Under these circumstances the value of silver would fall with that of gold, and the ratio of exchange between the two metals would not be likely to change very much. It is possible, however, that the decrease in the demand for silver, due to its inferior monetary utility, under the conditions supposed, would offset, in whole or in part, the tendency of debtors to make payments in silver. For the real cheapness of a money material in a given society depends not only on its cost of acquisition, but also on its monetary efficiency.

If, on the other hand, the supply of the cheaper metal, silver, should increase, the value of the whole monetary mass would fall farther than before, and the demand for silver for payments would decrease, while that of gold would increase, since its monetary utility would be higher. Consequently the metals would separate in value, because the influence of the demand for the money of the greater monetary utility would be against the maintenance of the ratio under conditions which increased the supply of the cheapening metal. Therefore, an increasing demand for a money material of a higher monetary utility is bound to work against the demand for a cheaper metal by debtors, and lessen the influence of that demand in retarding the fall of the price of the cheaper metal, and, in so far, again, defeat the purpose of the bimetallic system. However, the causes just described would operate thus only during a period of rapidly increasing wealth. During prolonged periods of slow economic development the ratio of exchange between the metals might be kept steady.

5. Bimetallism and Fluctuations of the Price Level. — If we admit that the ratio can be maintained in the bimetallic system, and that bimetallism is therefore practicable, it remains to consider whether the advantages claimed for it are really attainable, and of as great importance as bimetallists have claimed. There is little doubt that a steady ratio would keep the value of the metals approximately constant with reference to each other, but would it keep the value of both steady with reference to goods? It is claimed that an increase of the volume of money would diminish the fluctuations of the price level on the theory that a larger volume of money is less sensitive to changes in supply and demand than is a smaller quantity. Water which is sufficient to overflow a pond would scarcely be noticed in Lake Michigan or the ocean; and a drouth which would dry up the pond would lower the level of the lake but a fraction, and that of the ocean not at all. So, it is argued, the larger volume of money will show fewer changes of value by reason of an increasing, or a lessening, demand for it in the shape of goods; and a smaller change, also, from an increasing supply of the metal due to changing conditions of production. For it is not unlikely that what we may call the accidents of mining, whereby one metal or the other is produced in unusually large quantities for a time, may offset one another. When a new gold mine is discovered, the production of silver may decrease, and *vice versa*.

The argument adduced in favor of bimetallism goes to show that in all probability the degree of fluctuation of changing prices would be less, but that the fluctuations would be greater in number, provided the conditions prevailing at the time the system was put in operation continued. That is to say, if the demand for the medium of exchange remained about the same, and its supply were increased, as it would be under the bimetallic system, obviously the degree of change in the value of the medium of exchange would be lessened. This would be true not only because of the increase in the mass of exchange medium, but because prices would always follow the cheaper metal,[1] since it is with the cheaper metal that payments are made. If the system succeeded at all, then, strictly speak-

[1] Cf. Jevons, "Money and the Mechanism of Exchange," p. 138.

ing, the standard of value would alternate from one metal to the other with every variation in the ratio of exchange of the metals. Prices will not soar so high as the value of the cheaper metal would make them go if it were used by itself, nor so low as the value of the dearer metal would drive them if it alone were in use. Therefore the fluctuations would, probably, be of smaller range, but of greater frequency. It is claimed, however, that frequent small changes would be less detrimental to business than a smaller number of changes of considerable magnitude. This claim is of very doubtful validity. For the period of a large volume of debts, and of by far the greater number of productive and mercantile transactions, is short — too short to be seriously affected by a change of much magnitude in the purchasing power of money. The time necessary for such a change would overlap a series of periods of debt and of manufacturing and trade activity. To increase the number of fluctuations of the price level would be to introduce some, or many, within the debt periods and the cycles of production and trade. Business would be exposed to more uncertainty by such procedure, and such changes would be harder to forecast and to discount than would be a change in one direction through a portion of its progress.

Moreover, even if frequent small changes were less harmful than occasional large ones, it is questionable whether the condition of greater frequency and less degree could be permanent. The argument which supports it ignores the influence of the supply of goods on prices. The upward impulse which the bimetallic system would give to the price level would in time stimulate industry, and, by increasing the supply of products, bring about a new fall of prices. It is very likely that under the modern system of credit, the impulse given to production by a rise of prices might cause an expansion that would overshoot the mark, and thus produce a reaction that would more than offset the gain which had been made. Although, then, bimetallism would probably give a higher range of prices, at least at first, there is no reason whatever for assuming that the higher level would be, in the long run, any steadier than the one which it supplanted.

6. Bimetallism as a Relief from the Burden of Debts. — If the argument just set forth is correct, it follows that the claim that bimetallism would relieve debtors, loses much of its force. The real cause of hardship to debtors, the thing which the argument for bimetallism assumes to be of greatest importance, is not a high or low level of general prices, but the changes in these. The mere fact that the price level is high or low is not, of itself, important for either debtor or creditor, for producer or consumer; but the change from one price level to another is a very different matter. Now, in so far as bimetallism failed to restore the old price level completely, it would fail to justify its adoption; for it would simply substitute a new series of changes in the value of money, reckoned from a higher base line of prices. Nor could bimetallism correct these transient variations in prices which are due to the oscillations of credit. Indeed, it is not unlikely that the larger money reserve which bimetallism must bring into use, in order to be successful, would produce an extension of credit that would increase the number of these transient variations. Moreover, the effect of a change in the demand for either one of the metals could not be felt over the whole bimetallic area at once. It would be felt in one place sooner than in another. There would be opportunity, therefore, for loss or gain on transactions between places in which the effect is first felt and those which the movement reached later. Like the effects of a new supply of money, every variation under the bimetallic system would propagate itself, as it were, by jerks, and the results would be unequal in different places. But it is of the essence of the system that it must operate over a large area. Consequently, it would be much less likely to be of service to particular classes of debtors, or to particular communities.

In the interest of debtors, it is important to determine, also, what price level bimetallism would establish. Would it be the price level of five years before the adoption of the system, or that of ten years before? No evidence has ever been adduced to show that the price level which the bimetallic system would establish would be that which it was desired to restore. A larger volume of money might raise prices, but a definite increase is necessary to raise them to a particular level. Now it is impossible to show that the increased amount of money which the adoption of bimetallism would put into circulation would restore the price level of any particular year, or of any particular decade. Debts are not all of the same age. The restoration of the prices of one year, therefore, might prevent loss on debts contracted in that year, but it would not do so for the debts of longer or shorter standing. Consequently, it is impossible that the price level established by the bimetallic system could restore just relations between all debtors and their creditors. If it overshot, or undershot, the old price level, it would transfer from one party to the other whatever burden the change involved. The system might, indeed, check a fall, and substitute a rise, in the value of money; but it offers no plan for controlling the extent of the rise, or of insuring that it shall go only far enough to be just, and no farther. At best, the system could only be a palliative of any hardships caused by debts on a falling price market.

7. Bimetallism would not provide a Slowly Depreciating Currency. — There is no assurance that the bimetallic system would stimulate business by furnishing a slowly depreciating currency. Aside from the fact that the importance of such stimulation is usually exaggerated, the stimulus given to production might cause the supply of goods to gain upon the supply of money, and in that way check depreciation. The fall of value of the whole mass of money material caused by the use of the two metals would act as a check on the production of both, and retard any increase in their supply. The supply being practically constant, or of slow increase, while the volume of products constantly swelled, the value of the money mass would rise in time, and the world would then have another era of monetary appreciation, with a greater distance for prices to fall. The tremendous amount of the annual production of both gold and silver in recent years lends countenance to this argument. For the new supply has undoubtedly had considerable effect in lowering their value, and to check this production would check that fall.

8. Obstacles to International Bimetallism. — Bimetallism, to achieve any success at all in steadying the ratio of exchange between silver and gold, would have to be international in its scope. This requirement interposes insuperable obstacles to its adoption. International prejudice, the patriotic desire of the people of each country to have their own system of coinage, the difficulty of changing the ratios of coinage already existing in different countries, the shock to credit, and the disturbance which the change would produce in existing contracts and prices, as well as many other causes, stand in the way of the necessary international agreement. If a country which was poor and economically backward at the time of the adoption of the system became rich and economically strong, its people would need, and would try to secure, the metal of higher monetary utility. But the international agreement would stand in its way and, in a measure, check its industrial progress. Such a country would be impelled to break away from the system, and adopt the metal best suited to its changed condition. This was the experience of France. In 1803 she adopted the system of free coinage of both metals at the ratio of 15½ parts of silver for one part of gold. For nearly half a century, the conditions of demand and supply were such that the ratio was fairly well maintained, and the policy of France conferred on the world whatever benefits this steadiness of ratio offers, but at the expense of her own people. The change in the relative values of the two metals, caused by the discoveries of gold in Australia and California, made it impossible for France to persevere in her policy, except at a tremendous cost to herself. She was compelled to debase her fractional silver in order to save it, and in 1865 joined with Switzerland, Belgium, and Italy to form what is known as the Latin Union, for the maintenance of the bimetallic system. Under this union the great bulk of the coinage, especially of the principal coins, was gold. The monetary utility of silver was too low for economical use in France under the changed conditions. So her people saw, with equanimity, her principal coins changed to gold. When, a few years later, the ratio of exchange turned again in favor of silver, and gold once more became dearer, France protected herself against the loss of the money of higher utility, because her industrial condition required a money convenient for large payments. Such, too, was the experience of the United States, and such, it would seem, would be the experience of every progressive country, even under international bimetallism.

Finally, the arbitrary violation of all existing contracts by the establishment of bimetallism is a serious objection. Even if much of the claim were true, that gold monometallism at times bears harshly on debtors, it is more than doubtful whether the evil effects of the arbitrary violation spoken of would not create far greater hardships. The inviolability of contracts is an essential condition of progress. In the interests of business security and development, they must be kept, even when to keep them is an unexpected hardship on one of the parties.

9. The Increase in Gold and the Bimetallic Agitation. — The progress of events in recent years has quieted the demand for the establishment of bimetallism. The production of gold has increased so rapidly that the most ardent advocates of monetary expansion have every reason to be more than satisfied with the situation. It is not improbable, indeed, that the volume of money is greater than it would be, if, without the extension of gold production, the world were living under the bimetallic régime.

This progress in the production of gold, however, is not an accident. It is doubtful whether it is a proper use of language to say that there ever was any real scarcity of gold in the period of falling prices after 1873. The true explanation of falling prices, as has already been said, is probably to be found in the fact that whatever loss the world suffered from falling prices was not enough to offset the gain received from expanding production, so that it paid to let prices fall rather than to turn capital to producing gold. As soon as the point was reached where the profit from expanding production was not great enough to offset the loss from the appreciation of gold, it became profitable to turn part of the capital which had been hitherto devoted to producing other things to the production of more gold. The inventive genius of mankind was turned to the solution of the problem, and gave the world chemical and mineralogical discoveries which have increased the world's stock of money far beyond the dreams of the bimetallist. The movement has been, therefore, the result of curative causes whose operation bimetallism would have checked. The increase of the supply of gold has come about, in a sense, automatically, in response to increased pressure for more exchange medium. The establishment of bimetallism would have been, so to speak, an artificial cure of the difficulty, and, like other artificial cures of social ills, it probably would have created difficulties of its own. Indeed, we might say that the conclusion of the whole matter is, that while bimetallism would undeniably offer some advantages, it is more than questionable whether these would not be offset by the evils which it would fail to cure, added to those of which it would itself be the direct cause.

10. Symmetallism. — In its original form, bimetallism contemplated the separate use of gold and silver in the form of coins. A modification of this plan has been at various times proposed whereby the two metals would be united in a single coin, in some proportion, such, for example, as that indicated by the ratio established between them. That is, instead of calling 23.2 grains of gold, or 371.25 grains of silver, one dollar, we might say that 11.6 grains of gold and 115.6 grains of silver make a dollar. This system is known as symmetallism. It is difficult to say what advantage this plan has over the simpler bimetallic method. It would give us a system cumbersome and complicated for making payments, if the value of either metal should change; and it would offer opportunities for the abuse of coinage by governments that were not overscrupulous in the matter. Variations in the value of coins due to wear and tear would be difficult to detect, and the poor and ignorant would be more easily imposed upon. Practical difficulties of coinage also would stand in the way, and altogether the system has little to commend it.

11. Neo-bimetallism. — More scientific and practical is the more recent form of bimetallism, or neo-bimetallism, as it is called. According to the neo-bimetallist, the best way would be to issue paper currency based upon gold and silver. Notes of given denominations would call for gold or silver, at the option of the holder. This plan would give the public all the advantage that comes from the use of paper money, and would at the same time not interfere with the working of the bimetallic system if it should be adopted.

Instead of bimetallism at a fixed ratio, the free coinage of gold and silver at shifting ratios has been suggested. After what has been said of the simpler form of bimetallism, little need be added about this proposal. It does not avoid any of the disadvantages of free coinage at a fixed ratio, and it introduces new elements of uncertainty and variation. The system would be complicated, and impossible of regulation. For it would require constant government supervision of price changes, implying a knowledge of business movements, and a power to forecast their effects, that no government could by any possibility possess. The plan assumes the possibility of offsetting, by momentary acts, a series of forces acting, through a period, without any known relation between these forces and the act. This is impossible. The forces might cease to act before the remedy was applied, or they might then be operating in an opposite direction, and the situation would be made worse. The plan presupposes, too, common action by different countries. But if the nations of the world cannot agree to establish international bimetallism in its simple form, they will certainly never adopt a scheme against which exist all the reasons for their refusal in the other case, together with many which spring from the complex and changing conditions under which free coinage at a shifting ratio would have to be administered.

12. Commissions to regulate the Price Level. — Akin to bimetallism in its purpose is the proposal which has sometimes been made to keep prices steady by the injection or withdrawal of money from circulation at intervals, as prices fall or rise. To carry out this proposal it is suggested that a government commission, national or international, be established, whose duty shall be to compile tables of index numbers as a means of measuring the price changes. A base is to be selected, consisting, for example, of the average of prices for a series of years. This average is to be called 100, and changes in the level are to be computed periodically. According to the direction in which the price level has changed, the commission will then add or withdraw money from circulation.

The proposal is, in substance, an attempt to create a money whose value would be invariable, and it rests for support upon the crudest form of the quantity theory of money. It is a naïve conception, as has been remarked, that the addition or subtraction of currency necessarily has any effect whatever on the price level, or that there is any direct relation between its supply and the value of standard money. It is equally naïve to suppose that it would be possible to get a commission wise enough, or honest enough, to carry such a project through successfully for a considerable period of time. The history of the conduct of governments in the regulation of money does not inspire one with confidence in their possession of either the ability or the honesty to administer such a plan. But we do not need to rest our rejection of the scheme upon the difficulty of securing an honest and wise commission, for the plan is unsound in theory. This commission must inject and withdraw either standard money or government paper. If it added government paper to the circulation of a particular country, it would drive out standard money, and no effect would be produced on prices, but the country would soon be brought to an irredeemable paper basis. If, on the other hand, the commission injected or withdrew standard money, where would it get this money? It must obtain money either by taking it out of circulation, by taxation, or by the sale of bonds, or else the government must control the product of the mines. In either case the plan would cause the very condition which it intended to prevent or to remedy. To take the money out of circulation would be to contract the currency, in order later to expand it. To control the production of the mines would be to withhold the supply of money, in order latei to contract or expand it. If the amount of gold added to the existing stock from year to year were not sufficient to prevent a fall of prices, how could it be made sufficient simply by passing it through the hands of a commission?

It has been suggested[1] that international paper money, issued in quantities sufficient to neutralize the causes of fluctuation as soon as they should arise, would retain a constant value and thereby keep the general price level steady. But the proposed plan takes no account of causes of price changes arising on the side of goods. It is not the case that a change in the money supply will reverse such changes, irrespective of their source and causes. The addition or subtraction of a given quantity might merely alter the relation between the volume of exchanges settled by cancellation through credit paper and the volume settled by direct money payments, without affecting the price level at all. In short, as already said, price movements cannot be reversed by action that has no regard to their causes, nor can occasional action neutralize the effects of varied forces acting continuously and in constantly changing directions. If at any time a quantity of money were injected to cure appreciation, there would be no means of

[1] Gide, "Principles of Political Economy," 2d Amer. ed., Transl. by Veditz, p. 227, foot-note.

knowing whether the movement that had caused appreciation had come to a stop before the injection was made, or whether it was to continue, or whether the current of events was to change and depreciation set in. Consequently, a commission would be setting in motion a force inadequate to cure the alleged difficulty without any knowledge whether it would continue, or be replaced with a force of an opposite character. Therefore the addition or withdrawal of a given quantity of money at any time would be as likely to aggravate as to remedy the difficulty it was intended to cure. Moreover, a measurement of the price changes by means of index numbers is a necessary feature of the scheme, and what has been said in criticism of this method of measurement would be valid against this plan. The plan is an excellent one to promote speculation in stocks, and to put the money market at the mercy of gamblers; but it could have only a vicious effect on legitimate business.

CHAPTER XV

SOME FACTORS WHICH MODIFY THE INFLUENCE OF PRICE CHANGES

REFERENCES: Clark, J. B., The Gold Standard of Currency in the Light of Recent Theory, Pol. Sci. Quar., September, 1895; Emery, H. C., The Place of the Speculator in the Theory of Distribution, Amer. Econ. Assoc. Pub., 3d Ser., Vol. I., No. 1, pp. 103 ff.; Fisher, I., Appreciation and Interest, Amer. Econ. Assoc. Pub., Vol. XI., No. 4; Taussig, F. W., The Silver Situation in the United States, Amer. Econ. Assoc. Pub., Vol. VII., No. 1, pp. 91–118; Wells, D. A., Recent Economic Changes; White, H., The Gold Standard, The World's Congress of Bankers and Financiers, pp. 84–87.

1. Cause of the Demand for Steadiness of the Price Level. — We have seen that the demand that price level, or the purchasing power of money, be kept steady, has arisen more from a desire to keep the value of debts unchanged than from a wish to distribute the current product of industry equitably. That is, emphasis is usually laid upon money as a means of discharging debts, rather than as a medium of exchange or of distribution of product. This emphasis is doubtless due to the fact that sympathy naturally goes out to people who suffer hardship from the burden of their debts, whether that burden has been brought on by their own negligence, by misfortune, or by social changes over which they have no control. The feeling probably springs from the old-time notion that people are debtors because they are poor; that debts are contracted mainly for purposes of consumption. We have seen that this is to a large extent a mistaken view. It is much more important in this age to take care that the laborer shall not lose by any change in the purchasing power of money, than it is to provide against the appreciation of debts. Now it is for the advantage of the laboring class to have money which appreciates with respect to goods and depreciates with respect to labor. The laborer gains if a dollar will purchase more goods and less labor to-day than it would yesterday. If money appreciates in a proper degree, it gives the laborer his due share of the benefits of industrial progress. There is some reason to think that gold, in spite of the vicissitudes of its value, comes pretty near doing this.[1] In any case, it would seem that the purchasing power of gold, in the long run, falls with respect to labor, and rises with respect to goods.

2. Industrial Improvements diminish the Burden of Debts of Producers. — There are some considerations, however, which indicate that the loss to debtors from the appreciation of debts, caused by a fall in the price level, is less than at first view appears. Debtors lose, indeed, when they have to pay in products whose prices have fallen; but this loss

[1] See J. B. Clark, *Pol. Sci. Quar.*, September, 1895.

may be offset, in part at least, by a reduction in the cost of production of the goods which the debtor produces. Economic progress implies increased labor efficiency, and this, at first at any rate, is likely to benefit the producer as distinct from the laborer. It implies, also, improvements in industrial organization and in machinery, the advantages of both of which are bound in the first place to accrue to the producer. He cannot, of course, long retain this advantage, nor is it likely to be in its amount sufficient to offset the loss due to appreciation of money. Nevertheless, so far as it goes, it certainly does act as a buffer between the debtor producer and the burden of his debts.

Moreover, the debtor shares as a buyer the advantage of lower prices of goods other than his own, whether he buys for consumption or for further production. If his purchase of goods is for further production, the advantage is equivalent to a reduction of the cost of his own articles, and the saving is of the kind referred to in the preceding paragraph.

3. The Debtor Class also a Creditor Class. — In the third place, it must not be forgotten that nowadays the debtor class is also, to a considerable extent, the creditor class, and that their debts and credits are, in large degree, simultaneous. This is especially true of business debts, which form the great bulk of modern indebtedness. Business today is largely carried on by borrowed capital, and business which is not so carried on has current debts as well as unpaid accounts. Hence, any loss which business men suffer as debtors is offset partly, or wholly, by their gains as creditors, and *vice versa.*

4. Debts contracted for Profit. — Moreover, debts are contracted now more for the purpose of securing additional profits than from poverty. Business men contract obligations for the purpose of extending their business and enlarging their incomes. Farmers put mortgages on their farms more often in order to buy new land, or to make improvements on their old land, than because the owners lack money to till the land they already have. In other words, most debtors to-day are debtors for profit, not from necessity; and they are able to take care of themselves. Hence, to a not inconsiderable extent, any loss which they incur by appreciation of debts would mean a loss of expected profit, rather than a loss of principal.

5. Effect of shortening the Period of Debts. — Still further, it is a fact that a great volume of current indebtedness is contracted for short periods, so that the adjustment of the purchasing power of money to offset the changes in the burden of debts is less necessary. This statement, again, is especially true of business debts. Bank loans, which constitute so large a part of the volume of debts, usually run for a few days, or months at the most. The short-time loans of the banks constitute about sixty per cent. of the whole, and only a small portion of bank loans run over six or nine months. The life of farm mortgages in the United States, about the burden of which so much was written when prices were still tending downward, a few years ago, did not average more than four or five years.[1]

A gradual fall of prices running through a series of years would be distributed, therefore, among several groups of debtors, so that it is incorrect to assume, as so many times has been done, that the burden laid by falling prices upon a particular group of debtors is to be measured by the change in the purchasing power of money during the whole period of the fall. The loss is likely to be so distributed among successive debtors that the burden on each is trifling. This fact lessens whatever hardship the change brings, but does not altogether remove it. A hardship is not less a hardship because it is small in amount; yet where the loss is less, the suffering is also less.

There is, however, a fixed burden of indebtedness which is long standing and permanent in character. This is true of most public debts, and their burden, therefore, cannot be lightened by the cause just described. But we shall see that this burden is somewhat diminished by the payment of lower rates of interest, secured by means of frequent conversions.

[1] G. K. Holmes, Bulletin of the United States Department of Labor, November, 1895, p. 48.

6. The Influence of the Speculator in diminishing the Effect of Price Changes. — Whatever burden is placed upon debtors by falling prices is diminished, moreover, by the influence of speculation. It has been pointed out that the speculator in a measure guarantees stability of prices by discounting their changes, especially for short periods. What, in the absence of the speculator, would be a violent price change is likely to be converted through his influence into a number of successive small fluctuations, so that the descent from a high level to a low level of prices is by a series of short steps. In other words, the speculator discounts the fall, so that he saves the entrepreneur from a loss due to unexpected changes in prices through a period of time corresponding to the cycles of business movements. If prices are falling through a long period, this fall need not embarrass producers, since all they care for is to be guaranteed against loss during the comparatively short period of the producing processes.

7. The Influence of the Rate of Interest on the Burden of Debts. — Still again, the burden of indebtedness is lightened, as has been pointed out, by a fall in the rate of interest. It has been pretty conclusively shown by Professor Irving Fisher,[1] that the rate of interest tends in the long run to accommodate itself more or less closely to the changed value of money, and therefore to offset,

[1] "Appreciation and Interest," *Amer. Econ. Assoc. Pub.*, Vol. XI., No. 4.

in part at least, the loss caused by changes in the value of the principal of the debt. It is evident enough that if we could know beforehand that the purchasing power of money was to fall steadily at a definite rate through a known series of years, the changes would be discounted from year to year, from month to month, or from day to day, in the prices of commodities, and in the rates of interest paid on loans. The changes, however, cannot be thus clearly and definitely foreseen, nor are they gradual and regular. For example, to mention only one cause of irregular fluctuations, the new methods of mining gold and the discovery of new mines would alone make it impossible to foretell exactly what the changes of a given decade, or a given year, might be. Nevertheless, even the irregular changes are more or less made up for in changing rates of discount, and this can be done more and more exactly the shorter the debt period and the more frequent the conversions.

What creditors wish to have returned to them by debtors is such an amount of real capital as will yield them an amount of enjoyment equal to what they would have obtained by the consumption of their principal, plus a sum equal to their estimated loss by deferring that consumption, and their share of the advantage of economic progress, during the period of the loan. What lenders and borrowers are primarily interested in, then, is not the rate of interest, but what has been called the ratio of accumulation, or the amount (principal plus interest), of the loan. What the lender wants is a return which will be the ratio of accumulation that he would get irrespective of any change in the value of money. The loan will be discharged by a sum of money which will purchase this amount (principal and interest), or ratio of accumulation, of the goods loaned. If, now, the value of money has changed, the amount to be returned in terms of money must change so that it shall be equivalent to the amount, or ratio of accumulation, in terms of goods,—or better, of satisfaction, assuming that it can be measured. The sum necessary to do this will be less if money has appreciated, and more if it has depreciated. But of the amount of the debt to be returned in money, the principal is fixed; hence the whole change must fall on the portion of the amount allotted to interest. That is, the rate of interest must change, falling as money appreciates and rising as it depreciates. Professor Fisher has proven that high prices and rising prices are directly correlated with high rates of interest, and low or falling prices with low rates, and that an adjustment of interest to price movements takes place constantly, but for short periods is not so exact as for long ones. He has constructed the following table[1] of interest rates to show that experience confirms his theory:—

[1] "Appreciation and Interest," *Amer. Econ. Assoc. Pub.*, Vol. XI., No. 4, p. 55.

State of Prices	1824 to 1831 Incl.	1832 to 1841 Incl.	1842 to 1851 Incl.	1852 to 1861 Incl.	1862 to 1871 Incl.	1872 to 1881 Incl.	1882 to 1891 Incl.
London, High prices	3.8	4.4	3.6	5.4	5.1	3.7	3.0
Low prices	3.2	3.2	2.6	3.0	2.6	2.5	2.5
New York, High prices				9.1	7.4	7.0	5.3
Low prices				9.1	6.7	5.1	5.1
Berlin, High prices					4.6	3.7	3.3
Low prices					3.4	3.2	2.7
Paris, High prices						4.1	2.6
Low prices						2.4	2.6
Calcutta, High prices						6.2	5.4
Low prices						5.6	6.2
Tokyo, High prices,						12.3	10.1
Low prices						12.0	10.1
Shanghai, High prices							6.0
Low prices							5.7

"Of the 21 comparisons contained in this table, 17 show higher rates for high-price years than for low-price years, 1 shows the opposite condition, and 3 show equal rates in the two cases. As the table covers 68 years for London, 40 for New York, 30 for Berlin, 20 for Paris, 19 each for Calcutta and Tokyo, and 9 for Shanghai, or 205 years in the aggregate, the result may be accepted with great confidence that high and low prices are usually associated with high and low interest, respectively."[1]

The reasons for the lack of exactness in adjustment are to be found in the unequal ability of

[1] "Appreciation and Interest," *Amer. Econ. Assoc. Pub.*, Vol. XI., No. 4, p. 56.

investors to discount changes in the price level, and in the fact that time is necessary for the adjustment. The imperfectness of adjustment for short periods is not of much importance, since the change in the value of money through short periods is likely to be inconsiderable. Of course, a change in the rate of interest, operating in behalf of debtors, does not decrease the burden of debts which have been contracted at a fixed rate and cannot be converted at a lower rate. In these cases the burden must be borne, but the long-period debts whose conversion is not practicable are fortunately a small proportion of the whole, and are likely to become less as loanable capital increases. Consequently, speaking generally, the burden imposed on debtors by falling prices is more or less lightened by a falling rate of interest. "We thus see that the farmer who contracts a mortgage in gold is, if the interest is properly adjusted, no worse and no better off than if his contract were in a 'wheat' standard or a 'multiple' standard."[1] Whatever loss he incurs arises from the slower movement of the interest rate, as compared with that of the value of money.

8. Difficulty of doing Justice by Artificial Corrections of Price Changes. — Finally, it is at least questionable whether a correction of any given change in the purchasing power of money would not do as much harm as good, because a correc-

[1] "Appreciation and Interest," *Amer. Econ. Assoc. Pub.*, Vol. XI., No. 4, p. 16.

tion that was made for debts of one duration would not do for those of another. If we could create a price level which would relieve the burden of debts running for three years, we might be adding to the burden of those which run for some longer period. This is true, altogether apart from the social loss that would be caused by abandoning the principle of the inviolability of contracts.

Moreover, we must distinguish carefully between hardship and injustice. The debtor who suffers hardship on account of a fall in the price of his goods at a time when he is in debt, does not necessarily suffer injustice thereby. In contracting his debt, it may be for improvements or for the enlargement of his business, he takes his chances of such a change and such loss, and society requires him to estimate its probability fairly and to discount it correctly.

9. Gold Monometallism Probably does Substantial Justice in the Long Run.— In the light of all the considerations going to show that the effects of gold monometallism, in varying prices and in enhancing the pressure of debts, are far less evil than is often claimed, and in view of the impossibility of finding a standard which would not be open to even greater objections than is the gold standard, especially as any evil results of the latter to debtors are offset by the other influences that we have discussed, it is safe to conclude that the common judgment of the most progressive countries in favor of the gold standard is undoubtedly wise. Theory leads, on the whole, to the same conclusion as experience has done; and while, in the future as in the past, there will be times when the vicissitudes of life will give rise to demands for scaling debts and for relieving some people from burdens which they have been either unfortunate enough, or foolish enough, to put themselves under, yet, all things considered, the maintenance and extension of gold monometallism promises more of good and less of harm than any other system thus far proposed. The system is simpler, the monetary utility of the metal is high enough to meet the demand of economic progress for such a money, and the fluctuations in its value cause no greater difficulties, in the long run, than would occur in prices under the bimetallic system. Moreover, a sufficient supply of gold is certain enough. A relative lessening of the annual product, under some conditions of mining, does not mean that the supply is, or is likely to be, exhausted; but only that new processes are needed for the extraction of the metal. Surely the experience of the nineteenth century in invention and discovery justifies one in believing that the difficulties caused by a relative scarcity will be duly met by new discoveries.

CHAPTER XVI

INCONVERTIBLE PAPER MONEY

REFERENCES: Hepburn, A. B., Contest for Sound Money, Pt. I., Chs. 4–11; Jevons, W. S., Money and the Mechanism of Exchange, Ch. 18; Knies, K., Das Geld, pp. 344 ff.; Knox, J. J., United States Notes, Chs. 1–3, 13; Laughlin, J. L., Principles of Money, Chs. 13–14; Mill, J. S., Principles of Political Economy, Bk. III., Ch. 13; Noyes, A. D., Thirty Years of American Finance, Ch. 1; Pareto, V., Cours d'Économie Politique, Vol. I., § 327 ff.; Ricardo, D., Works (McCulloch's ed.), Ch. 27; Scott, W. A., Money and Banking, Ch. 6; Sumner, W. G., History of American Currency; Walker, F. A., Money, Pt. II.; Money, Trade, and Industry, Chs. 8–9; White, A. D., Paper Money Inflation in France; White, H., Money and Banking, 2d ed., Bk. III., Chs. 1–6.

1. Kinds of Paper Money. — The idea of supplanting metal with paper money for use in making exchanges is not modern. It is true, of course, that the ancient world did not know how to make paper, but they used articles like papyrus, the bark of trees, skin, leather, and other available substitutes. Paper money was used in China as early as the ninth century, and probably long before, and there is reason for believing that its use was not unknown in ancient Assyria and Babylon. Paper money may be, as we have already noted, of three kinds: representative; convertible, redeemable, or fiduciary; and inconvertible, or irredeemable. Representative paper money is simply certificates of deposit, or receipts, certifying that so many dollars, or pounds sterling, or marks, have been deposited with the issuer of the paper, returnable to the owner on presentation of the receipt. They are more convenient to use than are coins, especially for large sums, and are in all respects the exact equals of the specie they represent. They are, so to say, representatives plenipotentiary of specie. They may be issued by banks or by governments.

2. Meaning of Convertibility. — By convertible paper we mean notes issued by an individual, or by a public or private corporation, or a government, promising to pay the value expressed on the paper in coin, and redeemable in coin as a matter of fact on presentation, without demur or delay. The term is not correctly applied to paper which is payable in anything else than legal tender coin. Notes which promise to pay so many acres of land, or so many bushels of wheat, or so many tons of coal or iron, would not be convertible, in the proper sense of the word. Convertible paper must at all times, and under all circumstances, be instantly mutable into the money which is the standard legal tender of the country in which the paper is issued. Whether or not the notes bear on their face a promise to pay in specie, in land, or in goods, unless they are as a matter of fact paid in specie on demand, they are inconvertible paper. It is important to emphasize this point, —

that notes to be convertible must be payable in legal tender specie, — because the advocates of fiat money sometimes urge that if paper is payable in goods or land, it has the attribute of convertibility. This, however, is not a correct statement. Such notes are redeemable in the goods which they call for, but they are not in any proper sense of the word convertible paper. The word "convertible" is restricted in monetary science to redeemability in legal tender standard money, and in that alone. This is the case because what business men need, if they use paper money in making payments at all, is a kind of paper immediately exchangeable for something which they can use at once where paper money itself will not pass. The only kind of money available for this purpose is standard metallic money. No security of land or goods can take the place of the standard metal for this purpose. What is wanted is that the paper shall be exchangeable for a given amount of metal money at once on demand, and not at some future time, after the lapse of the period necessary to sell the land or goods which are held as security for the paper.

3. Characteristics of Irredeemable Paper. — Irredeemable, or inconvertible, paper money consists of notes for which specie is not obtainable on demand. This, too, may be issued either by governments or by banks. It may consist of notes which, although originally convertible, have lost their convertibility through the insolvency of their issuers, or it may consist of paper originally issued without the expectation or intention of paying it in specie. The latter form is properly called fiat money. The two kinds of inconvertible paper differ in their mode of issue only; in their behavior and effects they are in all respects the same.

A government may issue inconvertible paper money on the security of government land, or on the security of taxes specially assigned to redeem it. On the other hand, such paper may be issued without security, and put into circulation by political authority. If a government is sufficiently autocratic and strong, it may for a time force such paper upon a people unwilling to receive it. We recall that the sole condition of the use of any article as money is that it shall be generally accepted in the discharge of obligations, the payment of purchases and of debts. Its general acceptability is a result either of social habit or convention, of custom, of law, or of the credit of the issuer. Gold and silver pass current by force of social habit, due to their capacity for directly satisfying human desire. A check, or a bill of exchange, is accepted in payment because the maker of the paper commands the confidence of those who receive it. Inconvertible paper money issued by a government passes from hand to hand, if it passes at all, either because the people have no better money, and the quantity of it is so limited that its evils do not yet appear, or because the government is strong enough to compel its citizens to accept the paper. Since it answers their purpose, the people are content to use it.

4. Benefits and Dangers of Irredeemable Paper. — The advantages, as well as the dangers, of irredeemable paper money have been many times recited. Paper money has been likened by Adam Smith to a wagon way through the air, the use of which leaves the land under it available for raising produce to satisfy human wants. That is to say, paper money makes it unnecessary for society to invest real capital for the sake of getting a medium of exchange. Gold and silver are expensive to produce. The necessary amount of them requires the labor of many people and the consumption of much wealth. If a way is devised which makes it unnecessary to use gold and silver in exchange, clearly the labor and the goods formerly used in their production can be devoted to the production of goods that are directly consumable, the wealth of the community would be increased, and the general standard of consumption would be raised. If paper, whether convertible or inconvertible, is issued by a country which already possesses metallic money sufficient for its needs, the specie will partly or wholly cease to be used. Some of it will be diverted to use in the arts, and some will be exported to places where perhaps it can be of more service. A displacement of metallic money in use by paper money is, therefore, beneficial only if not done by all countries at once. If all countries attempted to secure this benefit at the same time, no saving of real capital would result, because the capital necessary to produce the existing specie has been invested already. The only advantage would be to divert a larger amount of the money metal to the arts. A real saving would be made, however, by the universal issue of paper, in so far as it rendered unnecessary the further investment of capital for additions to the metallic money supply to meet the needs of expanding trade. The perception of this saving of real capital by the use of paper money has led men and nations often to pass the danger line of issue, on the supposition that because a certain quantity of paper money was a good thing, its use for all purposes of exchange and payment would also be good.

A second advantage to society in the use of paper money lies in saving the wear and tear to which the metals are subjected when used as a means of exchange. The loss from this source is considerable. Moreover, paper money is more convenient for individuals to handle; it is easy to make large payments with it, because a note for $1000 is as easily carried and transferred as a note for $1; and finally, paper money is more convenient for making payments in distant places. The expense of sending it is less, as is also, perhaps, the risk of loss.

The fiscal advantage of paper money should not be passed by. When a government finds its credit so low that it cannot borrow money to meet its expenses, unless, perhaps, at exorbitant rates of interest, it sometimes can find a less expensive way to secure what it needs by issuing notes. It can do this successfully only if the circulating medium of the country is wholly, or largely, composed of specie which the paper can replace.

Paper money is, of course, far less stable in value than gold money. As we have seen, its circulation depends, in the last analysis, on the confidence reposed in the political authority which issues it, whereas that of gold is based on social habit of universal and perennial prevalence. Consequently, the area of acceptability of paper money is restricted. Such money is, generally speaking, national money, without value beyond the boundaries of a particular country. Its smaller area of acceptability makes the demand for it variable, and its value uncertain and changeable. Additions to the supply are dependent on the caprice, or the policy, of a government, while additions to metallic money are obtained only at a cost; and this difference causes greater variations in the value of the paper.

5. Influence of the Issue of Irredeemable Paper on Specie. — In a purely metallic monetary system, when a country is using metal which is used elsewhere as money, any surplus of money which it may have is at once revealed by the higher prices which prevail in its markets, and is turned into the channels of trade of other countries; while any deficiency from which it may be suffering, under similar circumstances, will be supplied from the circulation of foreign countries. Not so with fiat paper. Business may be stagnant, the demand for money may be small, and prices may fall, so that less money really would be needed, and yet the flood of inconvertible paper may rise in ever swelling proportions. When a country with metallic money begins to issue paper, the first result is to drive the specie out of circulation. The metallic money may be taken by the government in payment of taxes, and used to defray those public expenses which must be met in gold. It may be reduced to bullion for use in the arts, because the enlarged supply available has lowered the price and increased the demand. It may be hoarded in the form of coin by people who are afraid to part with it, or who look for the return of better times when it will be once more available to make payments. Or, finally, it may be exported to discharge foreign indebtedness.

If the amount of the medium of exchange demanded by the business of the country does not increase as fiat money comes into use, the metallic money will disappear as fast as the paper goes into circulation. If the need for the medium of exchange increases in the meantime, the specie may not disappear so rapidly, and the total volume of the means of exchange in the country, paper and metallic, will increase. During this process the money of the country will be mixed paper and coin. If, however, the output of paper money be persisted in, it will in time become sufficient to perform by itself the exchanges of the country, all the coin will be melted, hoarded, or exported, and the currency of the country will consist wholly of paper. No positive harm may be done up to this point of the process. But if the issue of the paper becomes still larger, its mischievous effects will be at once felt. In other words, the positive harm arises from over-issue, or the output of a quantity larger than the specie it displaces. The paper, unlike the gold and silver, cannot be exported, nor diverted to use in the arts. The merchants of foreign countries cannot use it, and will not accept it in payment. After the paper has driven out the coin, further issues go to swell the volume of home currency and accumulate like water in a pond that has no outlet.

6. Signs of Excessive Issue. — The first effect and the first sign of an issue in excess of the whole volume of metallic money displaced, or of the amount of exchange medium needed by the country, is a premium on gold. Speaking broadly, the issue of the paper does not alter the exchange relation of gold and goods. Payments for goods bought abroad, and for some other purposes, must continue to be made in gold. But if the gold is no longer in circulation, it must be bought in the form of bullion, and a premium will be paid for it in terms of the new paper money. This premium will show itself in a rise in the rate of foreign exchange. Foreign business indebtedness is ordinarily discharged by means of bills of exchange, but bills of exchange are quoted in terms of gold. If, on a specie basis, a bill of exchange for £1000, drawn in London on New York, can be paid by $4870, it would require $4969 to pay it if the currency of the United States were paper which had depreciated two per cent. That is, the American importer will have to pay $4969 in paper money, in order to buy a bill payable in gold to the amount of £1000. Now, such a condition is extremely bad for the foreign trade of the country in which gold is at a premium. It must make its foreign payments with one kind of money, and discharge its domestic obligations with another. The greater its balance of foreign indebtedness, the more heavily does the burden of the premium on gold diminish the profits of its exports and render its trade unremunerative. On so small a margin is trade carried on, that, in some cases, the premium on gold would turn an expected profit into a loss. Consequently, a small premium, or, indeed, the mere likelihood of a premium on gold, makes the foreign creditor demand a more favorable exchange in order to offset the premium, or discount the risk of loss involved in its possible appearance. The domestic importer, being subjected to a loss, will try to recoup himself by raising the prices of his goods in the home currency. This step in the process brings us to a consideration of the second evil of inconvertible paper money.

When the specie has been driven out of circulation, prices are no longer quoted in gold, but in paper. That is, they rise as the value of the paper falls. Thus the paper becomes a kind of secondary monetary standard. If the excess of paper over the specie displaced is small, it is possible that no change in the prices of goods will be noticed. For the force of custom on prices, in some places and for some articles at least, is very strong. It is a sort of economic friction, which interferes with the freedom of the price movement. An excess of paper great enough to show itself in a slight rise of the foreign exchanges may not manifest itself, therefore, in general prices. But the appearance of the premium on gold as shown in the exchanges is proof that inflation of prices and depreciation of the paper, in goods as well as in gold, is close at hand, and that ere long the price level in the country of issue will be different from that of the rest of the world; or, more accurately, will not bear the same relation to the world price level as existed under the specie régime.

7. The Relation of the Quantity of Inconvertible Paper to its Value. — It is important to discover how far prices respond to an increase in the paper-money issues after these exceed in amount the specie they displace. We have seen in another connection[1] that it is with inconvertible paper money that the so-called quantity theory of prices, within certain limits, holds true. Paper money

[1] See pp. 139–141.

derives its value solely from the demand for it for exchange purposes. Its marginal utility is always merely the reflected marginal utility of the goods it exchanges for. If the marginal composite unit of goods exchanges for a certain amount of paper, thus fixing the price level, that marginal unit will call for double the quantity of paper money if the whole volume of paper be doubled; provided, in the meantime, the total quantity of commodities has not changed, and credit transactions and the efficiency, or rapidity of circulation, of the paper money are constant. That is, under the fixed conditions assumed, the value of the paper money varies inversely as its quantity. Such is the accepted theory. Of course these fixed conditions are never realized, and the quantitative relation cannot be proved or disproved, statistically. But the statement that the value of the paper depends on its quantity, is not altogether correct, under any conditions. It depends partly upon the confidence of the community in the power of the paper to continue to circulate, and this confidence becomes less as the volume of the paper enlarges. If the depreciation is slow and approximately regular, prices and other conditions will accommodate themselves to the increasing quantity. But if the depreciation be very rapid, people lose confidence in their ability to pass the paper without considerable loss, many of them will refuse to accept it, and its value will fall more rapidly than in the proportion of the increased output. To pay $1000 for a breakfast, as Secretary Chase thought might be possible from the issue of United States notes in the early days of the Civil War, would so demoralize men's confidence in the stability of the money as to cause a fall in its value altogether disproportionate to its increase of quantity. Moreover, as confidence that others will take the money grows less, on account of the increasing quantity, the danger of loss from this fact is discounted by the present sellers of goods, and the purchasing power of money is still further decreased. The marginal utility of the instrument of utility for use falls more rapidly the nearer we approach surfeit, just as the marginal utility of consumable goods does under like circumstances. The relation between the value and the quantity of paper money could be true, then, only under impossible conditions, and only if its quantity were either fixed or increasing very slowly.

8. The Effect of an Issue of Paper Money on the Price Level. — An output of paper money in one country at first gives an upward impulse to the world's level of prices. The truth of this statement does not depend upon the truth or falsity of the quantity theory of the value of money, at any rate, as usually stated. All that the statement assumes is that *some* relation exists between the supply of money and its value, just as in the case of other commodities. A change in the supply, unless so small as to be entirely checked by economic friction, must always have some effect, although it may not appear in a modification of prices, but be entirely lost to view by concomitant changes in credit exchanges, in barter exchanges, in the efficiency of money, or in the volume of goods put upon the market.

Let us suppose that the metallic money of the United States were arbitrarily and instantaneously withdrawn from use, and an equal amount of paper money substituted. No reason appears why such a change should occasion any alteration in the price level of the world's goods. Let us suppose, further, that this change having been made, the gold which was withdrawn is arbitrarily and suddenly put into circulation in those countries which retain their metallic money. So far as concerns this change alone the level of the world's prices will tend to rise, and the prices in the United States, under its régime of paper money, will share in the upward swell. If, instead of the arbitrary withdrawal of specie, we have a gradual exportation of it, as paper money is put out in increasing volume, until all the gold has been driven out, the character of the result is not changed although the degree may differ much. As a matter of fact, gold, when supplanted with paper, disappears in several ways. The release of the metal from the service of demand for a means of payment lowers its value, and some of it is consequently attracted to use in the arts. Some, too, may be hoarded, and some will undoubtedly be exported to specie-using countries. Whatever the division of the amount between the uses, the value of the metal is lowered in consequence of the cessation of its use in one country. In some measure, therefore, does the level of prices throughout the world tend to rise. If, in accordance with our first supposition, the specie pushed out went out of use altogether, the amount of paper money which would be needed to replace it in order that prices should not be affected by the change, considered by itself,[1] would be exactly the amount of specie displaced. But as paper comes in specie does not go out of use, but simply changes its location, raising the price level as it goes. Hence the amount of paper which a country can issue, without causing its price level to vary from that of the world at large, must be greater than the amount of specie displaced, by a degree dependent on a change in the world's price level. The amount of paper which will exactly displace the specie, as the latter goes into use elsewhere, is greater than the amount which would replace it if it were suddenly destroyed. In the latter case, the price level which prevailed under the use of specie would remain; in the former case, a higher one would take its place; in both cases, the price level in the paper-using country would be the world level. Therefore, an amount of paper equal to the specie displaced would be excessive, on the old price level.

It follows from what has been said that the

[1] Irrespective of any impairment of public confidence.

fluctuations of prices, to which a country using inconvertible paper money is subjected, have three sources. First, the prices of its goods are subject to the same fluctuations as are those of gold-using countries, due to the progress and vicissitudes of trade and industry. No country can escape these unless the excessive use of inconvertible paper diminishes its business. Such a country must suffer, in the second place, from the fluctuations in prices caused by the varying value of its paper money in terms of gold; and, in the third place, from variations due to speculative attempts on the part of business men to protect themselves by discounting future changes in the value of the paper.

9. The Premium on Gold and the Depreciation of Paper in Commodities. — The amount of inflation of prices of goods, in terms of paper money, is the measure of the depreciation of the paper. Since a given quantity of goods is exchangeable for a certain amount of gold as well as of paper, it would seem, at first thought, that the depreciation of the paper money in terms of goods would exactly equal the premium on gold. In other words, it would seem that the paper price of bullion would be greater than the mint price, by an amount equal to that by which the foreign exchange is below the real exchange.

It has long been a matter of remark, however, that the premium on gold does not exactly measure the amount of depreciation of the paper, or the inflation of prices. The purchasing power of inconvertible paper money is a little less, when measured in goods than it is when measured in gold. There are several possible reasons for this difference. In the first place, the difference between the depreciation of paper in gold and the inflation of prices is probably enhanced by the probable risk of an increase in the quantity, and of future changes in the purchasing power of the paper. It might seem that the discount of this risk would affect gold and other goods in equal degrees. But the prices of other commodities cannot be changed as quickly as can the price of gold. Hence they cannot adapt themselves so quickly as can gold to changes in the supply of paper. The period for which the risk of change must be discounted is, therefore, longer for other commodities than for gold, and the amount of discount larger. Consequently the total depreciation of paper money in goods is greater than in gold.

A second cause of the difference in the amount of depreciation of paper in terms of gold and other goods, respectively, is found in the lower value of gold caused by its ejection from the country which adopts paper. As we have seen, the export of the gold raises the world level of prices; that is, it lowers the value of gold. Since prices are expressed in paper money, in the country which has adopted it, an increase of paper lowers its own value in gold and goods, or raises their value in terms of itself; but gold has fallen from its previous value, and this fall in a measure offsets the rise due to the increase of the paper. As nothing of the kind happens to commodities, their prices show the full rise due to the increase of paper. Thus gold suffers a double fall in price as against one fall suffered by other commodities. If, on the other hand, paper money contracts, its value rises as compared with goods and gold.

Another cause of the difference in depreciation as measured by gold and by goods, respectively, is found in the fact that the inconvertible legal-tender paper serves as a basis of credit. Besides the increased money demand for goods, caused by the additional issues of paper, there is also a credit demand due to the credit based on these extra issues. Hence the demand for goods is increased by more than the amount of the paper, and prices rise in a greater degree than the extra paper of itself would warrant. But no such twofold demand acts on gold. Hence an extra issue of paper does not cause the value of gold to rise so much as that of other goods, and therefore the paper depreciates more in terms of the latter than in the former. Suppose now that the excess of notes is withdrawn. The credit demand based on these must also be withdrawn. Prices of goods will fall under the twofold influence. Gold will fall under the influence of the retirement of the notes only.

The degree of depreciation of an inconvertible paper currency is affected by several circumstances, aside from its quantity. If it be issued in increasing quantities at a time when the demand for a medium of exchange is growing fast enough to absorb it, it will not depreciate. If the demand for currency happens to be decreasing, the depreciation will be increasing. If, again, the issue be made when for some reason gold is being hoarded, as in a time of war, or of a great commercial panic, depreciation might not ensue. There is never any certainty, however, that the issue of paper money will be timely, and no confidence can be felt beforehand that the evil effects of excessive issues would be counteracted by the influences mentioned.

10. Special Provision for maintaining the Value of Irredeemable Paper. — It sometimes happens that an attempt is made to give artificial value to fiat money by making it receivable for taxes. The effect of such a measure is temporary and, unless the quantity is carefully regulated, very small. If the amount of paper money issued is larger than the amount of metal displaced, by a quantity just equal to current government income, the excess over and above the demand needed for effecting exchanges is the amount which the government withdraws from circulation. The effect of receiving this excess in payment of government dues is precisely the same as the current redemption of the excess, provided it is held in the treasury after it is received. This could occur only if it were surplus revenue. If, however, the excess, over and above the amount equal to the metal displaced, is greater than the current government revenue calls for from day to day, then this channel of overflow for surplus paper money is choked, and the effect is the same as if the current redemption were not large enough to take care of the excess. Beyond this point the course of the purchasing power of the paper money will be unaffected by the fact that it is receivable for government dues.

It is further urged at times that if the people have confidence that the money will ultimately be redeemed by the government that issues it, its value will be sustained. This belief is utterly without foundation, except so far as the belief in ultimate convertibility leads to hoarding. The value of a promise to pay may be sustained under such circumstances if the paper is held as an investment, but its value as a medium of exchange will not be affected at all. The purchasing power, which is an essential characteristic of a medium of exchange, is present, not future, purchasing power. It is what a piece of money will buy now that determines what it will pass for. If the paper were at a discount, and the certainty of redemption were established at a period not too remote, a portion of the paper would probably be withdrawn from circulation as money, and held as an investment, and the purchasing power of the remainder would thereby be raised. Aside from this probability the certainty of ultimate redemption would have no effect.

11. The Evils of Irredeemable Paper. — The evils of depreciating and fluctuating paper money cannot easily be over-emphasized. Inflated prices introduce an element of uncertainty into business. Business men cannot be sure that the prices at which they contract to sell or buy will remain the same from the time the contract is made until the transaction is closed. Speculation of the worst kind becomes a feature of business life. Business sagacity is thwarted, and the spirit of prudence gives place to that of gambling. Risks of change, the probability of inflation or contraction, must be discounted, with a wide margin. The result is to produce greater changes in prices than the mere difference in the amount of money would of itself cause. Moreover, the speculative fever thus engendered introduces a demoralizing influence into a community; a desire to get rich quickly is stimulated, to the detriment of that security and steadiness which are essential to sound business methods and morals. Expensive living becomes the fashion. The nominal price of all property rates so much higher than it formerly did that people regard themselves as grown suddenly rich, forgetting that the change is a nominal, and not a real one. When a contraction of the paper money flood takes place, these changes are reversed; but as it is so much harder to retrench the expenses of living, and to think of one's self as becoming poor by the fall in nominal values, the feeling of sacrifice and loss engendered depresses a community, and for a time deadens enterprise. Moreover, the fluctuations of the value of inconvertible paper defraud creditors or debtors, according to the direction of the movement, without any corresponding advantage or offset, and they bear down severely on wage-earners. Wages are paid in paper, and, since wages do not rise as early or as rapidly as prices do, the cost of living is increased to all wage-earners.

12. The Fiscal Advantage of Irredeemable Paper. — The fiscal advantage which the government has in securing a loan without interest, by the issue of such paper, is dearly bought by the community. It is, in effect, an unjust method of taxation; for it strikes hardest the poor and ignorant, and it makes the burden of taxation variable and uncertain. When a government once yields to the temptation to issue inconvertible paper, it has entered upon a path that is likely to lead it downward in the scale of political integrity and national honor. The amount of paper money which a government is likely to issue depends primarily on its need for revenue.

It is a fiscal need, rather than a business need, that determines what the quantity of this kind of money shall be. Yet money is, first and foremost, a tool of the business world. Its quantity must depend on the demand for a means of exchange, its value must not be caused to vary any more than the accidents of business bring about, and, above all things, should be free from the variations due to forces outside of business and altogether unconnected with the service which money is intended to render. When once paper money has been issued in excess of the needs of a community, and the price level has begun to rise in consequence, demoralization is inevitable. Fiat paper has been well called the alcohol of commerce, whose fumes, entering the brains of individuals and of government officers, seem to make them incapable of sober judgment or self-restraint in the matter of further issue and further demoralization.

13. Motives to the Issue of Irredeemable Paper. — While the fiscal necessity of a government is generally the primary cause of issuing fiat money, the ease with which the money is obtained and the apparent temporary profit which it brings to the government easily create a popular demand for its continued and larger use. It is not evident to the people at large that the temporary benefits of paper issues have a very definitc limit, and that the use of fiat paper beyond this limit will cause only harm and loss.

Besides the fiscal motive for the use of fiat money, pressure for its increase comes from the debtor class. When the paper has driven up prices, debtors find it easier to pay debts which were contracted when prices were low. Of course, payment in depreciated paper is not an equitable return ; but as long as human nature is as it is, there will always be some who are ready to take advantage of any means for escaping their just burdens.

Still another reason which makes it difficult for a country to stop short of disaster when once it has entered upon a career of depreciated paper, is found in the proper and honest desire of many people to secure for the people at large whatever saving is effected by the use of paper money. In the view of these people, money is a tool of society, and the community as a whole should obtain whatever advantage comes from the improvement of it. The purpose of this demand is entirely proper, but the use of fiat paper money to effect this saving is very questionable, in view of the dangers which it invites. There are ways of securing to the public whatever benefit there is in the use of paper money without inviting the dangers of depreciation.

14. Some Noted Historical Examples of Irredeemable Paper. — The most noted instances of inconvertible paper money are the French assignats and mandats, the notes of the Bank of England during the so-called period of restriction following the Napoleonic wars, the notes issued by the Continental Congress, and the greenbacks issued by our government during the Civil War.

The assignats were issued by the revolutionary government of France in 1789. These were legal tender notes secured by the lands confiscated from the clergy. That is, these lands were pledged for the ultimate redemption of the notes. To facilitate their circulation, moreover, bank-note issues were prohibited; but they fell rapidly in value because of excessive issue, and in 1796 a one-hundred-franc note was worth one-third of a franc in gold. They were replaced later with the so-called mandats. These differed from the assignats only in the respect that for their payment specified portions of land were assigned.

The first issue of paper money by our Continental Congress was in 1775, to the amount of $10,000,000. These were not made legal tender by the Congress, although they were made so later by the various colonies. Before the time of the Declaration of Independence $15,000,000 had been issued. Within four years the volume of inconvertible paper rose to more than $240,000,000, and its value fell so rapidly that by 1781 it was worthless. This fall took place in spite of many efforts of the public and the legislature to prevent it.

The United States greenbacks, or legal-tender notes, were first authorized by Congress in 1862, to the amount of $150,000,000. Within four months $150,000,000 more were authorized. The maximum sum issued during the war was $450,000,000. They fell to 35 cents per $1 in 1864, and fluctuated at various rates until the resumption of specie payment in 1879. The amount outstanding is $346,681,016.

15. Regulation of Irredeemable Paper. — Waiving the question, which many people answer in the negative, whether it is ever really necessary for the government of a wealthy country to resort to fiat paper, it is important to determine some means of regulating the amount of issues so as to avoid the evils of depreciation and inflation. We have seen that some people think it possible to measure the fluctuations in prices and to enlarge or contract the amount of paper money accordingly. Aside from the unsound theory which underlies this proposal, the measurement proposed is practically impossible.

A premium on gold, however, is a sure sign of excess of issue of paper. Therefore, the quantity of paper should be so regulated as to prevent the appearance of this premium. The most successful instance of the management of paper issues in this way is that of the Bank of France during and after the Franco-Prussian War.

CHAPTER XVII

CONVERTIBLE PAPER CURRENCY

REFERENCES: Conant, C. A., History of Modern Banks of Issue, Ch. 1; Dunbar, C. F., Theory and History of Banking, Ch. 5; Gilbart, J. W., History, Principles, and Practice of Banking, Vol. I., Ch. 10; Jevons, W. S., Money and the Mechanism of Exchange, Chs. 16, 17; Laughlin, J. L., Principles of Money, Ch. 13; Macleod, H. D., The Theory and Practice of Banking, Vol. I., Ch. 4; Nicholson, J. S., Banker's Money; Scott, W. A., Money and Banking, Chs. 7–9; Walker, F. A., Money, Pt. III.; White, H., Money and Banking, 2d ed., Bk. III.

1. By whom Convertible Paper Notes are Issued. — By convertible paper currency is meant paper for which the party who issues it will pay specie on demand. The holder, therefore, has a medium of payment of the same value as the amount of gold called for, and is saved the inconvenience of handling the metal. Paper payable with any other commodity than specie is not properly called convertible. Such paper may, as a matter of fact, pass in exchange for gold, or goods, without depreciation; but the cause of its so passing is not that it is secured by land, goods, or what not.

As to its origin, convertible paper is usually put out by banks. Sometimes, however, it is a government issue, like our own United States notes or greenbacks, at the present time. In the latter case, the action of the government in issue and redemption partakes of the nature of banking, and the government is said by critics of this service to be in the banking business.

Convertible paper currency, when issued by a government, may be put out against the specific deposit of a sum of gold, or silver, as the case may be, equal to the amount called for by the notes and actually held on deposit for their redemption; or it may be issued without specific pledge, on the general credit of the government. The former notes are really certificates of deposit, of the nature of warehouse receipts, and constitute what is called representative money in this book. The gold and silver certificates issued by the United States Treasury are good examples of this kind of paper. In the case of treasury notes, like the greenbacks, the government does not keep specie equal to the value of the outstanding issues, nor does it retire the notes when presented for redemption or in payment of public dues. It treats them as money, paying them out again in discharge of its obligations, but guarantees their redemption in metallic money on demand, and keeps on hand a certain amount of specie for this purpose.

2. The Advantages of Government Convertible Currency. — The advantages to the people, of the use of government convertible currency, are those common to all paper money: the saving of capital in the production of gold and silver, the prevention of wear of the coins, and the greater convenience of paper. The advantage to the government is the fiscal one of securing a certain amount of revenue without resorting to ordinary forms of taxation. Over against this fiscal advantage must be set the expense of getting and maintaining the specie reserve necessary to insure prompt redemption of the notes. This expense increases the more frequent and large the presentation of notes for redemption. Moreover, the likelihood of frequent and voluminous redemption endangers the whole system of government note issue. For the specie reserve cannot be quickly increased to meet unusual demands. It can be enlarged only from taxation, or from the sale of bonds; but taxation, aside from being too slow to answer the purpose, would have to be increased to meet the extra payments and would thus wipe out the profit of note issue. The sale of bonds would be open to the same objections. The interest charges would very likely be much greater than any profit arising from the paper issues.

In order to avoid the danger of being confronted with a demand for redemption beyond the power of the treasury to meet, the amount of convertible paper is usually limited by law. This limitation, together with the mode of issue, deprives government paper of the power automatically to vary in volume with the need of business men for currency. The treasury notes are put out in payment of government dues; they cannot be put into circulation as loans to people who need more money to carry on trade. Hence they lack a very important characteristic which attaches to convertible paper issued under suitable provisions by banks. Government paper does not possess the quality of elasticity; bank paper does.

3. Convertible Bank Paper. — A bank note is a note given out by a bank, promising to pay in standard, or in legal-tender, money, the amount specified on its face. These notes get into circulation in this way: a customer may deposit metallic money with his bank and receive in exchange the more convenient notes; or, more commonly, he may give his own promissory note, or a bill of exchange to his banker, and receive in exchange the notes of the bank. In doing this he exchanges his own credit for that of the bank. Being a merchant, for example, he has incurred debts which he cannot at the moment pay. He could offer his creditors his promissory notes; but they, like him, are in debt, and want a medium of payment which they can pass on to their creditors in turn. His credit is not well enough established, or known, to admit of his notes passing current. But it is well known at the bank, and that of the bank is well established throughout the community in which the circle of indebtedness just described prevails. Hence the promissory notes of the bank will be accepted widely in payment. Therefore the merchant in question exchanges his promissory notes for those of the bank in convenient denominations, and with them pays his debts. The process is simply an exchange of credit of narrow circulation, or acceptability, for credit of wider circulation or acceptability. The bank notes therefore pass from hand to hand and perform the services of exchange, as does standard money. Of course the bank keeps on hand a sufficient reserve of specie to redeem these notes as they are presented to it.

Bank notes are now commonly issued in the second way described, that is, by way of discount. Business men in need of cash take their promissory notes, or bills, to the bank. The bank buys these with its own notes, charging for the exchange the interest on the amount at current rates for the period during which the customer's notes run. This charge is collected in advance and is called discount, and the process is known as discounting the customer's notes or bills. The term "discounts" is also applied to the advances thus made by the bank.

4. The Meaning of the Term "Elasticity" as applied to Convertible Paper Currency. — It is evident that the amount of the bank's discounts is determined by the volume of the notes and bills offered by its customers for bank notes. That volume depends, in turn, on the need of business men for currency. Hence the note issues of the bank are ultimately fixed by the demand of the business of the community, and vary with this demand. This power of bank notes to adjust their volume to the need for currency is called elasticity.

The exact meaning, the desirability, and, indeed, the existence of what is called elasticity have long been much disputed. It was the debate on this topic, and on its corollary doctrine of the true theory of the management of paper issues, which occurred in England during the second decade of the nineteenth century that gave to the world the famous Report of the Bullion Committee; and, a little later, a series of papers on the subject unsurpassed for the brilliancy and exhaustiveness of their treatment. By elasticity is commonly meant the quality of a body by virtue of which it can resume its previous size and shape, when these have been changed by temporary pulling or compression. If applied strictly to money, the term, accordingly, should mean that the existing volume of money should do more service under the tension of additional demand, and less on the relaxation of demand. As ordinarily used, however, elasticity of money means the power of the volume of money to increase and decrease with changing demand. These two meanings are not the same, and some confusion has arisen from failure to notice their difference. The difficulty arises from using the terms of physics in connections where their use can be only figurative.

When a demand for money becomes more intense at one place than at another, under a system of metallic money, the metal leaves the place of less intense for that of more intense demand. Its total quantity, however, is not increased. Under a system of convertible paper, an increased local demand for money is met by the issue of *more* paper, not by the transfer of some from another place. If we are to resort to physical analogies, the proper term for the characteristic under discussion would be fluidity, or mobility, in the case of the metallic money, and variability of volume in the case of paper. The so-called elasticity of gold money means a changed distribution; that of paper money implies a larger or smaller volume than before, in some place or places, but not at the expense of the supply of any other place. Metallic money has fluidity, not elasticity; convertible paper money has fluidity only to the extent that it flows to its centres of redemption and not to centres of demand for money, if this demand is elsewhere than at the points of redemption. If, then, either kind of money has elasticity, in the sense of variability of volume under pressure, it is convertible paper. It is the possibility and desirability of this quality of variability over and above, or otherwise than, that of metallic money that has been the subject of warm discussion in the theory of convertible paper money.

5. On the Desirability of Elasticity.—Of the desirability of having a currency that is elastic, or variable in volume, rather than merely fluid, or mobile, there is little doubt. There are certain local needs for an increased amount of money, dependent on the seasons and the kind of industry. The seasonal demands of agricultural communities have long been well known. With an elastic currency, like bank credits, these demands can be met without an extra strain on the money supply elsewhere, and without the expense of transferring specie. Bank notes serve the purpose better than deposits subject to check, because the people who want the seasonal extra supply of currency are too far from banks; they receive and spend sums too small to make their accounts profitable to a bank, and they are more or less unaccustomed to the business procedure connected with keeping active bank accounts. The currency is wanted largely to pay wages and small accounts.

It is urged by those who oppose elasticity of the medium of exchange, that these local and seasonal demands do not occur everywhere at the same time; that when the demand for the medium of exchange at one place is strong, it is weak at some other place. Hence, it is argued, no addition to the currency, but simply a transfer of part of it, is necessary. There is some force in this statement, but the fact that money may flow from a place of slack demand to one of intenser demand does not disprove the advisability of supplying additional currency, unless it can be shown that the amount transferred is sufficient, without causing strain elsewhere. Moreover, the expense of transfer may be greater than that of additional local bank issues, and the necessary supply should come by transfer only if that be less expensive; otherwise, additional issues should be made.

It is also urged that the stronger demand for money will cause a greater rapidity of circulation of the existing money supply, and therefore make an additional supply unnecessary. This is true, provided the increased efficiency of the existing money supply suffices to satisfy the demand. But this argument, like the preceding, simply says that there are other ways of meeting the demand. The reply is that from the variety of ways society will choose the one which is adequate and most effective, its expensiveness being considered.

It is argued further, that no attempt should be made to supply the demand for extra medium of exchange for seasonal and similar reasons, because it is better to let the stringency be felt in order to check speculation. This contention also has some force; but these demands are not always speculative, and in so far as they are not, the argument is beside the point.

6. The Banking Theory and the Currency Theory of Note Issue. — The different opinions held concerning the elasticity of bank notes have given rise to two theories of the proper mode of issue and management of such paper. One theory holds that the paper issues, if kept always convertible, cannot be issued in excess; that, consequently, they cannot depreciate, and that they will, under this condition, behave just as a like amount of metallic money would do, and, with good banking, will always be safe. This is known as the banking theory. According to this theory, if the notes are always kept convertible, and are in fact constantly redeemed in specie, no precaution is necessary to prevent their excessive issue and depreciation, except good banking, the refusal to discount paper which is not wholly good, based on sound trade transactions, and made by men of integrity in business.

Opposed to this view is the theory that bank paper can vary in volume independently of the gold and silver whose place it takes; that it can be put in circulation in excess of the specie which would replace it in a wholly metallic system, because as fast as it is put out it will inflate prices in proportion to its quantity and so cause a demand for additional issues. This is known as the currency theory.

The currency principle insists, contrary to the banking principle, that good banking and constant convertibility are not sufficient to prevent over-issue, depreciation, and inflation; that, on the contrary, the great influence of banks enables them to put their notes into circulation in excess of the specie which these displace; and that consequently the mixed currency of gold and paper will vary in purchasing power in a way different from that which would be shown by the purely metallic currency to whose behavior, according to the theorists of both schools, the mixed paper and gold currency ought to conform. According to this theory, bank currency must, therefore, be regulated so as to prevent its issue in excess of the specie it displaces, or represents. From the view-point of the currency theorist the function of the bank, as a note-issuing agency, is merely to exchange credit for specie and specie for credit. To prevent the issue of notes beyond the specie displaced, the amount must be restricted by requiring some kind of special security.

7. The Power of a Bank to force its Paper into Circulation. — Despite the clearness and conclusiveness of the proof of the truth of the banking principle, and despite its acceptance by most authorities on the subject, it is the currency theory which has in the main been put into practice. The Bank of England, the Reichsbank of Germany, and the national banks of the United States are all organized, as note-issuing institutions, on the currency theory. Their issues are limited and safeguarded by various devices. The Bank of France, on the other hand, is an excellent illustration of an institution founded on the banking principle. The experience of all these banks has furnished evidence so strong as to be conclusive in support of the truth of the banking principle, and the fallacy of its rival. The aim of the banks operated on the currency theory is to exchange paper for gold and gold for paper, to let no paper into circulation except as gold is taken out, and to issue no gold except in exchange for notes paid in, so that the stock of money may be kept exactly the same as it would be if wholly metallic. It is not necessary to quote figures from the history of the currency-theory banks to show that they have not been able to do this; nor to recite all the arguments whereby the Bullion Committee and their adherents proved that it could not be done. These arguments got their color from the fact, which somewhat obscured the points in dispute, that note issue was a far more important form of discount at the time of the great debate than it is now.

At that time it was the note-issuing function of banks that was thought to be their most important social, and their most profitable private, service. The belief in the potency of bank notes to affect the public welfare was long the chief inspiration of bank legislation, and led to the enactment of many laws directed to control the banks in the exercise of this power. Long rows of Blue Books and congressional documents and treatises on this subject fill the shelves of our libraries, silent witnesses to the belief of our fathers and grandfathers that as banks increased, so, too, would grow the importance of this particular function. How different is the fact from the expectation! The check, not the note, is to-day the symbol of banking progress, the instrument of large exchange. On January 22, 1904, the outstanding notes of the national banks of the United States amounted to $380,992,307, while the individual deposits, subject to check, were $3,300,619,898. It is the deposit and the check that we must reckon with to-day. But the change of form of the bank function has not changed its character. When a bank buys a piece of mercantile paper, by discounting a bill of exchange or a promissory note, it creates a debt against itself, whether it gives its customer notes, or credits him on its books. To discount a piece of mercantile paper by issuing notes in payment for it, differs in no respect from discounting the same paper and crediting its seller with a proper amount as a deposit to be drawn out by checks at the convenience of the holder. To ask, therefore, whether a bank can issue its notes in excess is to ask whether it can sell its credit in excess of the demand therefor. The answer of the adherents of the banking principle is in the negative; that if the bank discounts good paper, and meets all demands in it for the redemption of its notes, it cannot issue notes or create deposits to a degree to inflate prices. For banks can sell their credit only by purchasing securities, mercantile or other. Merchants will not borrow unless their business makes borrowing profitable, nor will they continue to pay interest on loans, whether of notes or deposits, longer than they must. Increase of trade, and of the volume of payments, is not caused by an enlarged demand for currency; the enlarged demand for currency is a consequence of the larger volume of business. To say that currency can be issued in excess of the demands of business is therefore to reverse cause and effect. If business grows and the volume of payments to be made enlarges, more means of exchange must be obtained to settle obligations, whether the currency in use be specie or paper, and the increase of the medium of exchange would come in either case. There can be no difference. It is true that banks sometimes lend incautiously, that they sometimes discount paper based on hazardous undertakings, and that the stimulation of industry of which such enterprises are the cause and the sign is followed by, or accompanied by, an increase in the emission of bank paper. But this larger emission is a response to the demand for increased means of payment which such enterprises create. An expansion of bank credits can come, therefore, only as a result of an expanded demand and a higher price scale, and they cannot exceed in amount the specie they represent, for this is the amount needed to do business on the higher price scale.

The proper means of preventing enlarged emissions is to prevent the unhealthful stimulation of trade which causes them. True, it may be said that the inability to secure a larger volume of currency would check the unsound business undertakings. But it would also check new enterprises that were legitimate and sound. The limitation of issues in order to prevent inflation from unsafe enterprises would at the same time deprive the community of the very important advantages which elasticity of the currency confers. It is an act of questionable wisdom to cure one set of ills by creating others, when the good can be obtained in other ways without incurring the harm. Moreover, the banker's interest works against over-issue. If he grants credit in excess of the legitimate need of business for it, the excess will return to him, for deposit at interest, or, failing that, for exchange into specie. He will therefore subject himself to loss.

8. Some Practical Considerations which modify the Above Conclusions. — Such is the reasoning of the banking theory, and it is without a logical flaw. Experience tells us, however, that banking is not always sound and careful; that men are sometimes carried away by extravagant expectations of business growth; that banks and bankers can, and do, stimulate this speculative feeling by making discounts easy and by lending on business ventures that have no substantial basis of success; that men are not always careful to insist on the instant and full convertibility of bank notes; that banks can sometimes create a feeling in the community against insistence on convertibility; and that, in consequence of all these facts, bank issues of notes or of deposits may possibly exceed the due needs of legitimate business, and subject the community to the evils of a depreciated currency. For this reason some strength is lent to the demand that measures be taken to prevent the undue expansion of bank credits, of whatever form; and although, as we have seen, there is no difference in character between bank notes and bank deposits, considered as forms of credit, nor in the principles which should guide banks in regulating them, their behavior after issue may differ so much as to make different treatment necessary.

The banking principle may be safely relied on for the control of the vast and ever changing accumulation of bank deposits, the result of the discount of commercial paper. The world over, these deposits are the property of people who are keen and able in the protection of their own interests. The depositor chooses his bank and the form of credit which he will take from it. He is in a position to judge, with at least reasonable certainty, of the soundness of his bank and the character of its management. He is in close touch with it, he can close his account with it at short notice, with little trouble. Deposit currency, in short, is perfectly suited to a commercial community, with its highly organized business relations, the close contiguity of its members, and its rapid means of communication. For these conditions, which are the very ones that need and favor a currency of the highest mobility, furnish at the same time protection against its possible evils.

The case of note issues is somewhat different. The notes, if they are to answer their purpose, will frequently, indeed usually, come into the hands of people who have no means of judging whether they are good or bad, and may never have heard of the bank which put them out. It will not do to say that people are not obliged to take bank notes, because to refuse them would be, in many instances, to injure themselves in a business way.

Wage-earners, for example, would find it rather hard to refuse such paper. But it is precisely the economically helpless in such matters who are most commonly the victims of fraud or error. For these reasons the note form of bank credit, if abused by bad management or over-confidence, is likely to do more harm than is the deposit form. "In a country where there is one chief bank, possessing an immense capital and unbounded confidence, the notes of such a bank, even if payable in gold, may be issued to such an extent as to cause an advance in prices, until an unfavorable course of the exchange shall cause payment of the notes to be demanded in gold."[1] The same condition may be brought about where the banks of issue are numerous and possess the confidence of the community. The notes get into the hands of people who have no interest in demanding redemption. They are scattered through the community in comparatively small amounts, so that an individual holder would gain nothing by depositing his holdings. Moreover, the trouble of making the deposits, where population is scattered, would act as a check on contraction. These conditions are more likely to be found in an agricultural community than elsewhere, and probably had much to do with the inflation caused by the wretched issues of our earlier state banks.

Practical necessities, therefore, justify the demand for some safeguarding of convertible bank

[1] Gilbart, "History, Principles, and Practice of Banking," Vol. I., p. 150.

paper, the need for which the economic principle correctly enough denies. The theory is sound and its principle is the one which must be followed to enable banks to accomplish the purpose of their existence. But human nature and some social conditions may interfere with its operation, and some people who are expected to be guided by it may occasionally find their temporary interests promoted, or apparently promoted, by violating it. The public evils that flow from its violation, or from friction in its working, justify the community in insisting on safeguards against them. On these grounds only can be found any defence for the claims of the currency principle that note issues should in some way be regulated by law.

9. Provision of Proper Safeguards for Note Issue. — All these arguments, however, do not justify the requirement of the currency theorists that the amount of convertible paper currency should be fixed by law. They justify merely the insistence on safeguards which will leave issues free for all legitimate business needs, while providing against the evil effects of expansion to meet illegitimate needs. The arguments justify regulation, not *a priori* definite limitation. For the legislator cannot determine beforehand what issues are proper and what are not. He must leave that to the banker to decide as occasion arises. The banker must be left unhampered to extend his credit, whether by note issues or deposits, to whatever amount is called for by the securities created by commercial transactions, and presented to him for discount. The owners of the securities, the business men of the community, are the best judges of what form should be taken by the bank credit which they want. The only interference which is economically justifiable, then, is the institution of proper safeguards against the abuse of the credit-issuing power of banks, and against the evil effects of this abuse on the public when it occurs. The whole matter has to do, not with limitation, but with the insistence that the banker shall regulate his note issues properly.

10. Regulation of Note Issues by limiting their Volume. — There are many methods of regulating convertible note issues in the interest of safety, but the principal ones may be grouped into these classes: those which act directly on the notes; those which, without limiting the volume of issue, provide for its safety by acting on the reserve; those which provide special security, apart from the reserve; and those which support the notes simply with the general credit of the issuer.

The plan of regulation which acts directly on the notes consists merely in fixing a maximum limit to their volume. The theory of this limitation is that a certain amount of money is always needed by the business community; that this amount, of whatever kind of currency it may consist, will always be equivalent to gold, because it never exceeds the demand for money on the prevailing scale of prices. This money, it is said, may as well be paper, since there will never be any call for its conversion into gold to any large extent, and the other kinds of currency in use furnish all the leeway necessary to accommodate changes in trade and in demand for specie for export. It is on this principle that the government of Canada supplies the small bills current in daily business, and restricts the bank to the issue of notes of denominations of over five dollars. Our own greenbacks now occupy a somewhat similar place in our monetary system. The objection to this mode of regulation has already been set forth in the criticism of the currency theory. The currency thus furnished has no elasticity, and no real correspondence with the demands of trade.

11. Regulation of Note Issues by controlling Reserve. — The second group of methods for regulating convertible paper money consists of those which operate on the reserve, instead of directly on the issues. The law may require banks to protect their notes by keeping on hand a fixed minimum amount of specie, or a stock of specie equal to the notes afloat, or equal to a certain proportion of these notes. Instead of specie, the law may require the holding of a reserve of securities, as bonds, stocks, and commercial paper. The amount of these paper securities may be, as in the case of a specie reserve, a fixed minimum, or equal to the whole issue, or to a certain proportion of it. As Professor Jevons has pointed out, these methods of regulation may be combined in various ways.

12. The Minimum Reserve Method.—The minimum reserve method of regulation, which requires that a fixed amount of specie shall be on hand at all times, whatever the amount of notes afloat, is prejudicial to good management, and under some conditions affords but slight protection. The purposes of a reserve are to protect the bank against danger of failure to redeem its obligations, and to afford relief to people who need money when it is hard to get. If, however, the bank be required to keep its reserve intact, these purposes are defeated at the time when the need for their accomplishment is greatest. Such a plan virtually means that banks must redeem their obligations until their reserves fall to a certain point, and must not do so beyond that point. It may, of course, be said that the bank is legally and morally bound to keep its reserve at sufficient height to preclude the danger of its falling to the fixed minimum. Yet there is a certain inconsistency in saying that a reserve sufficient for all demands must always be kept; but if it should not be sufficient, then redemption must cease. It is like telling a boat load of shipwrecked people that they may row for the shore while they have two oars, but must cease their efforts if one of them is lost or broken. Such a restriction on redemption would very likely increase the difficulties of the community in a time of business distress. If, at such a time, the reserve held against the notes approaches the minimum fixed by law, the fear of some people that the notes they have may not be redeemed will cause a sudden increase of the demand for redemption, and precipitate the evil the reserve is designed to prevent.

13. Proportional Reserve Method. — Similar objections may be made to the proportional reserve method. A demand for the payment of a considerable amount of notes may reduce the reserve to a quantity equal to the legal proportion of the notes still left in circulation. In that case no more could be paid, and the proportional reserve would be virtually a fixed minimum reserve. For example, if the amount of notes in circulation is $60,000, and the reserve required by law is one-third of the issue, or $20,000, the redemption of $15,000 of the notes would reduce the outstanding amount to $45,000; but the reserve would be lessened by a similar amount and would become $5000, an amount less than the legal requirement. Whatever advantage the proportional reserve method has over that of a minimum reserve comes from fixing the reserve at a high proportion of the total issue. But while a large reserve would better insure the safety of the notes, it would *pari passu* defeat the main purpose of using paper, namely, the saving of investment in metallic money.

14. Simple Deposit Method. — The plan of keeping on hand a stock of specie equal to the whole amount of notes issued, known as the simple deposit method, gives the notes the character of warehouse receipts, or certificates of deposit, which have been already described. Such paper is certainly safe if the warehouse man is honest; but it possesses none of the advantages claimed for bank money, except the mere saving of the wear of the coins. Moreover, under an autocratic government, or a government which can control the management of the bank of issue, such a stock of specie is a sore temptation to the authorities in times of treasury distress. Historical instances of the seizure of such deposits are not wanting. Those of the Bank of Amsterdam were secretly loaned to the government of Holland prior to the French invasion of 1795. The English government borrowed the gold of the Bank of England in 1797 by causing a suspension of specie payments; and that of France took a similar step with reference to the specie in the Bank of France in 1870.

15. The Partial Deposit Method. — By what Jevons has called the partial deposit system, a certain part of the notes are issued against stocks, bonds, and other securities, and further issues must be protected by the deposit of specie, dollar for dollar. This is the method employed by the Bank of England, which is permitted by law to put out a maximum of £17,500,000 [1] of notes on the security of government bonds. One advantage

[1] The amount was originally £14,000,000, but has been increased by the lapsed circulation of country banks which have ceased to issue notes.

of this system is that as the amount of outstanding notes increases, the proportion of specie reserve to the whole issue increases, and thus insures greater safety to the whole. But this safety is obtained at the expense, to some extent, of whatever advantage in the way of elasticity is furnished by bank notes proper.

16. The Bond-deposit Method.—Under the bond-deposit system the notes are secured by the stocks and bonds of governments. The notes of the national banks of the United States are thus secured. The banks are required by law to purchase bonds of the United States with their capital stock. These bonds are deposited with the treasurer of the United States at Washington, and the banks receive in return notes equal in amount to the par value of the bonds, but not in excess of their market value, nor of the capital stock of the bank.

There are several serious objections to the plan of securing note issues with public stocks. In the first place, the bond security, by itself, does not insure convertibility in the proper sense. It provides for ultimate redemption, but not for that immediate payment in gold, on demand, which is essential to business. Our own national bank notes may be paid in treasury notes, and these in turn may be presented to the treasury for gold. Evidently the bank notes command gold only so long as the treasury notes do so. Hence, our bank notes are convertible, not because their redemption as bank notes is properly provided for, but because the government is solvent. However, even if the law did not provide for the payment of national bank notes with government paper; if, in other words, the banks were required to redeem their notes directly in gold, the possession of bonds and other securities would not be a guarantee of their ability to do so, nor a sure means of enabling them to do so. The bonds would have to be sold to get gold to pay the notes. At a time of monetary stringency the holders of the notes present them to get gold because the need for the metal is great. If the banks must sell their securities to get this gold, the price of the securities is likely to be forced down, and that of gold raised, at a time when the need for it is greatest.

A second objection to the bond-deposit system is that the purchase of the bonds uses the real capital of the bank in procuring its notes by investment, instead of leaving it free for discounting commercial paper, which is the purpose for which the bank is organized.

Further, a system of bond-secured issues is inelastic. The volume of notes depends primarily on the price of bonds, and not on the amount of commercial paper offered for discount. If business is expanding and the need for currency becomes greater, it can be supplied only by buying bonds. But the briskness of business which causes the demand for more currency also raises the prices of bonds, so that their purchase as a basis for new issues is less profitable. When business is dull, the prices of bonds fall and lead to an increased output of notes, although the need for more is less. Moreover, the enlargement and contraction of the circulation under this system is not immediate and automatic. Administrative machinery must first be put in motion, and this usually requires so much time that the pressure of demand may pass before it can be met.

Still further, under the bond-security system of note issue, the expansion and contraction of the currency may be adversely affected by local rates of discount. If the price of bonds is low, places in which the rate of discount is low may find it more profitable to buy bonds as a basis of further note issue; while other places, in which the rate of discount is high, and in which, therefore, there is need of an expansion of the currency, may find it less profitable to purchase bonds than to use their capital as an immediate basis of discount.

The compulsory investment of bonds under circumstances like the above, constitutes in effect a forced loan from the community where interest is high to one where interest is low. Those who are in need of all their capital are compelled, in other words, to share its use with people who are in less need than themselves.

Nor are notes secured by the deposit of bonds necessarily safer than issues based on a partial metallic reserve. For if the credit of the government is impaired, its bonds will sink in price, and the security will be lessened. "The issue of notes against deposited securities did not save the note-holders from loss before the war, while careful and intelligent systems of banking like those of Louisiana, Massachusetts, and the state banks of Indiana and Ohio did protect them fully."[1] Of course, these remarks about the safety of notes secured by government bonds lose much of their force in the case of a strong and wealthy popular government like our own. There is certainly no more danger — most of us will say far less — that the safety of our national bank notes will be imperilled by impaired national credit than there would be if their management were left wholly to the banks that issue them.

The bond-deposit system of security is also objectionable because it makes necessary a permanent public debt. The rapid retirement of United States bonds available as a basis of circulation has at times raised a question as to the permanence of our system of note issue. Indeed, resort to other kinds of bonds has at times been urged, such as bonds of states and cities, and of great corporations. Such a step is to be deprecated. No matter how great the care with which such bonds may be chosen, public confidence in them would never be so great as in those of the national government, and trust in our bank paper could not fail to be shaken by their use.

17. The Safety-fund Method.— Notes may also

[1] Horace White, *Annals Amer. Acad.*, March, 1893, p. 20.

be kept convertible by the creation of a common fund of specie by contribution from the note-emitting banks. This fund, called a safety fund, is deposited with some public officer, the Comptroller of the Currency, for example, and out of it are redeemed the notes of any banks which fail. If the fund is impaired by such redemptions, it must be restored by further contributions. The experience of forty years with our present national banking system has shown that the fund which would have been required to cover the losses on notes, caused by all the failures of the period, could have been provided by a tax of about one-fifth of one per cent. per annum on the circulation. A fund which would fully insure the safety of the notes could therefore be created and maintained by so small a tax on circulation that no bank could reasonably object to it.

The safety-fund system leaves the volume of notes absolutely free to respond to business needs for currency; it would leave the capital stock of the banks free for ordinary banking business, and it would provide as safe a currency as does our present system.

18. Notes issued on General Assets. — If no special provision is made for the security of notes, but they are treated simply as one of the liabilities of the bank, dependent on its property and general credit, the notes are said to be issued against general assets. This system properly regards notes and deposits subject to check as liabilities of identical character, and aims to provide for the proper protection of both indifferently. With good banking, this system is scientifically perfect; but, as has been pointed out, experience shows that bank managers cannot, any more than other industrial leaders, always be depended upon for unerring sagacity and continued honesty. Hence, bad banking occurs, and would be likely to cause greater hardship in case of a failure, under a system of asset issue. As a precaution, it is frequently proposed to make the notes a first lien on the assets. Doubtless this additional security would in most cases suffice. For the notes are becoming a much smaller proportion of total liabilities, because the growth of deposits, against which checks are drawn, is more rapid than the growth of notes. It is difficult, however, to convince the public that this is the case; and in the matter of note issue the establishment of public confidence is absolutely essential.

19. The Advantages of Combining Several Methods. — It is evident that no plan of insuring the immediate payment of notes in specie is free from objection. No plan can be devised for insuring escape from reliance, somewhere in the management, on the integrity and faithfulness of men. Two purposes, incompatible in their nature, are aimed at by every scheme for regulating bank credits. One is to secure for society the saving afforded by dispensing with gold; the other is to avoid the dangers of inflation and depreciation that accompany the use of paper. Now, it is idle to expect that the full benefits can be obtained at the same time that all of the danger is avoided. One might as well expect to secure the rapid transportation furnished by a modern express train, and at the same time suffer no greater loss or injury from its wreck than one would suffer if travelling in an ox cart that lost its wheel. The benefits of complicated machinery cannot be had without incurring risks of greater loss than was experienced under simpler conditions, when the storm and stress of life break upon the more complex arrangements of society. All that we can reasonably ask is to secure a balance of advantage and risk of loss. In the matter of paper money it is far better to aim at a small portion of the advantages of its use, and run but little risk of loss, than to try to secure a large advantage at great risk. For in case of the failure of any bank to pay its notes on demand, the loss falls on many innocent people, and is likely to be distributed much more widely than is the case with the benefits during a period of successful management.

In view of these facts, that system of management of bank issues is best which minimizes the danger of loss, whether by restricting the issues well within the limits of safety or by insisting on the provision of an adequate reserve. On the other hand, there is such a thing as making the notes too good. If they are put wholly beyond the risk of loss, their elasticity is interfered with.

While business people who receive notes will deposit them for the sake of receiving interest, this motive is of small force when the amount to be deposited is small. In such a case the paper is just as likely to be kept on hand by numerous small holders, if they feel that there is no danger at all that it will not be redeemed. If there are any notes which are not protected by their equivalent in metallic money, there is some risk. This danger is more or less, according to the amount of metallic reserve held. The amount left unprotected should be large enough to remind holders that it is to their interest constantly to demand redemption.

A specie reserve should actually be held somewhere. It is sometimes said that the reserve should be made profitable by investment, for example, in government bonds. But if it is so used, it is no longer a specie reserve. It is idle to try to devise a plan whereby a specie reserve can be kept for the purpose of redeeming notes, and used for profit at the same time. The two things are incompatible. There is no way of making a profit on idle capital, and money kept for reserve is idle capital; or, at any rate, capital which is productive only in an indirect way. It is productive only in the sense that it makes the employment of the rest of the capital safer, or lessens the probability of a loss.

20. Comparative Advantages and Disadvantages of Government and Bank Issues. — We have seen that paper money may be issued either by banks or governments. If the notes issued are generally acceptable, they will serve the purpose of a medium of exchange. Several reasons are advanced, however, against the exercise of the function of issue by governments. In the first place, it is argued that the issue of paper money is not a proper function of the government. We cannot here go into a discussion of the proper sphere of government, and it is well not to dogmatize about it. Whether or not the statement is true depends on one's ideas as to what are the proper functions of government. It may be said, however, without fear of successful contradiction, that the experience of governments that have issued paper money has been so generally disastrous as to establish in a high degree the improbability of success in maintaining the notes convertible at par in times of fiscal exigency. Experience, therefore, is against government issues. The argument that the issue of paper money is equivalent to coinage, and therefore is a sovereign function to be exercised by the government, is based on a wrong notion of the nature of coinage. The coinage of specie and the engraving of paper money differ in a very important particular, and that, too, a particular which justifies us in calling the issue of one a sovereign function and that of the other not so. Notes are a species of credit instruments ; gold is not. For the government to go into the business of issuing paper money is, therefore, to draw on its credit, and to lay itself open to the possibility of financial weakness in times of sudden fiscal stress. In performing the function of coinage proper, governments incur no liability; in issuing notes, they do.

The likelihood of excessive issues is greater with government paper than with bank issues. Officers of the government are likely to be influenced to issue paper money beyond the needs of business, by the necessities of the public treasury, or by public clamor, or by the ignorance and corruption of lawmakers. Yet it is also true that bankers have sometimes yielded to the same temptation for their own profit. It may be fairly said that, as a rule, we can expect as much honesty in the management of our public finances as has been shown by private corporations that have had the privilege of issuing paper money. It would be rash to say that the distress caused by our own early banking, or by the depreciation of Bank of England notes previously to 1819, was less than the evils caused over equal periods from excessive government issues. Therefore, no argument for or against government issues, founded on the honesty or efficiency of the government as compared with private corporations, is of much permanent weight. There is, however, a very strong argument in favor of private issues in the fact that they should come out in response to business demand, that the amount of notes should adapt itself to the need of the country for currency. It is easy enough for government issues to expand, but very difficult for them to contract. Hard measures, such as bond sales or higher taxes, are usually needed for contraction. But neither of these methods is directly related to business ; and contraction, when it comes, may be either more or less than business requires.

It has been suggested, even by so high an authority as Ricardo,[1] that a government commission for the regulation of paper money might successfully vary the currency in response to the ebb and flow of business demand. This, of course, is possible, provided that this commission acted as bankers. It is likely, however, that people would rely too much on such a commission, and so encourage speculation. The work which Ricardo proposes for such a commission is, of course, very different from what is in the minds of those people who propose a commission to vary the currency for the purpose of keeping the price level constant.

It is sometimes urged against private bank issues, that the conferring of the power of issue on banks is likely to create a money power whose interests run contrary to those of the people at large. This argument is not to be altogether ridiculed. It certainly is not true that the interests of the banks and the interests of the people are always identical. In a higher sense, indeed, they are so, in the long run, but at particular times they may be opposite. But this is really an argument for controlling banks, not for forbidding them to issue notes. Cer-

[1] Works, McCulloch's ed., p. 219.

tainly no one's rights are curtailed and no harm is done by a proper regulation of the power of issue. The gain allowed banks of issue for their services to the public should not be excessive, and they should be so restricted by law as to be continually reminded that they are in a measure public institutions bound to care for the public interests as well as for the interests of their private stockholders.

While, then, we may not admit that governments cannot take care of the interests of their people, even in the matter of the issue of paper money, it is better not to rely too much on their intelligence and wisdom in such a matter. We should aim to secure to the country as much as possible of the gain from the use of paper money, while avoiding as much as possible of the loss that comes from its excessive use. It is easier for the government to control the banks in their issues than it is to manage the business itself.

BIBLIOGRAPHY

Aldrich, W. Money and Credit. New York, 1903.

Alison, A. England in 1815 and 1845; or a Sufficient and Contracted Currency. 2d ed. Edinburgh, 1845.

Allard, A. Graphiques de la Crise Monétaire et de la Baisse des Prix, 1850–1892. Bruxelles, 1892.

Anon. A Discourse concerning the Currency of the British Plantations in America. Boston, 1740. Reprint, London, 1751.

Ansell, G. F. The Royal Mint. London, 1870.

—— Treatise on Coinage. London, 1862.

Appleton, N. Remarks on Finance and Banking. 3d ed. Boston, 1837.

Arendt, O. Die vertragsmässige Doppelwährung. Berlin, 1880.

—— Der Währungsstreit in Deutschland. Eine Antwort auf Erwin Nasse's gleichnamige Schrift. Berlin, 1886.

Arnauné, A. La Monnaie, le Crédit et le Change. 2d ed. Paris, 1902.

Auspitz, R., und Lieben, R. Untersuchungen über die Theorie des Preises. Leipzig, 1889.

Austin, W. On the Imminent Depreciation of Gold and how to avoid Loss. London, 1853.

Babelon, E. Les Origines de la Monnaie. Paris, 1897.

MONEY

Bagehot, W. The Depreciation of Silver. London, 1877.
—— A Practical Plan for assimilating the English and American Money as a Step toward a Universal Money. 2d ed. London, 1889.
—— Lombard Street. A Description of the Money Market. 10th ed. New York, 1892.
Bain, F. W. The Corner in Gold; its History and Theory. Oxford, 1893.
Baird, H. C. Money and Bank Credit. Philadelphia, 1891.
Bamberger, L. Reichsgold. Studien über Währung und Wechsel. Leipzig, 1876.
—— Die Schicksale des Lateinischen Münzbundes. Ein Beitrag zur Währungspolitik. Berlin, 1885.
Barbour, D. The Theory of Bimetallism and the Effects of the Partial Demonetization of Silver on England and India. London, 1886.
Barclay, R. The Silver Question and the Gold Question. 4th ed. London, 1894.
—— Disturbance in the Standard of Value. 2d ed. London, 1893.
Beaure, A. Théorie et Pratique de la Monnaie. 2 vols. Paris, 1898.
Berkey, W. A. The Money Question. Grand Rapids, Michigan, 1876.
Bever, C. F. Die Frage des Geldes und Silbers und ihrer Währungen. Magdeburg, 1880.
Biedermann, E. Die Statistik der Edelmetalle. Berlin, 1898.
Le Blanc, M. Traité Historique des Monnoyes de France, avec leurs Figures, depuis le Commencement de la Monarchie jusqu' à Présent. Paris, 1690.
Boissevain, G. M. The Monetary Question. London and New York, 1891.

BIBLIOGRAPHY

Bonnet, V. La Depréciation de l'Argent et la Question Monétaire. Paris, 1875.

Bosanquet, J. W. Metallic, Paper, and Credit Currency. London, 1842.

Breckenridge, S. P. Legal Tender; a Study in English and American Monetary History. Chicago, 1903.

Bronson, H. An Historical Account of Connecticut Currency, Continental Money, and the Finances of the Revolution. New Haven, 1865.

—— The Money Problem. New Haven, 1877.

Brough, W. Open Mints and Free Banking. New York, 1898.

—— The Natural Law of Money. New York, 1896.

Brückner, A. Finanzgeschichtliche Studien. Kupfergeldkreisen. St. Petersburg, 1867.

Brüel, L. A. Materialien für die zu erwartende Reform des deutschen Münzwesens. Hannover, 1831.

Bullock, C. J. Essays on the Monetary History of the United States. New York, 1900.

Bulow-Cummerow. Das normale Geldsystem in seiner Anwendungen auf Preussen. Berlin, 1846.

Burck, H. A. Beiträge zur Währungsfrage. Düsseldorf, 1880.

Burckhardt-Bischoff, A. Die Lateinische Münz-Convention und der Internationale Bimetallismus. Basel, 1886.

Büsch, J. G. Abhandlung von dem Geldumlauf in anhaltender Rücksicht auf die Staatswirthschaft und Handlung. 2 vols. Hamburg und Kiel, 1800.

Cairnes, J. E. Essays in Political Economy, Theoretical and Applied. London, 1873.

Cannon, J. G. Clearing Houses. New York, 1900.

MONEY

Carlile, W. W. The Evolution of Modern Money. New York, 1901.

Casasus, J. D. Le Problême Monétaire et la Conférence Monétaire Internationale de Bruxelles. Paris, 1893.

Cernuschi, H. Nomisma, or Legal Tender. New York, 1877.

—— M. Michel Chevalier et la Bimetallism. Paris, 1876.

—— La Monnaie Bimétallique. Paris, 1876.

Chalmers, G. Considerations on Commerce, Bullion, and Coin. London, 1811.

Chalmers, R. A History of Currency in the British Colonies. London, 1893.

Cheap Money Experiments in Past and Present Times. Reprints from the Century Magazine. New York, 1892.

Chevalier, M. Cours d'Économie Politique. v. 3, La Monnaie. Paris, 1866.

—— On the Probable Fall in the Value of Gold, the Commercial and Social Consequences which may Ensue, and the Measures which it Invites. Translated from the French, with preface, by Richard Cobden. New York, 1859.

Clarke, F. W. Weights, Measures, and Money of all Nations. New York, 1888.

Cobb, A. S. Threadneedle Street; a Reply to Lombard Street. London, 1891.

Cobbett, W. Paper against Gold. New York, 1844.

Coffin, G. M. Silver from 1849 to 1892. Washington, 1892.

Cooper, P. Ideas for a Science of Good Government in Addresses, Letters, and Articles on a strictly National Currency, Tariff, and Civil Service. 2d ed. New York, 1883.

BIBLIOGRAPHY

Cornwell, W. C. Sound Money Monographs. New York, 1897.

—— The Currency and Banking Law of the Dominion of Canada considered with Reference to Currency Reform in the United States. New York, 1895.

Cowperthwait, J. H. Money, Silver, and Finance. New York, 1892.

Crosby, S. S. Early Coins of America. Boston, 1873.

Crump, A. Investigation into the Causes of the Great Fall in Prices which took place coincidently with the Demonetization of Silver in Germany. 1889.

Dalsime, J. La Monnaie : Histoire de l'Or de l'Argent et du Papier. Paris, 1882.

Daniell, C. The Gold Treasure of India. London, 1884.

Darwin, L. Bimetallism. A Summary and Examination of the Arguments for and against a Bimetallic System of Currency. London, 1897.

Davis, A. McF. Currency and Banking in the Province of Massachusetts Bay. 2 vols. Publications of the American Economic Association. Third series, Vols. I.–II. New York, 1900–1901.

—— Tracts relating to the Currency of the Massachusetts Bay, 1682–1720. Boston, 1902.

Del Mar, A. History of Monetary Systems. London, 1895.

—— Money and Civilization. London, 1886.

—— A History of the Precious Metals from the Earliest Times to the Present. London, 1880.

Doubleday, T. A Financial, Monetary, and Statistical History of England. 2 vols. London, 1847.

Dunbar, C. F. Laws of the United States relating to Currency, Finance, and Banking from 1789 to 1891. Boston, 1891.

Edgcumbe, R. P. Popular Fallacies regarding Bimetallism. London, 1896.

Ehrich, L. R. The Question of Silver. New York, 1892.

Elliot, J. Funding System of the United States. Washington, 1845.

Ellstaetter, K. Indian Silver Currency. An Historical and Economic Study. Chicago, 1895.

Evans, G. G. Evans's Illustrated History of the United States Mint; and Descriptions of all American Coins Issued. Revised edition. Philadelphia, 1892.

Farmer, E. J. The Conspiracy against Silver, or a Plea for Bimetallism in the United States. Cleveland, 1886.

Farrer, T. H. What Do We Pay With? London, 1889.

—— Studies in Currency. London, 1898.

Fawcett, W. L. Gold and Debt. Chicago, 1877.

Feer-Herzog, C. Gold oder Silber? Erörterung einer Tagesfrage. Aarau, 1873.

Felt, J. B. An Historical Account of Massachusetts Currency. Boston, 1839.

Ferris, J. A. The Financial Economy of the United States Illustrated, and Some of the Causes which Retard the Progress of California Demonstrated. San Francisco and New York, 1867.

Fisher, I. Appreciation and Interest. Publications of the American Economic Association. Vol. XI., No. 4. New York, 1896.

Fitzgerald, A. L. The Thirty Years' War on Silver. Chicago, 1903.

Fleetwood, W. A Sermon against Clipping. London, 1694.

—— Chronicon Preciosum; or, an Account of English Gold and Silver Money. London, 1745.

Fonda, A. J. Honest Money. New York, 1895.

Forbes, W. A Methodical Treatise concerning Bills of Exchange, etc. Edinburgh, 1718.

Gallatin, A. Considerations on the Currency and Banking System of the United States. Philadelphia, 1831.

—— Suggestions on the Banks and Currency of the Several United States. New York, 1841.

Gibbs, H. H., and **Grenfell, H. R.** The Bimetallic Controversy; a Collection of Pamphlets, Papers, and Speeches and Letters, with Contributions from Others. Reprint from original. London, 1886.

Giffen, R. The Case against Bimetallism. London, 1892.

—— Essays in Finance. First series, 4th ed. London, 1886. Second series, 3d ed. London, 1895.

Gilman, T. Federal Clearing Houses. Boston, 1899.

—— A Graded Banking System. Boston, 1898.

Gordon, A. C. Congressional Money. An Outline of the Federal Money System. New York, 1895.

Goschen, G. J. The Theory of the Foreign Exchanges. 15th ed. London, 1892.

Gouge, W. M. A Short History of Paper Money and Banking in the United States. Philadelphia, 1833.

Graham, J. Coin and Currency. 2d ed. London, 1826.

Gray, J. Lectures on the Nature and Use of Money. Edinburgh, 1848.

Grimaudet, F. Law of Money. New York, 1899.

—— Law of Payment. New York, 1900.

Hallard, J. H. Gold and Silver. An Elementary Treatise on Bimetallism. London, 1897.

Hallock, J. C. Clearing Out-of-Town Checks in England and the United States. St. Louis, 1903.

Hamilton, R. Money and Value. London, 1878.

Hankey, T. Banking. Its Utility and Economy. London, 1860.

—— Principles of Banking. London, 1887.

Harper, J. W. Money and Social Problems. Edinburgh and London, 1896.

Harris, J. An Essay on Money and Coins. London, 1757–1758.

Harvey, J. Paper Money, the Money of Civilization. London, 1877.

Harvey, W. H. Money of the People. Chicago, 1895.

Haupt, O. Arbitrages et Parités. 8th ed. Paris, 1894.

—— Währungs-Politik und Münzstatistik. Berlin, 1884.

—— Die Stellung der Scheidemünze im Deutschen Münzwesen. Vienna, 1878.

—— L'Histoire Monétaire de notre Temps. Paris, 1866.

—— The Monetary Question in 1892. 2d ed. London, 1892.

—— La Réhabilitation de l'Argent. Paris, 1881.

Hawkins, E. The Silver Coins of England, etc. London, 1841.

Hayes, R. The Negotiator's Magazine, or the Most Authentic Account yet published of the Moneys, Weights, and Measures of the Principal Places of Trade. London, 1770.

Hazlitt, W. C. Coinage of the European Continent. New York, 1895.

Helferich, J. von. Von den Periodischen Schwankungen im Werte der edlen Metalle von der Entdeckung Amerikas bis zum Jahre, 1830. Nürnberg, 1843.

Helferich, K. Geschichte der deutsche Geld Reform. Leipzig, 1898.

Helm, E. The Joint Standard. London, 1894.

BIBLIOGRAPHY

Hepburn, A. B. History of Coinage and Currency in the United States. New York, 1903.

Hertzka, T. Währung und Handel. Vienna, 1876.

Hickcox, J. H. An Historical Account of American Coinage. Albany, 1858.

Hildebrand, R. Die Theorie des Geldes. Kritische Untersuchungen. Jena, 1883.

Hill, B. A. Absolute Money. St. Louis, 1875.

Hill, E. Principles of Currency. London, 1856.

Hill, G. F. Handbook of Greek and Roman Coins. New York, 1899.

Hoffman, J. G. Die Lehre vom Gelde. Berlin, 1838.

—— Die Zeichen der Zeit im Deutschen Münzwesen. Berlin, 1841.

Horton, S. D. Silver and Gold and their Relation to the Problem of Resumption. Cincinnati, 1877.

—— Silver in Europe. New York, 1890.

—— The Silver Pound. London, 1887.

—— A Survey of the Diplomatic Aspects of the Silver Question. New York, 1891.

Howarth, W. Our Clearing System and Clearing Houses. 3d ed. London, 1897.

Howe, J. B. Monetary and Industrial Fallacies. Boston, 1878.

—— The Political Economy of Great Britain, the United States, and France in the Use of Money. Boston, 1878.

—— Monometallism and Bimetallism. Boston, 1879.

—— The Common Sense, etc., of Money. Boston, 1881.

Howell, G. A Synopsis of the Final Report of the Royal Commission appointed to inquire into the Recent Changes in the Relative Value of the Precious Metals. London, 1889.

Hucke, J. Die Geld-Verrichtungen in der Preis-Lohn, und Zinsgestaltung. Berlin, 1897.

Indianapolis Monetary Commission. See Laughlin.

International Monetary Conference. Paris, 1878. Washington, 1879.

—— Paris, 1881. Washington, 1887.

—— Paris, 1892. Report of the Commissioners on Behalf of the United States. Washington, 1893.

Jacob, W. An Historical Inquiry into the Production and Consumption of the Precious Metals. 2 vols. London, 1831.

Jenkinson, C., Earl of Liverpool. A Treatise on the Coins of the Realm. London, 1880.

Jevons, W. S. Money and the Mechanism of Exchange. New York, 1889.

—— Investigations in Currency and Finance. London, 1884.

Joplin, T. An Analysis and History of the Currency Question. London, 1832.

Jordan, W. L. The Standard of Value. 6th ed. London, 1896.

Kellogg, E. A New Monetary System. New York, 1868.

Kleser, H. Die deutsche Währungs Reform und ihre Gegner. Köln, 1883.

—— Geld und Währung. Berlin, 1881.

—— Währungs-und Wirtschaftspolitik. Köln, 1885.

Kluber, J. L. Das Münzwesen in Deutschland. Stuttgart und Tübingen, 1828.

Knies, K. Weltgeld und Weltmünzen. Berlin, 1874.

—— Geld und Credit. 2 vols. Berlin, 1876–1885.

Knight, W. F. de, and Tillman, J. F. History of the Currency of the Country. Washington, 1897.

BIBLIOGRAPHY

Knox, J. J. United States Notes. 3d ed. New York, 1892.

Kral, F. Geldwert und Preisbewegung im Deutschen Reichs, 1871–1884. Jena, 1887.

Lahn, J. J. O. Der Kreislauf des Geldes und Mechanismus des Sozial-lebens. Berlin, 1903.

Lalor, J. Money and Morals. London, 1852.

Laughlin, J. L. The History of Bimetallism in the United States. New York, 1900.

—— Report of Monetary Commission of the Indianapolis Convention of Boards of Trade, etc. Chicago, 1898.

—— The Principles of Money. New York, 1903.

Laveleye, E. de. La Monnaie et le Bimetallism International. Paris, 1891.

Law, John. Money and Trade Considered, etc. Glasgow, 1750.

Lees, W. N. The Drain of Silver to the East and the Currency of India. London, 1864.

Lejeune, A. Monnaie, Poids et Mesures des Principaux Pays du Monde. Paris, 1894.

Lenormant, F. Essai sur l'Organization politique et économique de la Monnaie dans Antiquité. Paris, 1863.

Levasseur, E. De la Valeur des Monnaies Romaines. Paris, 1879.

Linderman, H. R. Money and Legal Tender in the United States. New York, 1879.

Lindsay, S. Mc. Die Preisbewegung der Edelmetalle seit 1850. Jena, 1893.

Locke, J. Some Considerations of the Consequences of the lowering of Interest, etc. London, 1692.

Loria, A. Studi sur valore della Moneta. Torino, 1891.

Lotz, W. Die drei Flugschriften über den Münzstreit der sächisschen Albertiner und Ernestiner um 1530. Leipzig, 1893.

Lowndes, W. A Report containing an Essay for the Amendment of the Silver Coins. London, 1695.

Lube, D. G. Argument against the Gold Standard. London, 1832.

Macleod, H. D. Indian Currency. London, 1898.

—— Bimetallism. 2d ed. London, 1894.

McPherson, L. G. Monetary and Banking Problem. New York, 1896.

Malon, M. J. Documents Relatif à la Question Monétaire. 3 vols. Bruxelles, 1874–1880.

Malthus, T. R. The Measure of Value Stated and Illustrated. London, 1823.

Mann, C. A. Paper Money the Root of Evil. New York, 1872.

Mannequin, T. Le Problème Monétaire et la Distribution de la Richesse. Paris, 1879.

Marie, L. Traité Mathématique et Pratique des Opérations Financières. Paris, 1890.

Masayostu, M. Report on the Adoption of the Gold Standard in Japan. Tokyo, 1899.

Mershet, R. An Attempt to explain from Facts the Effect of the Issues of the Bank of England upon its Own Interests, etc. London, 1826.

Meyer, J. Das Geld. Eine National-oekonomische Studie. Vienna, 1872.

—— Theory of the Coin, Coinage, and Monetary System of the World. Translated by Mrs. C. P. Culver. Miscellaneous Documents of 45th Congress, 3d session. Washington, 1878.

Meyer, M. Gold-oder Doppelwährung. Berlin, 1894.

BIBLIOGRAPHY

Mill, J. S. Principles of Political Economy. 2 vols. New York, 1895.

Miller, H. A. Money and Bimetallism. New York, 1898.

Miller, J. W. Distribution of Wealth by Money. London, 1894.

Mills, R. H. The Principles of Currency and Banking. London, 1857.

Mitchell, W. C. A History of the Greenbacks. Chicago, 1903.

Molesworth, G. L. Silver and Gold. Manchester, 1891.

Mommsen, T. Histoire de la Monnaie Romaine, Traduite de l'Allemand par le Duc de Blacas. 3 vols. Paris, 1865.

Morrison, W. H. Observations on the System of Metallic Currency adopted in this Country. London, 1837.

Muhleman, M. L. Monetary Systems of the World. New York, 1895.

Mulhall, M. G. History of Prices since the Year 1850. London, 1885.

Murhard, K. Theorie des Geldes und der Münze. Leipzig, 1817.

Mushet, R. A Series of Tables exhibiting the Gain and Loss to the Fundholder arising from the Fluctuations in the Value of the Currency from 1800–1821. London, 1826.

Nasse, E. Die Demonetisation des Silbers und das Werthverhältniss der edlen Metalle. Berlin, 1876.

Nebenius, F. Der offentliche Credit. Baden, 1820.

Nève, J. Éléments de la Question Monétaire. Brussels, 1894.

Newcomb, S. A Critical Examination of our Financial Policy during the Southern Rebellion. New York, 1865.

Newmarch, W. The New Supplies of Gold. London, 1853.

Nicholson, J. S. Principles of Political Economy. 3 vols. New York, 1893–1901.

—— A Treatise on Money, etc. 5th ed. New York, 1901.

—— Banker's Money. London, 1902.

Niendorf, M. A. Die Goldwährung im Scheitern und der Einzug der Reichspapierwährung. Munich, 1875.

Noel, O. La Question Monétaire et l'Union Latine. Paris, 1882.

Norman, J. H. Complete Guide to the World's Twenty-nine Metal Monetary Systems. London, 1892.

—— A Ready Reckoner of the World's Foreign and Colonial Exchanges. 2d ed. London, 1897.

Noyes, A. D. Thirty Years of American Finance. New York, 1898.

Nys, E. Researches in the History of Economics. London, 1899.

Obst, Georg. Organisation des Zahlungsverkehrs. Stuttgart, 1901. [Pamph.]

Parnell, H. Observations upon the State of Currency in Ireland. Dublin, 1804.

—— Observations on Paper Money, Banking, and Overtrading. London, 1827.

Patterson, R. H. The Economy of Capital, or Gold and Trade. London, 1875.

—— The New Golden Age and Influence of the Precious Metals on the World. 2 vols. Edinburgh and London, 1882.

Peffer, W. A. The Farmer's Side. New York, 1891.

Phillips, H., Jr. Historical Sketches of the Paper Currency of the American Colonies. Roxbury, Mass., 1865.

Phin, J. Common-Sense Currency. New York, 1894.

Poor, H. V. Money and its Laws. New York, 1877.

—— Resumption and the Silver Question. New York, 1878.

Prager, M. Die Währungsfrage in den Vereinigten Staaten von Nordamerika. Stuttgart, 1897.

—— Die Währungs-und Bankreform in den Vereinigten Staaten von Amerika. Berlin, 1900.

Price, B. Currency and Banking. New York, 1876.

Price, L. L. Money and its Relations to Prices. London, 1896.

Probyn, L. C. Indian Coinage and Currency. London, 1897.

Puynode, M. G. Du. De la Monnaie, du Crédit et de l'Impôt. 2 vols. Paris, 1852.

Raguet, C. A Treatise on Currency and Banking. Philadelphia, 1839.

Rauchberg, H. Der Clearing-und Giro-Verkehr. Vienna, 1886.

Ridgeway, W. The Origin of Metallic Currency and Weight Standards. Cambridge, 1892.

Roscher, W. Betrachtungen über die Währungsfrage der deutschen Münzreform. Berlin, 1872.

Rothwell, R. P. Universal Bimetallism and an International Monetary Clearing House. New York, 1896.

—— Bimetallism Explained. London, 1897.

Ruding, R. Annals of the Coinage of Great Britain and its Dependencies. 3d ed. 3 vols. London, 1840.

Russell, H. B. International Monetary Conferences. New York, 1898.

Schaeffle, A. E. Für Internationale Doppelwährung. Tübingen, 1881.

Schmidt, H. The Silver Question in its Social Aspect. London, 1886.

Schoenhof, J. History of Money and Prices. New York, 1896.

Schurtz, H. Grundriss einer Entstehungs geschichte des Geldes. Weimar, 1898.

Scott, W. A. Money and Banking. New York, 1903.

Sealy, H. N. A Treatise on Coins, Currency, and Banking. London, 1858.

Senior, N. W. Three Lectures on the Cost of obtaining Money. London, 1830.

Seyd, E. Bullion and Foreign Exchanges. London, 1868.

—— The Question of Seigniorage and the Charge for Coining. London, 1868.

—— The Decline of Prosperity. London, 1879.

Shaw, W. A. Select Tracts and Documents Illustrative of English Monetary History, 1626–1730. London, 1896.

—— The History of Currency, 1252–1894. 2d ed. London, 1896.

Sherwood, S. The History and Theory of Money. Philadelphia, 1893.

Simmel, G. Philosophie des Geldes. Leipzig, 1900.

Simon, J. An Essay towards an Historical Account of Irish Coins. Dublin, 1749.

Sinclair, J. The Approaching Crisis. London, 1818.

—— Observations on the Report of the Bullion Committee. London, 1810.

Smith, J. T. Remarks on a Gold Currency for India. London, 1868.

Snowden, J. R. A Description of Ancient and Modern Coins in the Cabinet Collection of the Mint of the United States. Philadelphia, 1860.

Soetbeer, A. Edelmetall-Produktion und Werthverhältniss zwischen Gold und Silber seit der Entdeckung Amerika's bis zur Gegenwart. Gotha, 1879.

—— Litteratur nachweis über Geld-und Münzwesen in besondere über den Währungsstreit, 1871–1891. Berlin, 1892.

—— Materialen zur Erlaüterung und Beurteilung der wirtschaftlichen Edelmetallverhältnisse und der Währungsfrage. 2d ed. Berlin, 1886.

—— Deutsche Münzverfassung. Erlangen, 1874.

Spaulding, E. G. History of the Legal Tender Paper Money issued during the Great Rebellion. 2d ed. Buffalo, 1869.

Stewart, J. Principles of Money applied to the Present State of the Coin of Bengal. 1772.

Stirling, P. F. The Australian and Californian Gold Discoveries and their Probable Consequences. London, 1853.

Stokes, A. P. Joint-Metallism. 5th ed. New York, 1896.

Suess, E. The Future of Silver. Washington, 1893.

Sumner, W. G. A History of American Currency. New York, 1878.

Swan, C. H. Monetary Problems and Reforms. New York, 1897.

Taussig, F. W. The Silver Situation in the United States. 2d ed. New York, 1896.

Taylor, J. An Essay on Money, its Origin and Use. London, 1832.

Thiers, A. The Mississippi Bubble; a Memoir of John Law. Translated by F. S. Fiske. New York, 1859.

Thornton, H. An Inquiry into the Nature and Effects of the Paper Credit of Great Britain. London, 1802.

Tooke, T. Considerations on the State of the Currency. 2d ed. London, 1826.

—— and **Newmarch, W.** A History of Prices and of the State of the Circulation from 1793 to 1856. 6 vols. London, 1838–1857.

Trenholm, W. L. The People's Money. New York, 1893.

Upton, J. K. Money in Politics. Revised edition. Boston, 1895.

—— A Coin Catechism: a Book of Facts, not Theories. New York, 1896.

de Viti de Marco, A. Moneta e Prezzi, ossia il Principio Quantitativo in Rapporto Alla Questione Monetario. Rome, 1885.

Wagner, A. Die Geld-und Credittheorie der Peel'schen Bankacte. Wien, 1862.

—— Für Bimetallistische Münzpolitik Deutschlands. Berlin, 1881.

—— Staatspapiergeld, Reichs-Kassenschemie und Banknoten. Berlin, 1874.

Waldron, G. B. Handbook on Currency and Wealth. New York, 1896.

Walker, F. A. Money. New York, 1877.

—— Money in its Relation to Trade and Industry. New York, 1888.

—— International Bimetallism. New York, 1896.

Walker, J. H. Money, Trade, and Banking. Boston, 1882.

Walras, L. Theorie de la Monnaie. Laussane, 1886.

Walsh, C. M. Measurement of General Exchange Value. New York, 1901.

—— Fundamental Problem in Monetary Science. New York, 1903.

Walsh, R. H. Elementary Treatise on Metallic Currency. Dublin, 1853.

Ward, J. A History of Gold as a Commodity and as a Measure of Value. London, 1852.

Ward, W. Remarks on the Monetary Legislation of Great Britain. London, 1847.

Watson, D. K. History of American Coinage. New York, 1899.

Webb, M. de P. The Great Power. London and New York, 1897.

Webster, P. Political Essays on the Nature and Operation of Money. Philadelphia, 1791.

Webster, S. The Misuse of Legal Tender. New York, 1893.

Weibezahn, H. Der Abschluss der deutschen Münzreform. Leipzig, 1873.

—— Deutschlands Münz-Einheit mit Goldwährung. Leipzig, 1871.

White, A. D. Fiat Money Inflation in France. Revised edition. New York, 1896.

White, H. Money and Banking. 2d ed. Boston, 1902.

Whitney, D. R. The Suffolk Bank. Cambridge, 1878.

Wicksell, K. Geldzins und Guterpreise. Jena, 1898.

Willis, H. P. A History of the Latin Monetary Union. Chicago, 1901.

Wilson, J. Capital, Currency, and Banking. 2d ed. London, 1859.

Wirth, M. Handbuch des Bankwesen. Köln, 1883.

Wolowski, M. L. (Editor). Traicte de la Première Invention des Monnoies de Nicole Oresme et Traité de la Monnoie de Copernic. Paris, 1864.

—— L'Or et l'Argent. Paris, 1870.

—— Le Change et la Circulation. Paris, 1869.

Wood, J. P. Memoirs of the Life of John Law of Lauriston. Edinburgh, 1824.

INDEX

INDEX

INDEX

INDEX

Printed in the United States of America.